GLOBAL HUMAN RESOURCES PERSPECTIVES

Jagdish N. Sheth
Brooker Professor of Research
Graduate School of Business
University of Southern California

Golpira S. Eshghi
Associate Professor of Management
Bentley College

ISBN: 0-538-80045-3

Library of Congress Catalog Card Number: 88-60623

1 2 3 4 5 6 7 8 M 3 2 1 0 9 8

Printed in the United States of America

PREFACE

International aspects of human resource practices and policies are becoming increasingly important in management. Virtually all profit and nonprofit organizations today either supply or demand products and services which have some foreign labor component. For example, most agricultural products grown and consumed in the United States have significant foreign or migrant worker employment. In the factories of Europe, "guest workers" from Italy, Turkey, and Pakistan build automobiles and produce steel. And more recently, increasing numbers of foreign workers are involved in software development as well as in building software factories in several countries, including Singapore and India.

Understanding and managing human resource issues in a global environment is important for several reasons. First, worldwide communication and information technologies enable us to exchange information rapidly throughout the world. Very few places in the world are inaccessible to worldwide communication and information; thus, the world is truly a global village.

Second, an increasing interdependence connects nations of the world both economically and politically. In addition to economic integrations such as the EEC and the ASEAN block countries, today we also have worldwide international trade between advanced and less developed countries, between Western bloc and Eastern block nations, and between Far East and Western nations.

Finally, the cross-cultural understanding of people's values, ethics, and attitudes is becoming increasingly necessary whether we deal with them as employees, suppliers, customers, or shareholders.

This volume is designed to supplement standard textbooks in required MBA courses on the management of human resources as well as at the advanced undergraduate level. It is intended to fulfill the accreditation requirements for internationalizing the business curriculum.

This volume is prepared to serve the following educational needs in human resource management.

- It explores the complexity of cross-cultural differences, especially with respect to employee selection, training, reward systems, and career advancement.
- It provides a managerial and strategic perspective on human resource issues.
- It investigates differences and similarities in human resource practices among the U.S., European, and Japanese multinationals. Also, it focuses on the tradeoffs in human resource practices that a global organization is likely to make.
- It provides an annotated bibliography, which will facilitate self-study or specify research projects related to international management.

A number of criteria were utilized in selecting the papers for this volume.

- They must be managerial in orientation.
- They must be written by authors who are recognized for their contributions to the field.

- The authors must represent a worldwide perspective rather than limit themselves to the U.S. perspective.

Although the volume is designed to supplement the management and human resource courses required in the MBA and advanced undergraduate progams, it can also satisfy the needs of the Executive MBA program and corporate executive seminars on global human resource management.

The editors and the Publishers are grateful to the authors and publishers who granted permission to reprint articles included in this volume.

Jagdish N. Sheth
Golpira S. Eshghi

CONTENTS

INTRODUCTION

Managing business is really managing people; it is not managing a laboratory, a factory, or money. The most difficult resource to manage is people! The task of managing people is more complex and difficult across national boundaries for a number of reasons.

First, government regulations vary significantly across national boundaries with respect to hiring, firing, training, or promoting employees. Second, labor relations, especially with unions, vary a great deal from country to country. Some have collective bargaining, others have shop stewards, and still others have no specific union laws. Furthermore, in some countries, unions tend to be militant, and in other countries they tend to be political.

Third, the economic infrastructure, including tax policy and wage guidelines, differs significantly across national boundaries. This requires significant adjustments in fringe benefits, salary structure and retirement procedures. Finally, management styles tend to vary across cultures. Some cultures prefer a paternalistic style of management, others tend to be highly task or merit oriented, and still others believe in social networks.

Why is Global Human Resource Management is Important?

Despite the complexity inherent in the global context, it is becoming increasingly inevitable that human resource managers must understand and appreciate global aspects of managing people. Figure I.1 summarizes four major reasons.

Figure I.1.

INCREASING IMPORTANCE OF GLOBAL HUMAN RESOURCE UNDERSTANDING

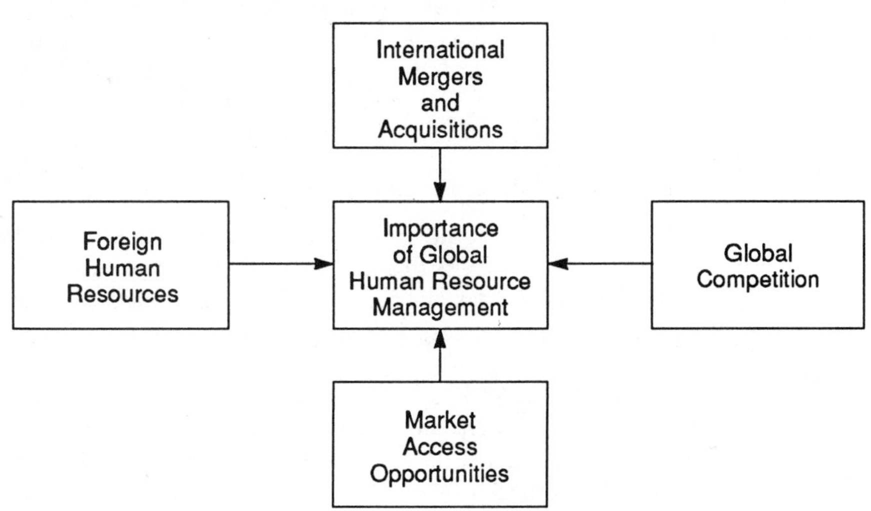

International Mergers and Acquisitions

In recent years, there have been a significant number of international mergers, acquisitions, and strategic alliances. For example, General Electric recently sold its U.S. based consumer electronics business to the Thomson Group from France and acquired the latter's European–based medical electronics business. Both corporations, must now learn to manage people with different technical and cultural backgrounds, different reward systems, and possibly different career aspirations.

Recently, some Japanese companies have learned the hard way that it is a lot harder to manage an acquired business than to start a new business. They had a difficult time reorienting American workers and managers to think like the Japanese.

Finally, several years ago, AT&T decided to establish a strategic alliance with Olivetti, the Italian office equipment and computer giant. AT&T was strong in telecommunications but weak in personal computers, and Olivetti was strong in Europe but relatively ineffective in the U.S. market. It seemed like a good strategic alliance between the two companies. But what was a good plan has become a complex and difficult implementation problem as people from two different corporate cultures try to work together as a team.

Global Competition

In the last twenty–five years, global competition has increased significantly among the multinationals of the triad power nations (Japan, North American, and Europe). They all compete in each other's markets across virtually all sectors of the economy, and it is becoming increasingly necessary for these to enter foreign markets simply to protect their domestic market. For example, when Michelin invaded North America with its radial tires by subsidizing the entry from its European operations, Goodyear was forced to retaliate by entering the European markets. Financially, it is less expensive to cross-subsidize a small foreign market from a large domestic market share than it is for a dominant market share holder to drop its prices in order to drive out the new entrant.

The same experiences have been observed in computers, peripherals, semiconductors, agriculture, specialty chemicals, and in the automobile industry. As companies expand their operations beyond national boundaries, they encounter human resource issues even if it is strictly an export operation. In other words, human resource management is central to any global presence.

Market Access Opportunities

A third major reason for the increasing importance of global human resource understanding is the access to emerging markets. As new nations and their economies become market opportunities, it becomes necessary to understand and manage business cultures, ethics, and negotiations particular to those countries and their markets.

While experienced multinations such as Boeing and IBM have learned this over many years, it is often a new experience for many other corporations. For example, since China has opened up its markets to the Western world, many U.S. corporations are learning, probably by much trial and error, how to do business in China. Indeed, popular executive training programs are offered on this topic by a number of universities and consultants. The same phenomenon is observed with respect to the India market. A more exciting, and probably more complex, opportunity is the Soviet Union's emerging market in Western Europe, North America, and Japan.

The key human resource issues are selecting, training, and supporting people (technical, legal, financial, and marketing) and helping them to understand the silent languages of doing business with overseas markets. Cultures vary significantly, especially in their business institutions, with respect to business ethics, symbols, and practices. For example, business people have different values for time, space, and material possessions. Similarly, they have different attitudes with respect to mixing friendship with business. And most importantly, what constitutes an agreement is radically different. In some cultures only a written legal contract constitutes an agreement whereas in other cultures it is considered an insult to one's integrity. We are all aware of the importance of the tea ceremony in Japan and the high degree of informality of the American business.

Foreign Human Resources

It is becoming increasingly necessary to search for human resources across national boundaries even if you do business only in a domestic market. In the United States, we are all aware of the migrant farm workers from Mexico and Central America. In Europe, especially in Germany, "guest workers" from Italy, Turkey, and Pakistan are a common resource.

While this has been true in the factory, it is becoming increasingly universal in white collar clerical, technical, and professional fields. For example, a number of temporary clerical help companies are actively searching for workers to work in corporations on a temporary basis. Recently, Microsoft went to India and hired a large number of computer programmers to work in the U.S. Over the years, an acute shortage of nurses and teachers in the United States has forced many organizations, and even governments, to seek foreign human resources.

More recently, foreign procurement of human resources is starting to occur among professionals. This also has some precedents. The French have traditionally exported military professionals to many parts of the world. The British even created a managing partner system: British professionals managed business enterprises of deposed colonial rulers and wealthy industrialists. More recently, this is happening increasingly with respect to investment banking, consulting, medicine, public accounting, and other professional services.

As corporations continue to recruit workers from other countries for their factories and offices, it will become increasingly important to understand the global nature of human resource issues.

Managing Human Resources in a Global Environment

Understanding global differences in human resources is important to any organization today because of increasing economic interdependence, instant worldwide communication, and emerging global migrant workforce. However, managing human resources globally is becoming equally important as both profit and nonprofit organizations expand their activities across national boundaries.

As organizations cross national boundaries, they encounter obvious trade-offs in human resource management. On one hand, it may be important to standardize human resources practices such as selection, training, rewards, and career planning across national boundaries for reasons of consistency and efficiency. On the other hand, it may be critical to localize human resource practices by country or region to meet union, government, and employee concerns related to job discrimination, especially in the management ranks. Recently, several Japanese multinationals have been publicly criticized for the lack of non-Japanese executives from North America, Europe, and Asia in their top management positions. Similar criticism was levied against several European colonial powers when they expanded their economic activities in less-developed countries or colonies.

What are the appropriate human resource management strategies in a global context? Figure I.2 provides a framework for developing specific strategies depending on the degree of trade-offs inherent between consistency and localization.

Consistency of human resources is extremely important in a number of situations. Most professional services including medical, legal, consulting, and banking require a high degree of consistency because of the expertise and influence they possess. Consistency of human resources is equally important in a highly capital-intensive manufacturing environment—including high tech industries. Finally, it is extremely important in industries like retailing where corporate image heavily depends on people.

Localization of human resources, on the other hand, becomes important when government rules and regulations across national boundaries differ with respect to wages, hiring, and firing of employees. For example, minimum wage, child labor, and environmental laws vary significantly from country to country. Second, the localization of human resource practices also become necessary when labor unions differ significantly in their philosophies, structures, and governance.

Third, cross-cultural differences of employees, shareholders, and customers often require making adjustments from country to country. For example, in some countries

Figure I.2

Need for Human Resource Consistency	Need for Human Resource Localization: High	Need for Human Resource Localization: Low
High	Umbrella Human Resource Management	Worldwide Human Resource Management
Low	Decentralized Human Resource Management	Ad hoc Human Resource Management

family is more important than career; therefore, it is difficult to implement job relocation, temporary overseas assignments, family relocation issues. Finally, ethnocentric values of countries are also different. National pride, local emphasis, and purity of the culture (values, language, religion) all require a multinational advisor to adjust its human resource practices to do business in that country.

When neither consistency nor localization is critical *ad hoc human resource strategy* is sufficient, at least with respect to international issues. It really does not matter whether an organization has a standardized or a localized human resource strategy. For example, export-oriented companies often experience this situation. It all depends on specific individuals and situations. Of course, this is likely to be less and less true as organizations globally expand their scope of business operations.

When the localization of human resource practices is important but the consistency of human resources is not critical, the best option is a *decentralized human resource strategy.* This is often true in joint ventures and licensing arrangements in which transfer of technology is a fundamental business proposition.

In other words, each joint venture or license has its own corporate identity and localized business practices are prevalent. This is often the case when the advanced countries enter the less-developed countries through a joint venture.

A third option is a *worldwide human resource strategy.* This is the best option when consistency of human resources is essential and the need for localization is not high. Examples include retail franchising, professional services, and highly skilled operations. Increasingly, more multinationals are moving toward a worldwide human resource strategy even if it requires changing local regulations, unions, and employee values. In a worldwide human resource strategy, it is a common practice to employ people from different parts of the world, move them around, and even encourage managing businesses in foreign countries. There is no domination of the host country expatriates; they come from all countries where the organization is engaged in business operations. For example, this is becoming increasingly true in consulting businesses and among the U.S. companies which emphasize consistency.

Finally and probably most realistically, both consistency and localization of human resources are important. This is the most difficult situation and requires a hybrid solution. We suggest an *umbrella human resource strategy* in which basic employee policies, processes, and procedures are standardized on a worldwide basis to provide umbrella guidelines. However, at the same time, either at a country level or a regional level, the international managers are given autonomy with respect to selection, training, promotion, and career advancement of their people. For example, IBM seems to follow this umbrella strategy.

Summary of the Book

The book is divided into four parts. The first part focuses on cultural, political, and economic issues which are important external forces for managing the human resources. In a very interesting and comprehensive paper, Hofstede suggests that four dimensions define national cultures: individualism vs. collectivism; social stratification; uncertainty avoidance associated with the future; and division of labor between men and women. As economic interdependence grows between the advanced and the less-developed nations, it is very likely that these cross-cultural differences will become increasingly important. Also important will be unemployment and underemployment of people in third world countries. Government policies, regulations, and practices are likely to be shaped by the fundamentals of supply and demand of labor.

In the second part, the book focuses on strategy and styles of human resource management. Human resource strategies including staffing, appraisal, rewards, training, and development become critical issues in the global strategic planning process. Many companies have discovered this the hard way by focusing too much on technology and finance and too little on people. The management styles vary strongly between the triad power nations (North America, Europe, and Japan) and within the European countries with respect to perceptions about what motivates people. Is it job security, recognition, or self-motivation? Furthermore, should a manager act informally or formally with his subordinates on the job or socialize with them outside the work environment become issues of management style.

Part three discusses implementation issues of selection and training of employees at all levels of management. Specifically, it deals with the issues of worker involvement in quality circles, selection criteria for overseas managers, and understanding human resource practices of the U.S., European and Japanese multinationals.

Part Four is reserved for special topics. We have selected three important and emerging human resource issues. The first deals with women managers and executives. A number of myths exist as to why we have fewer women in international management: women neither seek nor accept international management positions; North American managers are reluctant to send women overseas; and women would not be effective because foreigners are prejudiced against female managers. Apparently, these are more myths than reality because times have changed.

China is a large emerging market especially for advanced Western and Asian countries. Its unique ancient history and civilization as well as the communist policy and practices are likely to create significant differences in China's human resource practices. For example, when job security is guaranteed by the socialistic policy, how does one provide incentives to factory workers? Also, what is the role of labor unions with the local governments?

A third special topic relates to Japanese human resource practices and philosophy. Because Japan has demonstrated a superior system of management, it will become increasingly necessary to understand similarities and differences between the Japanese and non-Japanese organizations. The area we have chosen to focus is Japanese-owned companies and their attitudes toward unions in the United States.

In addition, the book includes an annotated bibliography for students to explore specific areas in more depth.

I The Global Environment for Human Resources

1. THE CULTURAL RELATIVITY OF ORGANIZATIONAL PRACTICES AND THEORIES

GEERT HOFSTEDE

Geert Hofstede is Director of the Institute for Research on Intercultural Cooperation at Arnhem, the Netherlands. He has worked as a manager in industry and as an academic teacher and researcher in a number of international institutes in Europe.

This paper summarizes the author's recently published findings about differences in people's work-related values among 50 countries. In view of these differences, ethnocentric management theories (those based on the value system of one particular country) have become untenable. This concept is illustrated for the fields of leadership, organization, and motivation.

Introduction

Management and National Cultures

A key issue for organization science is the influence of national cultures on management. Twenty or even 10 years ago, the existence of a relationship between management and national cultures was far from obvious to many, and it may not be obvious to everyone even now. In the 1950s and 60s, the dominant belief, at least in Europe and the U.S., was that management was something universal. There were principles of sound management, which existed regardless of national environments. If national or local practice deviated from these principles, it was time to change local practice. In the future, the universality of sound management practices would lead to societies becoming more and more alike. This applied even to the poor countries of the Third World, which would become rich as well and would be managed just like the rich countries. Also, the differences between management in the First and Second World (capitalist and socialist) would disappear; in fact, under the surface they were thought to be a lot smaller than was officially recognized. This way of thinking, which dominated the 1950s and 60s, is known as the "convergence hypothesis."

During the 1970s, the belief in the unavoidable convergence of management practices waned. It was too obviously in conflict with the reality we saw around us. At the same time supranational organizations like the European Common Market, which were founded very much on the convergence belief, had to recognize the stubbornness of national differences. Even within existing nations, regional differences became more rather than less accentuated. The Welsh, the Flemish, the Basques, the Bangladeshi, the Quebecois defended their own identity, and this was

Geert Hofstede, "The Cultural Relativity of Organizational Theories," *Journal of International Business Studies* XIV.2 (1983): 75–90. Reprinted by permission.

difficult to reconcile with a management philosophy of convergence. It slowly became clear that national and even regional cultures do matter for management. The national and regional differences are not disappearing; they are here to stay. In fact, these differences may become one of the most crucial problems for management—in particular for the management of multinational, multicultural organizations, whether public or private.

The Importance of Nationality

Nationality is important to management for at least 3 reasons. The first, very obviously, is political. Nations are political units, rooted in history, with their own institutions: forms of government, legal systems, educational systems, labor and employer's association systems. Not only do the formal institutions differ, but even if we could equalize them, the informal ways of using them differ. For example, formal law in France protects the rights of the individual against the state much better than formal law in Great Britain or Holland. However, few French citizens have ever won court cases against the state, whereas this happens quite regularly in Holland or Britain. Such informal political realities are quite resistant to change.

The second reason why nationality is important is sociological. Nationality or regionality has a symbolic value to citizens. We all derive part of our identity from it; it is part of the "who am I." The symbolic value of the fact of belonging to a nation or region has been and still is sufficient reason for people to go to war, when they feel their common identity to be threatened. National and regional differences are felt by people to be a reality—and therefore they are a reality.

The third reason why nationality is important is psychological. Our thinking is partly conditioned by national culture factors. This is an effect of early life experiences in the family and later educational experiences in schools and organizations, which are not the same across national borders. In a classroom, I can easily demonstrate the process of conditioning by experience. For this purpose I use an ambiguous picture: one that can be interpreted in 2 different ways. One such picture represents either an attractive young girl or an ugly old woman, depending on the way you look at it. In order to demonstrate the process of conditioning, I ask one half of the class to close their eyes. To the other half, I show for 5 seconds a slightly changed version of the picture, in which only the young girl can be seen. Then I ask the other half to close their eyes, and to the first half I show, also for 5 seconds, a version in which only the old woman can be seen. After this preparation, I show the ambiguous picture to everyone at the same time. The results are amazing: the vast majority of those "conditioned" by seeing the young girl first, now see only the young girl in the ambiguous picture; and most of those "conditioned" by seeing the old woman first can see only the old woman afterwards.

Mental Programming

This very simple experiment shows that, as a teacher, I can in 5 seconds condition a randomly taken half of a class to see something else in a picture than would the other half. If this is so, how much stronger should the differences in perception of the same reality be between people who have been "conditioned" by different educational and life experiences not for a mere 5 seconds, but for 20, 30, or 40 years? Through our experiences we become "mentally programmed" to interpret new experiences in a certain way. My favorite definition of "culture" is precisely that its essence is *collective mental programming*: it is that part of our conditioning that we share with other members of our nation, region, or group but not with members of other nations, regions, or groups.

Examples of differences in mental programming between members of different nations can be observed all around us. One source of difference is, of course, language and all that comes with it, but there is much more. In Europe, British people will form a neat queue whenever they have to wait; not so, the French. Dutch people will as a rule greet strangers when they enter a small, closed space like a railway compartment, doctor's waiting room, or lift; not so, the Belgians. Austrians will wait at a red pedestrian traffic light even when there is no traffic; not so the Dutch. Swiss tend to become very angry when somebody—say, a foreigner—makes a mistake in traffic; not so the Swedes. All these are part of an invisible set of mental programs which belongs to these countries' national cultures.

Such cultural programs are difficult to change, unless one detaches the individual from his or her culture. Within a nation or a part of it, culture changes only slowly. This is the more so because what is in the minds of the people has also become crystallized in the institutions mentioned earlier: government, legal systems, educational systems, industrial relations systems, family structures, religious organizations, sports clubs, settlement patterns, literature, architecture, and even scientific theories. All these reflect traditions and common ways of thinking, which are rooted in the common culture but may be different for other cultures. The institutions constrain and reinforce the ways of thinking on which they are based. One well-known mechanism by which culturally determined ways of thinking perpetuate themselves is the self-fulfilling prophecy. If, for example, the belief is held that people from a certain minority are irresponsible, the institutions in such an environment will not admit these people into positions of responsibility; never being given responsibility, minority people will be unable to learn it, and very likely they will actually behave irresponsibly. So, everyone remains caught in the belief—including, probably, the minority people themselves. Another example of the self-fulfilling prophecy: if the dominant way of thinking in a society is that all people are ultimately motivated by self-interest, those who do not pursue self-interest are considered as deviant. As it is unpleasant to be a deviant, most people in such an environment will justify whatever they want to do with some reference to self-interest, thereby reinforcing the dominant way of thinking. People in such a society cannot even imagine motives that cannot be reduced to self-interest.

National Character

This paper shall be limited to national cultures, excluding cultural differences between groups within nations; such as, those based on regions, social classes, occupations, religion, age, sex, or even families. These differences in culture within nations, of course, do exist, but for most nations we can still distinguish some ways of thinking that most inhabitants share and that we can consider part of their national culture or national character. National characters are more clearly distinguishable to foreigners than to the nationals themselves. When we live within a country, we do not discover what we have in common with our compatriots, only what makes us different from them.

Statements about national culture or national character smell of superficiality and false generalization. There are 2 reasons for this. First, there is no commonly accepted language to describe such a complex thing as a "culture." We meet the same problem if we want to describe someone's "personality": we risk being subjective and superficial. In the case of "personality," however, psychology has at least developed terms like intelligence, energy level, introversion-extroversion and emotional stability, to mention a few, which are more or less commonly understood. In the case of "culture," such a scientific language does not exist. In the second place, statements about national character have often been based on impressions only, not on systematic study. Such statements can indeed be considered false generalizations.

A Research Project Across 50 Countries

My own research into national cultures was carried out between 1967 and 1978. It has attempted to meet the 2 objectives I just mentioned: to develop a commonly acceptable, well-defined, and empirically based terminology to describe cultures; and to use systematically collected data about a large number of cultures, rather than just impressions. I obtained these data more or less by accident. From 1967 to 1971 I worked as a psychologist on the international staff of a large multinational corporation. As part of my job I collected data on the employees' attitudes and values, by means of standardized paper-and-pencil questionnaires. Virtually all employees of the corporation were surveyed, from unskilled workers to research scientists in many countries around the globe. Then from 1971 to 1973 the surveys were repeated once more with the same group of employees. All in all the corporation collected over 116,000 questionnaires which were stored in a computerized data bank. For 40 countries, there were sufficient data for systematic analysis.

It soon appeared that those items in the questionnaires that dealt with employee values rather than attitudes showed remarkable and very stable differences between countries. By an attitude I mean the response to a question like "how do you like your job?" or "how do you like your boss?" By a value I mean answers to questions of whether people prefer one type of boss over another, or their choice of factors to describe an ideal job. Values indicate their desires, not their perceptions of what actually went on. These values, not the attitudes, reflect differences in mental programming and national character.

These differences, however, were always statistical in nature. Suppose people were asked whether they strongly agreed, agreed, were undecided, disagreed, or strongly disagreed with a certain value statement. In such a case we would not find that all employees in country A agreed and all in country B disagreed; instead we might find that 60 percent of the employees in country A agreed, while only 40 percent in country B agreed. Characterizing a national culture does not mean that every individual within that culture is mentally programmed in the same way. The national culture found is a kind of average pattern of beliefs and values, around which individuals in the country vary. For example, I found that, on average, Japanese have a greater desire for a strong authority than English; but some English have a greater desire for a strong authority than quite a few Japanese. In describing national cultures we refer to common elements within each nation, but we should not generalize to every individual within that nation.

In 1971 I went as a teacher to an international business school, where I asked the course participants, who were managers from many different countries, to answer the same values questions we used in the multinational corporation. The answers revealed the same type of pattern of differences between countries, showing that we were not dealing with a phenomenon particular to this one company. Then in my later research, from 1973 to 1979, at the European Institute for Advanced Studies in Brussels, I looked for other studies comparing aspects of national character across countries. I found about 40 such studies comparing 5 or more countries which showed differences confirming the ones found in the multinational corporation. All this material together forms the basis for my book *Culture's Consequences* [Hofstede 1980]. Later, supplementary data became available for another 10 countries and 3 multi-country regions, thereby raising the total number of countries to 50 [Hofstede 1983].

Four Dimensions of National Culture

My terminology for describing national cultures consists of 4 different criteria which I call "dimensions" because they occur in nearly all possible combinations. They are largely independent of each other:

1. Individualism versus Collectivism;
2. Large or Small Power Distance;
3. Strong or Weak Uncertainty Avoidance; and
4. Masculinity versus Femininity.

The research data have allowed me to attribute to each of the 40 countries represented in the data bank of the multinational corporation an index value (between 0 and about 100) on each of these 4 dimensions.

The 4 dimensions were found through a combination of multivariate statistics (factor analysis) and theoretical reasoning. The cases analysed in the factor analysis were the 40 countries; the variables were the mean scores or answer percentages for the different value questions, as produced by the multinational corporation's employees within these countries. This factor analysis showed that 50 percent of the variance in answer patterns between countries on the value questions could be explained by 3 factors, corresponding to the dimensions 1 + 2, 3 and 4. Theoretical reasoning led to the further splitting of the first factor into 2 dimensions. The theoretical reasoning meant that each dimension should be conceptually linkable to some very fundamental problem in human societies, but a problem to which different societies have found different answers. These are the issues studied in primitive, nonliterate societies by cultural anthropologists, such as, the distribution of power, or the distribution of roles between the sexes. There is no reason why such issues should be relevant only for primitive societies.

The first dimension is labeled "Individualism versus Collectivism." The fundamental issue involved is the relation between an individual and his or her fellow individuals. At one end of the scale we find societies in which the ties between individuals are very loose. Everybody is supposed to look after his or her own self-interest and maybe the interest of his or her immediate family. This is made possible by a large amount of freedom that such a society leaves individuals. At the other end of the scale we find societies in which the ties between individuals are very tight. People are born into collectivities or ingroups which may be their extended family (including grandparents, uncles, aunts, and so on), their tribe, or their village. Everybody is supposed to look after the interest of his or her ingroup and to have no other opinions and beliefs than the opinions and beliefs in their ingroup. In exchange, the ingroup will protect them when they are in trouble. We see that both the Individualist and the Collectivist society are integrated wholes, but the Individualist society is loosely integrated, and the Collectivist society tightly integrated.

All 50 countries studied can be placed somewhere along the Individualist-Collectivist scale. On the basis of the answers obtained on the questionnaire in the multinational corporation, each country was given an Individualism Index score. The score is such that 100 represents a strongly Individualist society, and 0 a strongly Collectivist society: all 50 countries are somewhere between these extremes.

It appears that the degree of Individualism in a country is statistically related to that country's wealth. Figure 1 shows the list of countries used, and Figure 2 shows vertically the Individualism Index scores of the 50 countries, and horizontally their wealth, expressed in their gross national product per capita at the time the surveys were taken (around 1970). We see evidence that wealthy countries are more Individualist and poor countries more Collectivist. Very Individualist countries are the U.S., Great Britain, the Netherlands; very Collectivist are Columbia, Pakistan, and Taiwan. In the middle we find Japan, India, Austria, and Spain.

Power Distance

The second dimension is labeled "Power Distance." The fundamental issue involved is how society deals with the fact that people are unequal. People are unequal in physical and intellectual capacities. Some societies let these unequalities grow over time into inequalities in power and wealth; the latter may become hereditary and no longer related to physical and intellectual capacities at all. Other societies try to play down inequalities in power and wealth as much as possible. Surely, no society has ever reached complete equality, because there are strong forces in society that perpetuate existing inequalities. All societies are unequal, but some are more unequal than others. This degree of inequality is measured by the Power Distance scale, which also runs from 0 (small Power Distance) to 100 (large Power Distance).

In organizations, the level of Power Distance is related to the degree of centralization of authority and the degree of autocratic leadership. This relationship shows that centralization and autocratic leadership are rooted in the "mental pro-

Figure 1

THE COUNTRIES AND REGIONS

ARA	Arab countries (Egypt, Lebanon, Lybia, Kuwait, Iraq, Saudi-Arabia, U.A.E.)	JAM	Jamaica
		JPN	Japan
		KOR	South Korea
ARG	Argentina	MAL	Malaysia
AUL	Australia	MEX	Mexico
AUT	Austria	NET	Netherlands
BEL	Belgium	NOR	Norway
BRA	Brazil	NZL	New Zealand
CAN	Canada	PAK	Pakistan
CHL	Chile	PAN	Panama
COL	Colombia	PER	Peru
COS	Costa Rica	PHI	Philippines
DEN	Denmark	POR	Portugal
EAF	East Africa (Kenya, Ethiopia, Zambia)	SAF	South Africa
		SAL	Salvador
EQA	Equador	SIN	Singapore
FIN	Finland	SPA	Spain
FRA	France	SWE	Sweden
GBR	Great Britain	SWI	Switzerland
GER	Germany	TAI	Taiwan
GRE	Greece	THA	Thailand
GUA	Guatemala	TUR	Turkey
HOK	Hong Kong	URU	Uruguay
IDO	Indonesia	USA	United States
IND	India	VEN	Venezuela
IRA	Iran	WAF	West Africa (Nigeria, Ghana, Sierra Leone)
IRE	Ireland		
ISR	Israel	YUG	Yugoslavia
ITA	Italy		

gramming" of the members of a society, not only of those in power but also of those at the bottom of the power hierarchy. Societies in which power tends to be distributed unequally can remain so because this situation satisfies the psychological need for dependence of the people without power. We could also say that societies and organizations will be led as autocratically as their members will permit. The autocracy exists just as much in the members as in the leaders: the value systems of the 2 groups are usually complementary.

In Figure 3 Power Distance is plotted horizontally and Individualism-Collectivism vertically. The Philippines, Venezuela, India, and others show large Power Distance index scores, but also France and Belgium score fairly high. Denmark, Israel, and

Figure 2

THE POSITION OF THE 50 COUNTRIES ON THEIR INDIVIDUALISM INDEX (IDV) VERSUS THEIR 1970 NATIONAL WEALTH

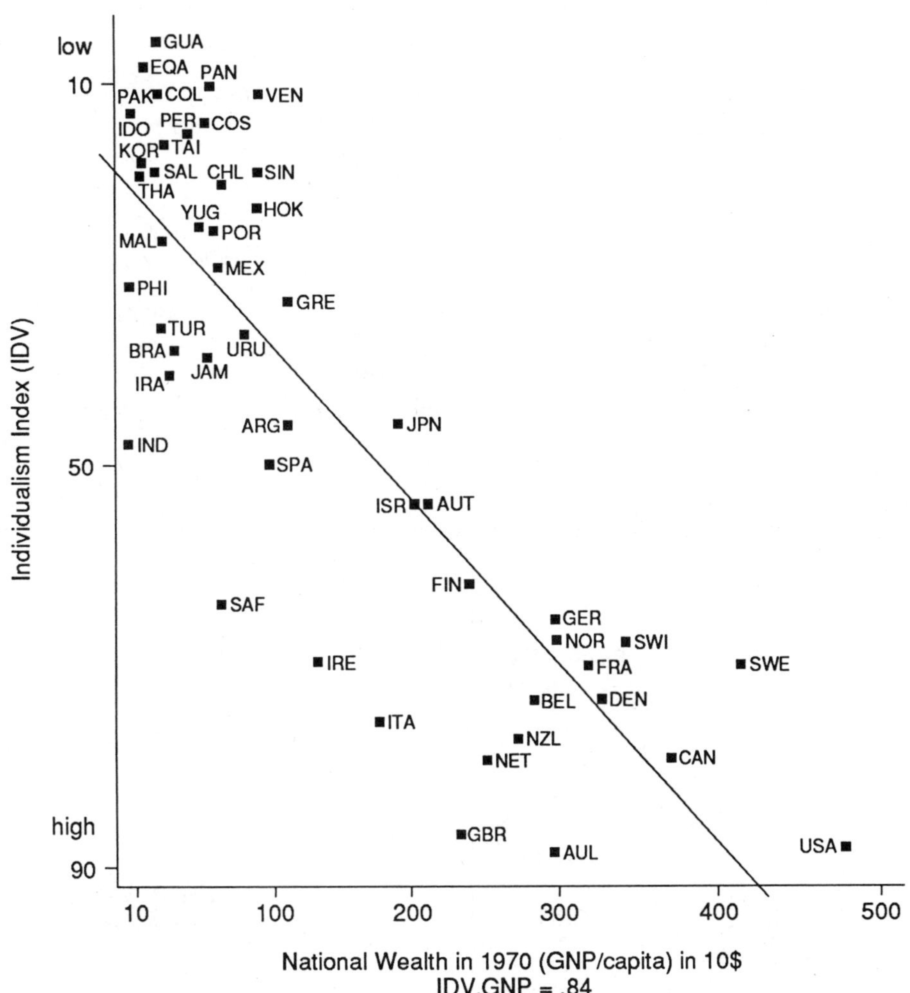

Austria score low. We see that there is a global relationship between Power Distance and Collectivism: Collectivist countries always show large Power Distances, but Individualist countries do not always show small Power Distances. The Latin European countries—France, Belgium, Italy, and Spain, plus marginally South Africa—show a combination of large Power Distances plus Individualism. The other wealthy Western countries all combine smaller Power Distance with Individualism. All poor countries are Collectivist with larger Power Distances.

Figure 3

THE POSITION OF THE 50 COUNTRIES ON THE POWER DISTANCE AND INDIVIDUALISM SCALES

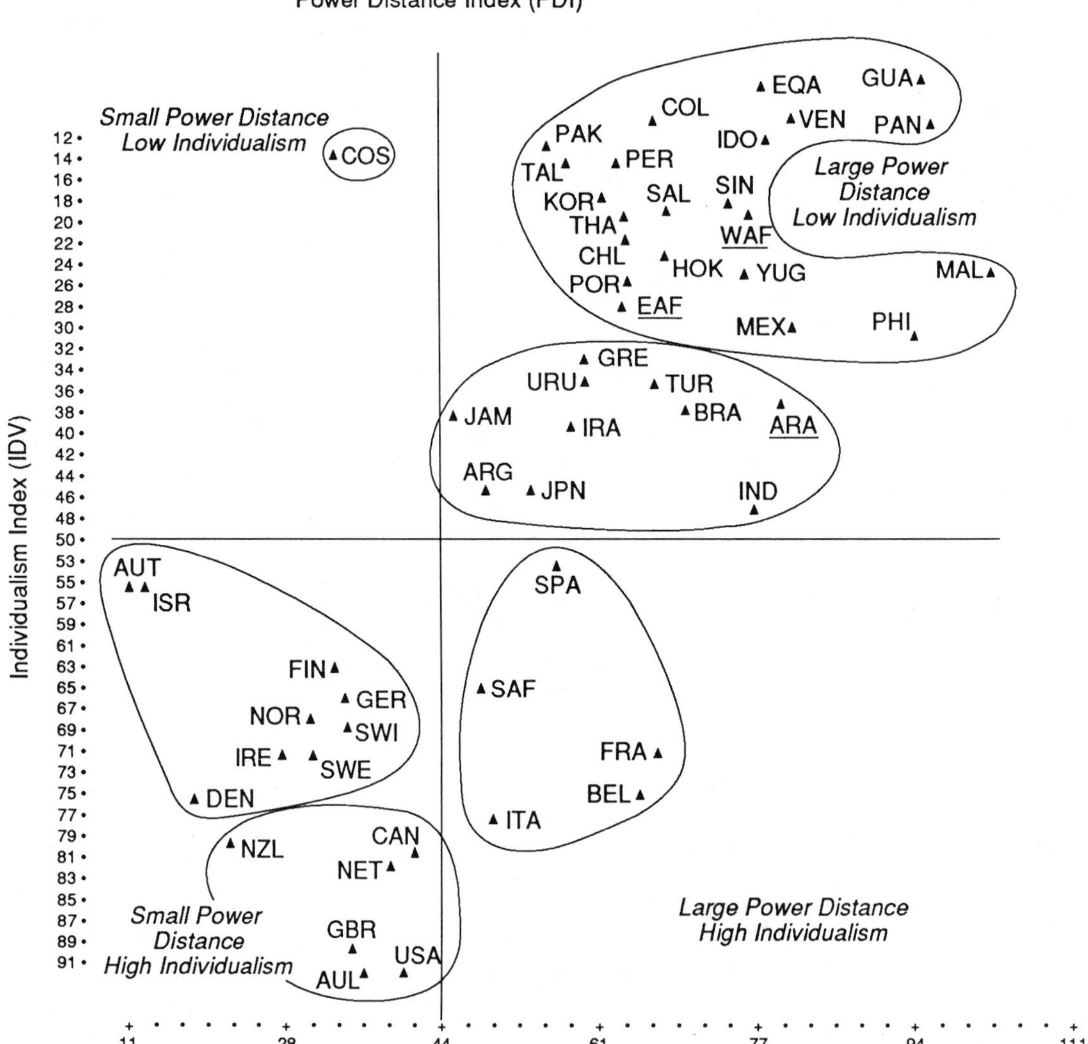

Uncertainty Avoidance

The third dimension is labeled "Uncertainty Avoidance." The fundamental issue involved here is how society deals with the fact that time runs only one way; that is, we are all caught in the reality of past, present and future, and we have to live with uncertainty because the future is unknown and always will be. Some societies socialize their members into accepting this uncertainty and not becoming upset by it. People in such societies will tend to accept each day as it comes. They will take risks rather easily. They will not work as hard. They will be relatively tolerant of behavior and opinions different from their own because they do not feel threatened by them. Such societies can be called "weak Uncertainty Avoidance" societies; they are societies in which people have a natural tendency to feel relatively secure.

Other societies socialize their people into trying to beat the future. Because the future remains essentially unpredictable, in those societies there will be a higher level of anxiety in people, which becomes manifest in greater nervousness, emotionality, and aggressiveness. Such societies, called "strong Uncertainty Avoidance" societies, also have institutions that try to create security and avoid risk. We can create security in 3 ways. One is technology, in the broadest sense of the word. Through technology we protect ourselves from the risks of nature and war. We build houses, dikes, power stations, and ICBMs which are meant to give us a feeling of security. The second way of creating security is law, again in the broadest sense of the word. Through laws and all kinds of formal rules and institutions, we protect ourselves from the unpredictability of human behavior. The proliferation of laws and rules implies an intolerance of deviant behaviours and opinions. Where laws cannot be made because the subject is too fuzzy, we can create a feeling of security by the nomination of experts. Experts are people whose word we accept as a kind of law because we assume them to be beyond uncertainty. The third way of creating a feeling of security is religion, once more in the broadest sense of the word. This sense includes secular religions and ideologies, such as Marxism, dogmatic Capitalism, or movements that preach an escape into meditation. Even science is included. All human societies have their religions in some way or another. All religions, in some way, make uncertainty tolerable, because they all contain a message that is beyond uncertainty, that helps us to accept the uncertainty of today because we interpret experiences in terms of something bigger and more powerful that transcends personal reality. In strongly Uncertainty Avoiding societies we find religions which claim absolute truth and which do not tolerate other religions. We also find in such societies a scientific tradition looking for ultimate, absolute truths, as opposed to a more relativist, empiricist tradition in the weak Uncertainty Avoidance societies.

The Uncertainty Avoidance dimension, thus, implies a number of things, from aggressiveness to a need for absolute truth, that we do not usually consider as belonging together. They appear to belong together in the logic of culture patterns, but this logic differs from our own daily logic. Without research we would not have found that, on the level of societies, these things go together.

Figure 4 plots the Uncertainty Avoidance index for 50 countries along the vertical axis, against the Power Distance index on the horizontal axis. We find several clusters of countries. There is a large cluster of countries with strong Uncertainty Avoidance and large Power Distance. They are: all the Latin countries, both Latin European and Latin American; Mediterranean countries, such as, Yugoslavia, Greece, and Turkey; and Japan plus Korea.

The Asian countries are found in 2 clusters with large Power Distance and medium to weak Uncertainty Avoidance. Then we find a cluster of German-speaking countries, including Israel and marginally Finland, combining small Power Distance with medium to strong Uncertainty Avoidance.

Figure 4

THE POSITION OF THE 50 COUNTRIES ON THE POWER DISTANCE AND UNCERTAINTY AVOIDANCE SCALES

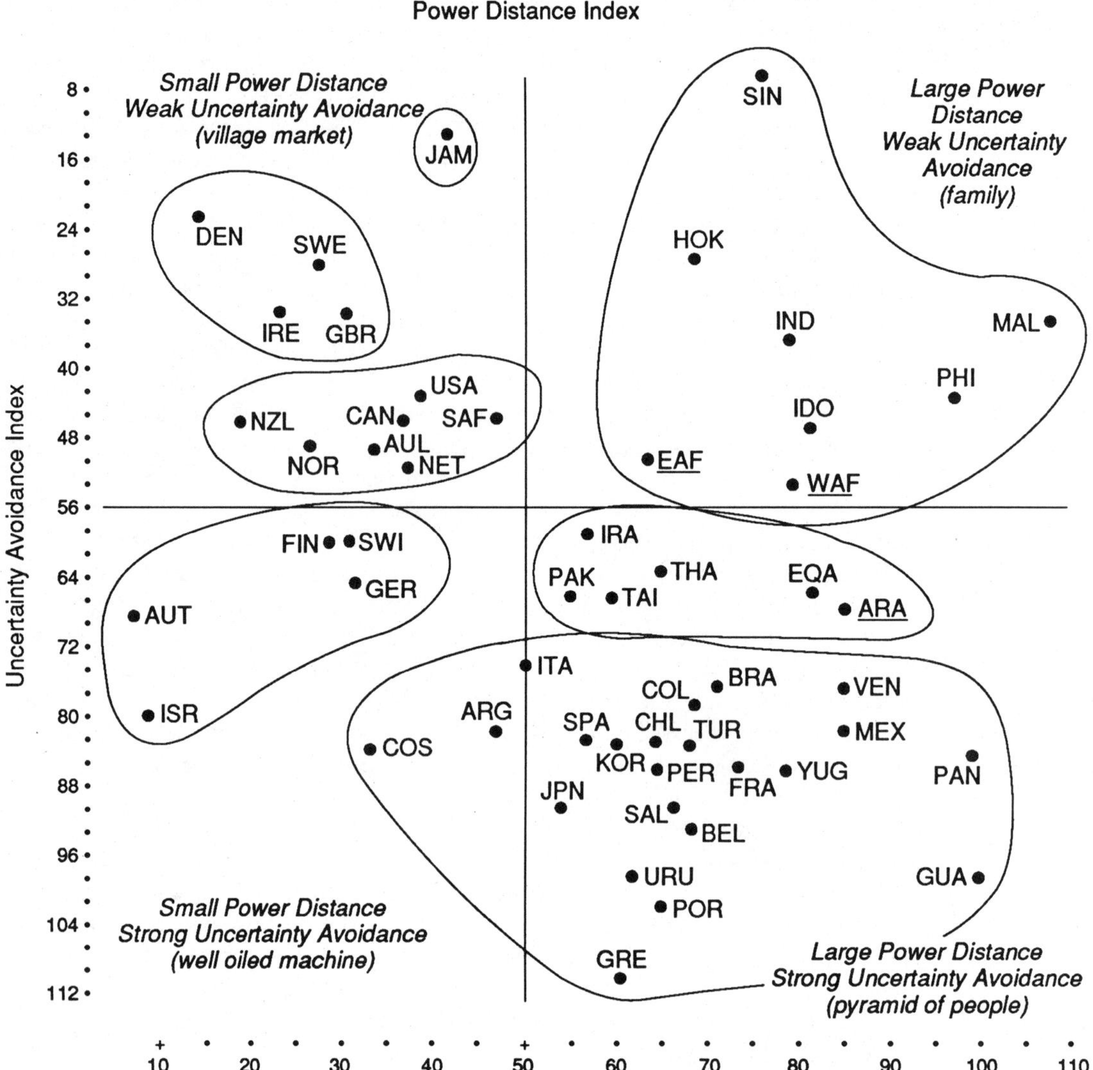

Both small Power Distance and weak Uncertainty Avoidance are found in Denmark, Sweden, Great Britain, and Ireland, while the Netherlands, U.S., Norway, and the other Anglo countries are in the middle.

Masculinity-Femininity

The fourth dimension is labeled "Masculinity versus Femininity." The fundamental issue involved is the division of roles between the sexes in society. All societies have to deal with the basic fact that one half of mankind is female and the other male. The only activities that are strictly determined by the sex of a person are those related to procreation. Men cannot have babies. Human societies, however, through the ages and around the globe, have also associated other roles to men only, or to women only. This is called social, rather than biological, sex role division.

All social role divisions are more or less arbitrary, and what is seen as a typical task for men or for women can vary from one society to the other. We can classify societies on whether they try to minimize or to maximize the social sex role division. Some societies allow both men and women to take many different roles. Others make a sharp division between what men should do and what women should do. In this latter case, the distribution is always such that men take the more assertive and dominant roles and women the more service-oriented and caring roles. I have called those societies with a maximized social sex role division "Masculine," and those with a relatively small social sex role division "Feminine." In Masculine societies, the traditional masculine social values permeate the whole society—even the way of thinking of the women. These values include the importance of showing off, of performing, of achieving something visible, of making money, of "big is beautiful." In more Feminine societies, the dominant values—for both men and women—are those more traditionally associated with the feminine role: not showing off, putting relationships with people before money, minding the quality of life and the preservation of the environment, helping others, in particular the weak, and "small is beautiful." In a masculine society, the public hero is the successful achiever, the superman. In a more Feminine society, the public sympathy goes to the anti-hero, the underdog. Individual brilliance in a Feminine society is suspect.

Following the procedure used for the other dimensions, each of the 50 countries was given an index score on the Masculinity-Femininity scale: a high score means a more Masculine, a low score a more Feminine country. Figure 5 plots the Masculinity index score horizontally and the Uncertainty Avoidance index again vertically. The most Masculine country is Japan; also quite Masculine are the German-speaking countries: Germany, Austria, and Switzerland. Moderately Masculine are a number of Latin countries, such as Venezuela, Mexico, and Italy; also the entire cluster of Anglo countries including some of their former colonies: India and the Philippines.

On the far end towards the Feminine side we find the 4 Nordic countries and the Netherlands. Some Latin and Mediterranean countries like Yugoslavia, Chile, Portugal, Spain, and France are moderately Feminine.

Some Consequences for Management Theory and Practice

The naive assumption that management is the same or is becoming the same around the world is not tenable in view of these demonstrated differences in national cultures. Consider a few of the ideas about management which have been popularized in the Western literature in the past 15 years; in particular, about leadership, about models of organization, and about motivation. These theories were almost without exception made in the U.S.; in fact, the post-World War II management literature is entirely U.S. dominated. This reflects the economic importance of the U.S. during this period,

Figure 5

THE POSITION OF THE 50 COUNTRIES ON THE UNCERTAINTY AVOIDANCE AND MASCULINITY SCALES

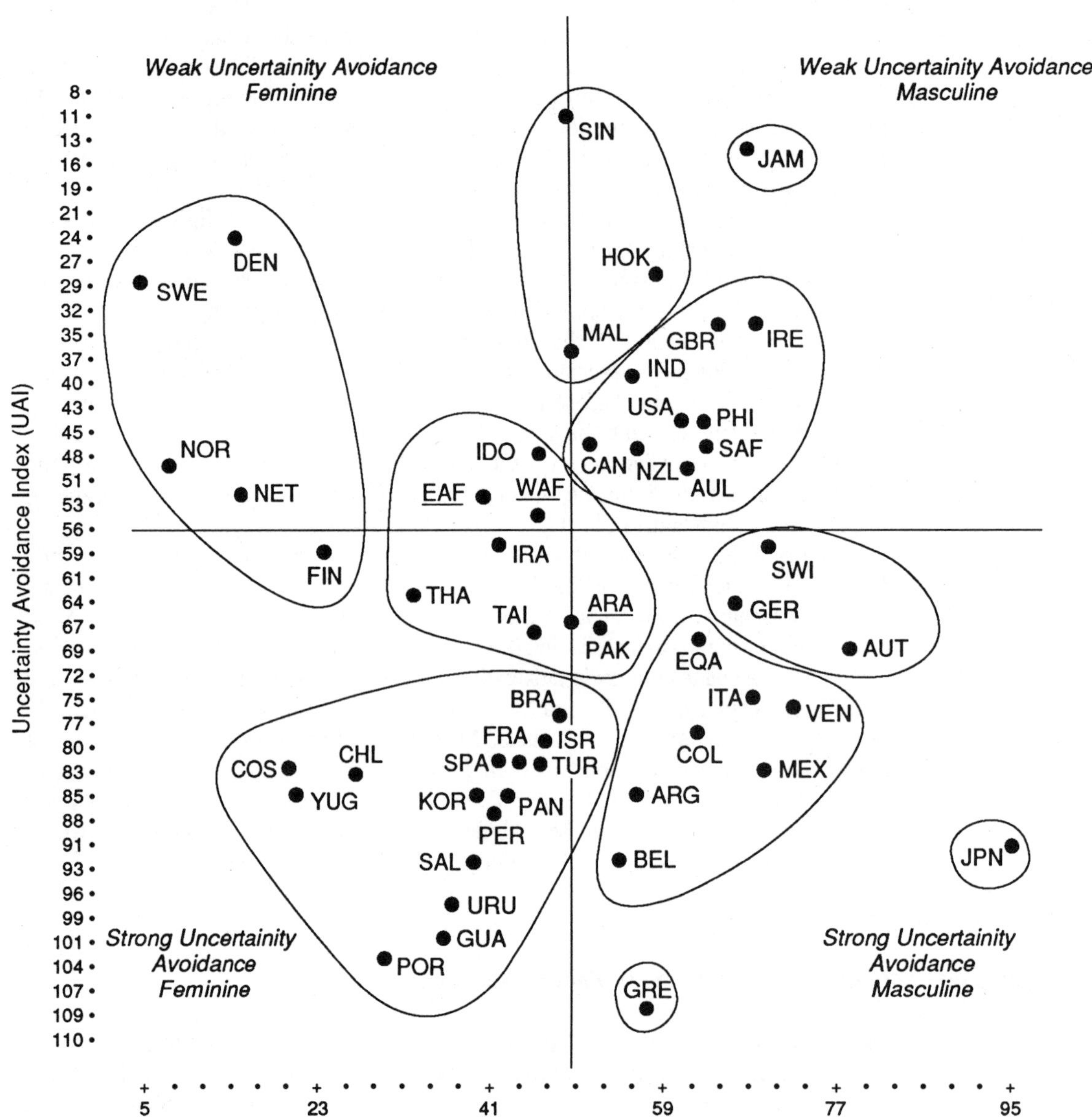

but culturally the U.S. is just one country among all others, with its particular configuration of cultural values which differs from that of most other countries.

Leadership

The most relevant dimensions for leadership are Individualism and Power Distance. Let us look at Figure 3 again. We find the U.S. in an extreme position on the Individualism scale (50 out of 50) and just below average on the Power Distance scale (16 out of 50). What does the high Individualism score mean? U.S. leadership theories are about leading individuals based on the presumed needs of individuals who seek their ultimate self-interest. For example, the word "duty," which implies obligations towards others or towards society, does not appear at all in the U.S. leadership theories.

Leadership in a Collectivist society—basically any Third World country—is a group phenomenon. A working group which is not the same as the natural ingroup will have to be made into another ingroup in order to be effective. People in these countries are able to bring considerable loyalty to their job, providing they feel that the employer returns the loyalty in the form of protection, just like their natural ingroup does.

Let us now look at the Power Distance dimension, in terms of participative leadership. What does participative leadership U.S. style mean?

Individual subordinates are allowed to participate in the leader's decisions, but these remain the leader's decisions; it is the leader who keeps the initiative. Management prerogatives are very important in the U.S. Let us remember that on Power Distance, the U.S. is more or less in the middle zone. In countries with higher Power Distances—such as, many Third World countries, but also France and Belgium—individual subordinates as a rule do not want to participate. It is part of their expectations that leaders lead autocratically, and such subordinates will, in fact, by their own behavior make it difficult for leaders to lead in any other way. There is very little participative leadership in France and Belgium. If the society is at the same time Collectivist, however, there will be ways by which subordinates in a group can still influence the leader. This applies to all Asian countries.

Let us take some countries on the other side, however: Denmark, Sweden, or Israel. In this case, subordinates will not necessarily wait until their boss takes the initiative to let them participate. They will, for example, support forms of employee codetermination in which either individuals or groups can take initiatives towards management. In these cultures there are no management prerogatives that are automatically accepted; anything a boss does may be challenged by the subordinates. Management privileges in particular are much more easily accepted in U.S. than in some of the very low Power Distance countries. A similar difference is found in the ratios between management compensation and subordinate compensation.

Organization

In organizations the decisive dimensions of culture are Power Distance and Uncertainty Avoidance. Organizations are devices to distribute power, and they also serve to avoid uncertainty, to make things predictable. So let us look at Figure 4 again. My former colleague, Professor James Stevens from *INSEAD,* once gave the same description of an organizational problem to separate groups of French, West German, and British management students. The problem described a conflict between 2 departments. The students were asked to determine what was wrong and what should be done to resolve the problem. The French in majority referred the problem to the next higher authority level. The Germans suggested the setting of rules to resolve such problems in the future. The British wanted to improve communications between the 2 department heads, perhaps by some kind of human relations training. My colleague concluded that the dominant underlying model of an organization for the French was a pyramid, a hierarchical structure held together by the unity of command (larger Power Distance) as well as by rules (strong Uncertainty Avoidance). The model for the Germans was a well-oiled machine; the exercise of personal command was largely unnecessary because the rules settled everything (strong Uncertainty Avoidance, but smaller Power Distance). The model for the British was a village market: no decisive hierarchy, flexible rules, and a resolution of problems by negotiating (small Power Distance and weak Uncertainty Avoidance). These models left one corner in the diagram of Figure 4 unexplained, but a discussion with an Indian colleague led me to believe that the underlying model of an organization for the Indians is the family: undisputed personal authority of the father-leader but few formal rules (large Power Distance and weak Uncertainty Avoidance). This should also apply in the Chinese culture city-states of Hong Kong and Singapore (see Figure 4).

The U.S. is close to the center of the diagram of Figure 4 and so are the Netherlands and Switzerland. This may explain something of the success of U.S., Dutch, and Swiss multinationals in operating in a variety of cultures; in the U.S. literature and practice, all 4 models of organization—the pyramid, the well-oiled machine, the village market, and the family—can be found, but none of them can be considered dominant.

Motivation

The theories of motivation (what makes people act) and the practices of motivating people can both be related to the Individualism-Collectivism dimension. In the U.S., the highest motivation is supposed to stem from the individuals' need to fulfill their obligations towards themselves. We find terms like "self-actualization" and "self-respect" on the top of the list of motivators. In a more Collectivist society, however, people will try primarily to fulfill their obligations towards their ingroup. This may be their family, but their collective loyalty may also be directed towards some larger unit: their enterprise, or their country. Such people do not seek self-actualization or self-respect, but they primarily seek "face" in their relationships with ingroup members. The importance of face as a motivator does not appear in the U.S. motivation literature at all. The distinction between "face" cultures and "self-respect" cultures is similar to the distinction between "shame" and "guilt" cultures identified by the anthropologist Ruth Benedict [1974].

Other dimensions relevant to motivation are Uncertainty Avoidance and Masculinity-Femininity. Let us look at Figure 5 again. The dominant theme of the U.S. literature of the past 20 years is that people are basically motivated by a desire to achieve something. We should, therefore, allow our people to achieve: give them challenge, and enrich their jobs if they do not contain any challenge. The idea of "achievement" and "challenge," U.S. style, implies 2 things: a willingness to take some risks (weak Uncertainty Avoidance) and a need to perform, to assert oneself (Masculinity). It is therefore no wonder that in the diagram of Figure 5 we find the U.S. in the weak Uncertainty Avoidance, Masculine corner. It shares this position with the other Anglo countries. Let us take the case of some other countries, however: Japan or Germany. These are also Masculine countries but with stronger Uncertainty Avoidance. This means that in these countries there is less willingness to take risks: security is a powerful motivator. People are very willing to perform if they are offered security in exchange. Interestingly, these security-seeking countries seem to have been doing better economically in the past 20 years than the risk takers; but the management theories that tell us that risk taking is a good thing were made in the U.S. or Great Britain, not in Japan or Germany.

If we go to the other corner of Figure 5, we find the Netherlands and the Nordic countries combining weak Uncertainty Avoidance with a more Feminine value system. Here, the maintenance of good interpersonal relations is a strong motivator, and people frown at competition for performance. In these countries we meet a powerful interpersonal motivation which is missing in the U.S. theories. There is striking difference in the forms of "humanization of work" proposed in the U.S. and in Sweden: a stress in the U.S. on creating possibilities for individual performance, but a stress in Sweden on creating possibilities for interpersonal solidarity. In the fourth corner of Figure 5, we find both security and interpersonal motivation; Yugoslav worker self-management contains both elements. We are far away here from the motivation to achieve according to the U.S. style.

Conclusion: The Cultural Relativity of Management and Organization Practices and Theories

Both management practitioners and management theorists over the past 80 years have been blind to the extent to which activities like "management" and "organizing" are culturally dependent. They are culturally dependent because managing and organizing do not consist of making or moving tangible objects, but of manipulating symbols which have meaning to the people who are managed or organized. Because the meaning which we associate with symbols is heavily affected by what we have learned in our family, in our school, in our work environment, and in our society, management and organization are penetrated with culture from the beginning to the end. Practice is usually wiser than theory, and if we see what effective organizations in different cultures have done, we recognize that their leaders did adapt foreign management ideas to local cultural conditions. This happened extremely effectively in Japan, where mainly U.S. management theories were taken over but in an adapted form. This adaptation led to entirely new forms of practice which in the Japanese case were highly successful. An example is the Quality Control Circle, originally based on U.S. impulses but adapted to the Japanese uncertainty-avoiding, semicollectivist environment. The Quality Control Circle has been so effective in Japan that now the Americans are bringing it back to the U.S.; but is doubtful whether most of its present U.S. protagonists realize the role that Japanese educational and social conditions play in the ability of Japanese workers to function effectively in a Quality Control Circle.

Not all other countries have been as fortunate as Japan in that a successful adaptation of American management theories and practices could take place. In Europe but even more often in Third World countries, foreign management methods and ideas were indiscriminately imported as a part of "technology transfer." The evident failure of much of the international development assistance of the 60s and 70s is at least partly due to this lack of cultural sensitivity in the transfer of management ideas. It has caused enormous economic losses and human suffering. Free market capitalism as practised in the U.S., for example, is an idea which is deeply rooted historically and culturally in Individualism. "Everybody for himself" is supposed to lead to the highest common good, according to Adam Smith [1970]. If this idea is forced upon a traditionally Collectivist society, it means that work organizations will be created which do not offer to employees the protection which they expect to get in exchange for their loyalty. The system itself in such a society breeds disloyal, irresponsible employees. Japan has not taken over this aspect of capitalism and has maintained a much higher level of protection of employees by their organization. Many U.S. managers and politicians have great problems with recognizing that their type of capitalism is culturally unsuitable for a more Collectivist society. It is for good cultural reasons that various forms of state capitalism or state socialism are tried in Third World countries.

Most present-day management theories are "ethnocentric," that is, they take the cultural environment of the theorist for granted. What we need is more cultural sensitivity in management theories; we could call the result "organizational anthropology" or "management anthropology." It is unlikely to be the product of one single country's intellectual effort; it needs by definition a synergy between ideas from different sources. The fact that no single country now enjoys a degree of economic dominance as the U.S. once did will certainly help: economic power is all too often related to intellectual influence. In a world in which economic power is more widely spread, we can more easily hope to recognize truth coming from many sources. In this process, the contribution of Japanese and Chinese scholars, for example, will be vital, because they represent sources of practical wisdom and ideas which complement practices and ideas born in Europe and the U.S.

The convergence of management will never come. What we can bring about is an understanding of how the culture in which we grew up and which is dear to us affects our thinking differently from other peoples' thinking, and what this means for the transfer of management practices and theories. What this can also lead to is a better ability to manage intercultural negotiations and multicultural organizations like the United Nations, which are essential for the common survival of us all.

References

Benedict, Ruth. *The Chrysanthemum and the Sword: Patterns of Japanese Culture*. New York, NY: New American Library, 1974 (1946), p. 222.

Hofstede, Geert. *Culture's Consequences: International Differences in Work-Related Values*. Beverly Hills/London: SAGE Publications, 1980.

______. "Dimensions of National Cultures in Fifty Countries and Three Regions." In *Expiscations in Cross-Cultural Psychology*, edited by J. Deregowski, S. Dziurawiec, and R. C. Annis. Lisse, Netherlands: Swets and Zeitlinger, 1983.

Smith, Adam. *The Wealth of Nations*. Harmondsworth, UK: Penguin, 1970 (1776).

2. EMPLOYMENT TRENDS IN DEVELOPING COUNTRIES, 1960–80 AND BEYOND

MICHAEL HOPKINS
International Labour Office.

The purpose of this article is to give a broad picture of what is currently happening to the levels and structure of employment in the Third World as well as of developments over the past 20 years or so. It is divided into five sections: the first examines a number of basic economic indicators for the major developing regions of the world; the second analyses trends in the structure of labour supply and economic output from 1960 to 1980; the third discusses available country-specific data concerning trends in the employment status of individuals; the fourth uses available data in order to assess the changes in both unemployment and underemployment in response to lower economic growth rates caused by the recession of the early 1980s; and a final section summarises the findings and draws some conclusions.

1. General Economic Situation

Table 1 presents some basic economic data for 92 developing countries (all countries in the developing world with more than 1 million people in the middle of 1979—China is excluded because of lack of data). It covers 2,254 million people, or 97 per cent of the developing world (excluding China). The regional classification of these 92 countries (see appendix) is not only geographical but also distinguishes between different levels of income and identifies major oil exporters in the Middle East and Africa. It can be seen that Latin America and the Caribbean (middle-income) and the major oil exporters in the Middle East and Africa account for slightly more than half the developing countries'[1] GDP with less than a fifth of their total population, while India and Asia (low-income) with more than half of the population have just over one-sixth of total GDP.

As well as the inequalities between regions, what is most revealing is the impact of the world recession on economic growth rates. On average the developing world's economies grew by around 5.5 per cent per annum between 1960 and 1980. However, for both 1981 and 1982 (forecast) growth was less than 1 per cent per annum for all developing countries taken together, despite the fact that population grew at

Michael Hopkins, "Employment Trends in Developing Countries, 1960–80 and Beyond," *International Labor Review* 122.4 (July-August 1983): 461–478.

The author wishes to thank Tita Mesa for assembling the data on which this article is based. He is also grateful to Farhad Mehran and James N. Ypsilantis of the ILO Bureau of Statistics for help in preparing some of the labour statistics, and to them and Jean Mouly, Rolph Van Der Hoeven, Peter Richards and Gerry Rodgers for comments on an earlier draft.

Table 1

ECONOMIC GROWTH IN DEVELOPING COUNTRIES, 1960–82

Region	% of Total Population In 1980[1]	% of Total GDP In 1980[2]	GDP/Capita In 1980[2] Rates (US$ 1975)	GDP Average Annual Growth 1960-70[3]	1970-80[4]	1980-81[5]	1981-82[3] (Est)	Annual Population Growth[3] (1970–80)
Latin America and Caribbean (middle-income)	13.8	35.9	1,333	5.6	5.6	1.0	−0.1	2.5
Latin America and Caribbean (low-income)	2.0	2.6	638	5.2	3.7	2.0	1.6	2.8
Asia (middle-income)	7.9	10.8	697	7.5	8.0	7.2	4.3	2.5
Asia (low-income)	20.8	8.3	204	4.1	5.8	6.5	5.0	2.3
India	30.3	8.6	145	3.2	3.6	4.5	3.2	2.2
Africa and Middle East (oil exporters)	4.6	14.3	1,593	8.9	7.3	−8.2 (−1.8)[6]	−2.6 (−6.1)[6]	3.4
Africa and Middle East (middle-income)	12.0	16.8	715	7.6	4.8	−0.2 (4.1)[7]	−0.1 (4.3)[7]	2.8
Africa (low-income)	8.5	2.7	163	3.4	1.8	2.2	2.3	2.7
Total or average (all regions)	100	100	355	5.9	5.5	0.82	0.77	2.4

Sources: [1]From United Nations Population Division. [2]Based on sources 3 and 4. [3]Based on GDP data from United Nations, Department of International Economic and Social Affairs. *Handbook of world development statistics, 1982* (New York, 1982). [4]From World Bank: *World development report*, 1982 (New York, Oxford University Press, 1982). [5]Estimates based on country growth rates from UNCIAD and ECLA data files in October 1982. [6]Excluding Iraq. [7]Excluding Iran.

around 2.4 per cent per annum between 1970 and 1980; in other words, if this population growth is continuing in the early 1980s, then per capita incomes are falling in developing countries—a situation that has occurred only in some parts of Africa over the past 20 years. Most seriously affected are Latin America and the Caribbean, Africa and the Middle East. In fact the Middle Eastern situation is somewhat confused, not only because of declining oil prices in the early 1980s (e.g. per capita income in Kuwait fell by 17.8 per cent in 1981 and was expected to decline by 14.2 per cent in 1982), but also because turbulence in Iran and Iraq and war between them led to serious instability in the region. (Iran, with a population of around 38 million, had a decline in GDP of 12.4 per cent in 1981 while in Iraq, with 13 million people, the decline was 40 per cent in the same year.)

The situation in Asia is somewhat brighter. The astonishing growth of the economies of six of the countries in middle-income Asia of 8.0 per cent per annum in the 1970s tapered off in 1981 to 7.2 per cent and, largely because of the recession, was expected to decline to about 4.3 per cent in 1982. This growth is still higher than their population growth rate (2.5 per cent per annum from 1970 to 1980). Asia (low-income) and India were expected to have economic growth rates in 1982 which exceed those for population, hence, on average at least, some increase in material prosperity can be expected. Even in middle-income Africa and the Middle East, when Jordan, Turkey and Iran are excluded, the economic growth rate for 1981 was 4.0 per cent and was expected to be 4.4 per cent in 1982. These rates, too, are likely to exceed population growth rates.

The above does not imply that even higher economic growth rates and lower population growth rates should be the main development objectives. Lower population growth usually follows and is accompanied by egalitarian development. Similarly, a move towards egalitarianism would reduce levels of underemployment in that it would share out a larger slice of the GNP cake while at the same time giving an impetus to economic growth by allowing untapped human resources a chance to contribute. Economic growth earned in this way may be sacrificed in the short term under certain conditions, but is likely to be more sustained and equitable in the long term.[2]

2. General Employment Situation: Labour Supply and Output[3]

Table 2 illustrates the major structural changes in the economics of the 92 developing countries (in this table some data are also shown for China). The most striking of these is the relative decline in the share of agriculture both as the major contributor of GDP and as a provider of jobs (as proxied for by labour force figures at least), a decline which is accompanied by an increase in the shares of industry and services. Particularly noteworthy is the rise in industry GDP in the industrialisation/import substitution phase of the 1960s (from 30 to 38 per cent), compared to the smaller change in industrialisation in the 1970s (from 38 to 39 per cent).

Another important phenomenon is the rise in importance of the service sector. Not only was it the largest source of GDP by 1980; it also provided a larger source of jobs than the industrial sector. If as countries develop they adopt the same structure

Table 2

STRUCTURE OF PRODUCTION AND LABOUR FORCE 1960, 1970 and 1980[1] (% SHARE OF TOTAL)

Region	Agriculture						Industry						Services					
	1960		1970		1980		1960		1970		1980		1960		1970		1980	
	GDP	LF	GDP	LF	GDP	LF	GDP	LF	GDP	LF	GDP	LF	GDP	LF	GDP	LF	GDP	LF
Latin America and Caribbean (middle)	16.0	45.6	12.8	38.9	10.5	31.8	35.9	20.7	38.4	22.4	38.5	25.8	48.1	33.6	48.8	38.6	51.0	42.4
Latin America and Caribbean (low)	25.7	63.5	21.7	56.6	16.7	49.3	27.8	14.8	30.8	16.3	32.0	19.8	46.5	21.7	47.5	27.1	51.3	30.9
Asia (middle)	35.1	68.0	26.6	60.0	18.1	52.5	21.0	12.2	29.0	15.9	36.2	19.4	43.9	19.8	44.4	24.2	45.7	28.1
Asia (low)	50.5	76.4	44.0	71.5	32.9	65.5	17.3	8.1	21.9	9.4	27.3	11.8	32.2	15.5	34.1	19.1	39.8	22.6
India	50.9	74.0	44.1	69.3	37.2	62.2	19.4	11.3	23.3	13.5	24.7	17.2	39.6	14.6	32.6	17.2	38.1	20.6
Africa and Middle East (oil)	28.8	68.8	13.7	60.0	7.9	51.8	48.1	11.2	67.5	14.7	62.5	18.3	23.1	20.0	18.8	25.3	29.6	29.9
Africa and Middle East (middle)	32.8	69.8	23.8	63.0	20.1	55.6	29.7	12.2	39.5	15.3	35.5	19.0	37.5	17.9	36.7	21.6	44.4	25.4
Africa (low)	54.7	87.6	44.5	83.7	41.0	80.0	13.2	5.1	17.3	6.8	16.6	8.6	32.1	7.3	38.2	9.6	42.4	11.4
China	–	74.8	–	67.8	31.0	60.0	–	15.4	–	20.4	47.0	25.8	–	9.8	–	11.9	22.0	14.1
Overall	30.9	72.6	22.9	66.4	17.3	59.1	30.0	12.8	38.1	16.0	38.5	19.9	39.1	14.5	39.0	17.7	44.2	21.0

[1]The composition of the three economic sectors is (1) *Agriculture:* agriculture, forestry, hunting and fishing: (2) *Industry:* mining and quarrying, manufacturing, construction and public utilities (electricity, gas, water and sanitary services): (3) *Services:* commerce, transport, storage and communications,and public and private services.

Sources: GDP: Same as source 3, table 1; China 1980 figures same as a source 4, table 1. Labour force (LF): ILO Bureau of Statistics.

as richer Third World countries, e.g. those in Latin America, then agriculture will be superseded as a provider of jobs and (relatively) as a source of GDP by the service sector (look, for example, at the structure of GDP and labour force in middle-income Latin America in table 2). In that case those who see agricultural development as the key to overall development are likely to be running against the course of history.[4] Hence it might be profitable to undertake new research on the dynamics of both the industrial and service sectors as major absorbers of manpower in the future and, in particular, to give more weight than hitherto to the relatively neglected service sector in developing countries.

All the regions reveal the same general pattern, although to different degrees. China, with labour increasingly being incorporated in the industrial and service sectors, is no exception. In the oil-exporting Middle East and Africa (Nigeria), the agricultural share of output drastically declined from 29 to 8 per cent in the period 1960-80. This is unsurprising because of the rise of oil prices and production. However, labour moved more slowly: 69 per cent of the labour force were in agriculture in 1960 and 52 per cent remained there in 1980.

The ratio of GDP to labour force provides a rough index of per capita labour income. Table 3 gives the change in labour income from 1960 to 1980.[5] It can be seen that overall labour incomes nearly doubled over the period, with the greatest increase arising from industry followed by services, with agriculture lagging behind. That the overall increase was greater than in individual sectors illustrates, again, the extent of labour migration from agriculture into the higher-paid sectors, industry and services. Individual regions followed the general trend, with only a few exceptions.

Table 4 gives some data showing the composition of the labour force by sex and how it has changed over time. In every region there are proportionately fewer women in the labour force (as conventionally measured) than men, ranging from around 38 per cent of the labour force in Asia (middle-income) to around 23 per cent in middle-income Latin America and the Caribbean. Taking all sectors together, it

Table 3

SECTORAL GDP INDEX AND AVERAGE INCOME[1] PER LABOUR FORCE MEMBER, 1980 (1960=100)

Region	Agriculture	Industry	Services	Overall
Latin America and Caribbean (middle)	166 (1,445)	153 (6,566)	150 (5,297)	178 (4,399)
Latin America and Caribbean (low)	128 (688)	132 (3,285)	119 (3,381)	154 (2,034)
Asia (middle)	174 (519)	279 (2,800)	190 (2,436)	259 (1,501)
Asia (low)	134 (249)	186 (1,145)	145 (870)	172 (496)
India	109 (214)	105 (512)	114 (662)	126 (358)
Africa and Middle East (oil)	102 (717)	222 (16,102)	240 (4,670)	279 (4,716)
Africa and Middle East (middle)	148 (749)	147 (3,858)	160 (3,613)	192 (2,067)
Africa (low)	92 (206)	82 (774)	95 (1,500)	111 (402)
Overall	130 (406)	165 (3,152)	153 (2,485)	191 (1,377)

[1]Average income figures for 1980 are given in parentheses (in 1975 $).
Sources: Labour force figures from ILO Bureau of Statistics. GDP from source 3, table 1.

Table 4

STRUCTURE OF LABOUR FORCE BY SEX, 1960, 1970 AND 1980
(% DISTRIBUTION BY SEX, SECTOR, YEAR AND REGION)

Region		1960				1970				1980			
		Ag	Ind	Serv	Total	Ag	Ind	Serv	Total	Ag	Ind	Serv	Total
Latin America and	M	92.8	83.8	66.9	82.0	93.2	83.8	62.2	79.2	91.8	84.7	61.7	77.2
Caribbean (middle)	F	7.8	16.2	33.1	18.0	6.8	16.2	37.8	20.8	8.2	15.3	38.3	22.8
Latin America and	M	82.7	77.0	54.0	75.7	85.4	78.3	55.5	76.2	85.7	79.4	56.2	75.4
Caribbean (low)	F	17.3	23.0	46.0	24.3	14.6	21.7	44.5	23.8	14.3	20.6	43.8	24.6
Asia (middle)	M	60.5	66.3	65.2	62.1	58.9	68.3	62.5	61.3	59.3	68.2	61.8	61.7
	F	39.5	33.6	34.8	37.9	41.1	31.7	37.5	38.7	40.7	31.8	38.2	38.3
Asia (low)	M	71.4	76.8	74.5	72.3	72.0	72.4	73.3	72.3	72.4	72.8	73.5	72.7
	F	28.6	23.2	25.5	27.6	28.0	27.6	26.7	27.7	27.6	27.2	26.5	27.3
China	M	55.0	80.0	83.7	61.6	56.2	71.3	79.5	62.1	55.9	69.4	77.3	62.4
	F	45.0	20.0	16.3	38.4	43.8	28.7	20.5	37.9	44.1	30.6	22.7	37.6
India	M	64.6	75.4	84.2	68.7	62.1	73.9	83.8	67.4	62.3	72.9	82.6	68.3
	F	35.4	24.6	15.8	31.3	37.9	26.1	16.2	32.6	37.7	27.1	17.4	31.7
Africa and Middle	M	64.0	80.7	61.5	65.3	67.2	75.4	59.3	66.4	68.8	75.9	59.2	67.2
East (oil)	F	36.0	19.3	38.5	34.7	32.8	24.6	40.7	33.6	31.2	24.1	40.8	32.8
Africa and Middle	M	71.4	85.7	83.7	75.4	72.1	85.5	80.0	75.8	71.3	85.6	78.8	75.9
East (middle)	F	28.6	14.3	16.3	24.6	27.9	14.5	20.0	24.2	28.7	14.4	21.2	24.1
Africa (low)	M	61.5	81.5	74.7	63.5	61.6	79.7	74.0	64.0	61.8	79.1	74.3	64.7
	F	38.5	18.5	25.3	36.5	38.4	20.3	26.0	36.0	38.2	20.9	25.7	35.3
Overall	M	63.3	79.0	76.9	67.3	63.5	74.3	74.1	67.1	63.6	73.5	73.1	67.6
	F	36.7	21.0	23.1	32.7	36.5	25.7	25.9	32.9	36.4	26.5	26.9	32.4

Source: ILO Bureau of Statistics.

can be seen that women's share of the labour force remained constant for all the developing countries over the period 1960-80 (32.7 per cent in 1960 and 32.4 per cent in 1980). Individual regions and sectors varied, however. From 1960 to 1980 female participation in the agricultural labour force increased in four regions and decreased in five, in industry it increased in six regions and decreased in three, and in services it increased in eight regions and decreased in one. The main change, therefore, is the relative increase of women in industry and services compared to men over time.

3. Status in Employment

Data for three status groups, namely self-employed, employees and unpaid family workers, are given in table 5 for 11 developing countries for which reasonably good data exist for years around both 1970 and 1980.

In general it can be seen that self-employment (i.e. the proportion of employers and own-account workers) decreased over the period in seven countries, the proportion of employees increased in all cases and the proportion of unpaid family workers decrease in eight out of 11 cases. This is true for women and men alike. However, women are more likely to be employees than men and this tendency is increasing over time. In addition, men are three times more likely to be self-employed than women and this relationship is quite stable over time.

An interpretation of these results suggests that the relations of production in the economies considered are becoming more capitalistic over time because wage labour is becoming much more important than self-employment or family work. In a sense, this means too that the economies are becoming more developed. The results cannot be generalised to all developing countries because most of the countries considered in table 5 have higher GNP per capita than the average for developing countries as a whole. Another interesting phenomenon is the extent to which female workers are entering into more formal employment relationships, as illustrated by their faster movement into wage labour than men.

4. Trends in Labour Force and Unemployment in Developing Countries

It would be useful to know what happened to unemployment in developing countries in the past, how the current world recession is affecting it, what will happen to the unemployed in the short to medium term, who are the most affected and what should be done about it. Unfortunately—although some people claim to have found the answer to the last question—there are a number of reasons why it is not possible to do what the OECD, for example, has done for industrialised countries. This is partly because unemployment is difficult to measure in developing countries—and is, in fact, rarely measured on a consistent basis—but also because there are conceptual, statistical, resource and political problems. The reasons for the last two types of problem are obvious enough. The poorest countries do not have the level of skilled manpower or the funds to carry out comprehensive labour force surveys

Table 5

STATUS IN EMPLOYMENT, CIRCA 1970 AND 1980 (% DISTRIBUTION)

Country		Circa 1970				Circa 1980			
		Self-Employed[1]	Employees	Unpaid Family Workers	Not Classified	Self-Employed[1]	Employees	Unpaid Family Workers	Non Classified
Costa Rica	M	19.9	69.3	7.0	3.8	.	.	.	.
	F	5.3	91.2	1.3	2.1	.	.	.	.
	T	17.1	73.5	5.9	3.5	19.6	75.3	3.9	1.3
El Salvador	M	28.0	55.8	12.3	3.9	23.4	63.3	13.0	0.4
	F	19.7	55.8	4.0	20.6	34.4	56.9	8.1	0.6
	T	26.2	55.8	10.5	7.5	27.0	61.1	11.3	0.5
Hong Kong	M	12.8	81.5	1.4	4.3	12.7	82.3	0.6	4.5
	F	5.5	86.3	3.7	4.5	4.2	88.8	3.0	4.0
	T	10.4	83.1	2.1	4.4	9.7	84.6	1.4	4.3
Indonesia	M	44.8	35.4	18.1	1.6	45.7	36.9	15.9	1.4
	F	29.1	28.2	39.8	2.9	26.5	31.3	41.0	1.2
	T	39.7	33.0	25.3	2.0	39.2	35.0	24.4	1.3
Republic of Korea	M	42.8	42.5	11.6	3.1	38.0	49.0	6.8	6.2
	F	17.4	29.6	51.4	1.7	22.4	38.0	36.1	3.4
	T	33.9	38.0	25.5	2.6	32.1	44.9	17.8	5.2
Pakistan	T	50.9	18.1	29.3	1.7	48.9	22.1	27.3	1.7
Panama	M	43.7	49.1	4.8	2.4	35.0	56.1	6.2	2.7
	F	14.4	73.0	5.0	7.6	11.3	80.3	2.0	6.4
	T	36.2	55.3	4.8	3.7	27.8	63.5	4.9	3.6
Philippines	M	42.7	39.4	15.1	2.8	44.2	42.9	11.4	1.5
	F	23.3	41.0	27.0	8.6	27.0	47.7	21.2	4.1
	T	36.5	39.9	18.9	4.7	38.8	44.4	14.5	2.3
Singapore	M	21.0	68.6	2.6	7.8	15.9	79.6	1.7	2.9
	F	8.5	68.4	5.1	18.0	5.1	87.4	4.0	3.5
	T	17.8	68.6	3.2	10.4	12.1	82.3	2.5	3.1
Thailand	M	45.4	19.9	32.6	2.2	44.9	23.4	30.7	0.9
	F	12.0	10.4	76.0	1.6	15.6	15.5	68.4	0.5
	T	29.6	15.4	53.0	1.9	31.2	19.7	48.4	0.7
Venezuela	M	36.4	54.8	1.2	7.5	.	.	.	.
	F	12.6	74.9	1.8	10.7	.	.	.	.
	T	31.1	59.4	1.3	8.3	26.5	64.2	3.2	6.1

[1]Includes employers and own-account workers only (unpaid family workers are shown separately).
Source: ILO: *Year Book of Labour Statistics* (Geneva).

and censuses, while politically the publication of unemployment data is always a sensitive issue.

Conceptually and statistically, the problem of defining who is in the labour force, what is the active population, and how someone can remain unemployed in the absence of social security has occupied labour statisticians for decades.[6] Some have even gone as far as to say that open unemployment in developing countries is a myth since a high proportion of the unemployed will be young and relatively well educated, or that the typical unemployed person is not badly off because his unemployment reflects both the ability of someone to maintain him and his high aspirations relative to the jobs available.[7] Clearly, where employment exchanges do not exist or cover only a small proportion of the workforce, as is the case in most developing countries, there can be no official unemployment count. This is not the place to go into a detailed analysis of concepts; suffice it to say that even when unemployment statistics are available in developing countries they give an unreliable and possibly misleading guide to what is happening to labour underutilisation there.[8]

What is done here is to obtain an estimate of labour productivity[9] and to apply this estimate to output in order to arrive at an estimate of persons employed. This is reported in table 6. Since output growth rates have been estimated and labour supply can be projected (see table 7), changes in labour demand and supply over time can be estimated, since the latter arise mainly from changes in population growth and participation rates, and the former largely from changes in output and productivity. Hence an index of "labour pressure" can be calculated in the light of changes in labour demand and supply. This is given in table 6. The index is set equal to 100 in the base year (1980) for all regions and varies with labour demand and supply in subsequent years. This method avoids the presentation of absolute magnitudes of unemployment, which are probably erroneous, but provides a good idea of how the pressure on the labour market evolves as the forces of supply and demand change over time.

This exercise shows that the lower growth rates in the early 1980s which are a result of (or, rather, describe) the world recession, have unsurprisingly led to higher unemployment rates (this could, perhaps, better be interpreted as a lower demand for employed persons). Overall, however, the effects are small, the rise in unemployment being 0.8 per cent for the period 1980-82 and estimated at 1.9 per cent for 1980-85 if the economic growth rates of 1980-82 continue. Individual regions vary, however, and the results bear out what one might expect, namely that those regions more integrated into the world economy—notably Latin America and the Caribbean (and in particular richer Latin America) and the Middle East oil exporters (plus Nigeria)—fare rather badly, although middle-income Asia is an exception here. The other parts of Africa and Asia are hardly affected by the recession in terms of increases in unemployment.

Whether the trend towards higher unemployment will continue to the year 2000 or not is a moot point. One major reason why it may is the higher growth of the labour force forecast for the next two decades of the century compared to the two previous decades. As shown in table 7, this phenomenon applies across all developing regions (except for China) and will occur as a result of the declining mortality rate that is itself due to the improvement in social conditions in many developing countries in the 1960s and 1970s.[10]

Table 6

TRENDS IN UNEMPLOYMENT IN DEVELOPING REGIONS, 1982-85

Region	GDP/Capita 1980 US$ 1975)	GDP Growth Rate[1] (% Per Annum) 1970-80	1980-82	Productivity[2] Growth Estimate 1980-85[2] (%)		Unemployment Indices[3] (1980 = 100) 1982		1985	
Latin America and Caribbean (middle)	1333	5.6	0.5	0	(−1.8)	104.2	(100.9)	110.3	(102.5)
Latin America and Caribbean (low)	638	3.7	1.8	0	(−0.4)	102.2	(101.5)	105.2	(103.5)
Asia (middle)	697	8.0	5.7	2.63		99.5		98.6	
Asia (low)	204	5.8	5.8	2.83		99.3		98.3	
India	145	3.6	3.9	1.49		99.7		99.2	
Africa and Middle East (oil)	1593	7.3	−4.0[4]	0	(−5.3)	111.8	(102.2)	126.6	(105.1)
Africa and Middle East (middle)	715	4.8	4.2[5]	1.43		99.9		99.7	
Africa (low)	163	1.8	2.2	0.24		100.5		101.4	
Overall average	355	5.5	0.8	0.91	(−0.51)	100.8		101.9	

[1]Geometric average of growth rates given in table 1. [2]Productivity (P = growth in output per employed person) has been estimated on the basis of the regression equation: $P = -1.38 + 0.77g - 0.000562x$ ($R^2 = 0.75$) where g = economic growth rate per annum, r = GNP per capita. Data came from 15 countries for which information was available for both 1970 and 1980. Hence, the equation is based on output growth and productivity growth estimates for the whole decade of the 1970s. As a rule of thumb, two estimates have been retained, one derived directly from the regression equation and the other set equal to zero when productivity growth estimates were negative. The reason for this is that it is thought unlikely that negative productivity growth, which is shown in parentheses, could continue for long. [3]Because of difficulties in comparing absolute open unemployment levels between countries and regions (see text), index numbers have been used to represent percentage changes in expected unemployment levels over time. The fact that all the index numbers start at 100 should not be taken to mean that unemployment is at the same level for each region in the base year 1980. See note 2 for explanation of figures in parentheses. [4]Excluding Iraq. [5]Excluding Iran.

Table 7

LABOUR FORCE GROWTH AND PROJECTIONS. 1980-2000 (93 LARGEST DEVELOPING COUNTRIES)

Region	Labour Force 1980 (000s)	Growth Rates (% Per Annum)	
		1960-80	1980-2000
Latin America and Caribbean (middle)	100,131	2.6	2.9
Latin America and Caribbean (low)	14,663	2.4	3.0
Asia (middle)	72,774	2.6	2.7
Asia (low)	165,992	2.0	2.5
China	421,904	1.4	1.3
India	266,103	1.9	2.2
Africa and Middle East (oil)	34,401	2.1	2.7
Africa and Middle East (middle)	86,427	2.1	2.8
Africa (low)	80,046	2.1	2.5
Total	1,242,441	1.9	2.1

Source: ILO Bureau of Statistics.

What the above analysis misses out, however, is the more important problem of poverty and underemployment in developing countries. The two concepts are closely related since the general consensus among labour statisticians is that the underemployed consist of those persons whose occupation is inadequate "in relation to specified norms or alternative employment, account being taken of [their] occupational skill",[11] and a distinction is drawn between visible and invisible underemployment. Visible underemployment is primarily a statistical notion denoting employment which is of shorter duration than normal, where the persons concerned are seeking or would accept additional work; invisible underemployment is an analytical concept referring to a situation reflecting low income levels and poverty, insufficient use of skills and low productivity.

In the case of invisible underemployment those who are really desperate are forced to work in some manner, often for long hours and meagre rewards. Such people suffer from lack of access to assets and services, have low or non-existent levels of education and are heavily concentrated in the rural areas. Altimir[12] quotes recent studies in Latin America which show how far the problems of poverty and underemployment overlap: there is a greater relative concentration of underemployment among poor groups, households with unemployed heads or non-active heads (housewives, disabled persons, persons living on transfers, etc.) and households with female heads. They also show that "households whose heads are visibly underemployed (up to 39 hours' work per week, but preferring to work longer) have a far higher than average probability of being poor". This leads Altimir to state that "the measurements of the extent of poverty may therefore be considered as approaches to the problem of underemployment from the welfare side, and open the way for treating the problem of poverty from the standpoint of inadequate use of human resources. In the final analysis, this approach is that of underdevelopment."

In an earlier article[13] I went further and defined all those families whose basic human needs have not been satisfied as being represented in the labour force by underemployed workers,[14] i.e. workers who do not earn enough to provide either themselves or their families with an adequate standard of living because they are unable to find work of a sufficiently remunerative and productive nature. This means that, if basic human needs are to be satisfied, either the existing jobs performed by the underemployed must be improved or new productive jobs must be created.

Using these arguments together with the estimates of poverty and underemployment in my previous article plus the recent estimates of economic growth given in the present one, I have reworked my old figures using the reduced economic growth rates over the period 1974-82 in order to take account of the current world recession. Table 8 gives estimates of the change in poverty and underemployment levels over the period 1974-82.[15]

These estimates have been based on the assumption that income distribution at the lower end remained unchanged over the period. Information on the distribution of income is rarely reliable even at a given point in time, and still less so over a period of years. It is particularly important to remember this here, since the crucial information required to estimate poverty is at the lower end of the distribution scale where self-consumption and production give rise to serious measurement problems and trends are correspondingly difficult to estimate. Nevertheless, for Latin America at least, Altimir felt confident enough to say that in the early 1970s, when economic growth was rapid, there was an improvement in the absolute level of consumption of the poor strata. On the other hand, the rise in per capita income did not reduce the relative inequality between strata but rather led to the "social stratification being reproduced on a dynamic basis". If these results are applied to underemployment it would seem that worsening income distribution might have increased underemployment if the trends of the early 1970s continued to the early 1980s but that improved levels of consumption may have checked its rise. Hence, the net effect from the mid-1970s to the early 1980s may have been small, in Latin America at least. The results for Latin America presented in table 8 support the above view with underemployment increasing modestly from 30 million in 1974 to 34 million in 1982.

Overall, underemployment in developing countries (excluding China) has slightly increased between 1974 and 1982—from 421 to 448 million—despite increases in per capita incomes of 1.8 per cent per annum. Nevertheless, the proportion of those underemployed in the population as a whole declined from 56 to 51 per cent during the period. Without the recession the total numbers in underemployment in 1982 would have been marginally higher than in 1974—422 million—if the growth rates of the period 1960-77 had continued until 1982.[16] This illustrates that, recession or no, the problem of underemployment is severe and unlikely to disappear without much greater increases in growth rates coupled with improvements in the distribution of income.

If we disaggregate the total figures for the numbers underemployed, we can see that underemployment worsened in all the developing subregions with the exception

Table 8

REGIONAL ESTIMATES OF ABSOLUTE POVERTY AND UNDEREMPLOYMENT, 1974 AND 1982

Region[1]	Population (Millions) 1974[2]	Population (Millions) 1982[3]	Numbers (Millions) And % In Basic-Needs Poverty[4] 1974	%	1982	%	Under-employed (Millions)[5] 1974	Under-employed (Millions)[5] 1982	% Population Growth, 1974-82 (Per Annum)[6]	% GNP Capita Growth, 1974-82 (Per Annum)[7]	
Latin America (middle)	210	256	65	(31)	69.9	(27.3)	21.0	22.6	2.5	1.8	(3.7)
Latin America (low)	97	121	29	(30)	35.3	(29.2)	9.2	11.2	2.8	0.4	(2.5)
Middle East and Africa (oil)	154	201	40	(26)	49.0	(24.4)	14.0	17.2	3.4	1.1	(4.7)
Asia (excl. China)	1,095	1,313	759	(69)	753.6	(57.4)	296.0	293.9	2.3	2.6	(2.1)
Africa (arid)	142	177	73	(51)	77.0	(43.5)	25.5	27.0	2.8	1.8	(1.5)
Africa (tropical)	161	199	132	(82)	181.4	(91.2)	55.4	76.2	2.7	−0.8	(1.6)
Total	1,859	2,267	1,103	(56)	1,166	(51)	421.1	448.1	2.5	1.8	(2.6)

[1]Regions correspond to those used in M. J. D. Hopkins: "A global forecast of absolute poverty and employment" in *International Labor Review,* Sep.-Oct. 1980 (henceforth MH80). A straight mapping has been made for most coefficients (e.g. growth rates) for all the regions except Asia, which is now an aggregation of Asia (middle), Asia (low) and Asia (India) in the previous tables in this article. [2]Population in 1974 from MH80, p. 574, table 4, column 1. [3]Population in 1982 is derived from 1974 population augmented annually by the average growth rates from 1970 to 1980. Since population growth rates rarely change quicklthis is a fair assumption. [4]The 1974 figures come from MH80, table 4, column 3. The 1982 figures have been estimated assuming that income distribution has remained constant over the period 1974-82 and assuming a linear relation between growth in GNP, population and basic-needs poverty. This was done as follows, Let r^2 = annual per capital growth rate 1974-82 as in MH80, p. 574, last column. Let r^4 = new annual GNP per capita growth rates. Both r^2 and r^4 are given as the last column in this table. See note 7 for description of calculations of these growth rates. Let d = old difference between numbers in basic-needs poverty between 1974 and 1982, as in MH80. Let x = new difference between numbers in basic-needs poverty between 1974 and 1982 with new growth rates taking account of the world recession. Then for each region-

$$x = d\,\frac{(1 + r^x)^8}{(1 + r^d)^8} \quad \text{(where } 8 = 1982 - 1974\text{)}$$

Knowing the numbers in basic-needs poverty in 1974 and knowing x then allows us to estimate the numbers in basic-needs poverty in 1982. [5]Following MH80 this simply applies the labour force participation rate in 1982 for each region to the numbers in poverty. Reading from top to bottom in the table, these rates were 32.3 per cent, 31.8 per cent, 35.0 per cent, 39.0 per cent, 35.0 per cent, 42.0 per cent, 38 per cent. They were calculated from country data available in the ILO Bureau of Statistics. [6]From table 1 taking into account note 1 above. [7]The growth rate is a geometric average of GDP per capita growth rates 1970 to 1980 taken from table 1 (assumed to apply to period 1974-80) and GDP per capita estimated for 1980-82, table 1. Note that growth rates for GNP and GDP have been used interchangeably. Errors here are minor and can be ignored.

of Asia, where some improvement occurred. This improvement is largely due to the impressive growth records of certain Far Eastern countries (Hong Kong, Republic of Korea, Malaysia, Singapore) although even there economic growth is substantially less in the early 1980s than it was in the 1970s; it is also due to the fact that India is scarcely touched by the world recession because its trade with the rest of the world is insignificant compared to domestic production. The poorest countries in tropical Africa, however, saw a substantial leap in the numbers in underemployment, from 55 to 76 million.[17]

5. Summary and Conclusions

The data available on employment-related statistics for a large number of countries in the developing regions of the world are poor and make difficult, if not foolhardy, an assessment of trends in the composition of the labour force, sectoral employment demand, unemployment and underemployment. Available data, however, suffer as much from weakness in conceptualisation—clearly the case for employment and closely related poverty statistics—as from past shortcomings in the prevailing development model that led to the failure to collect certain types of statistics both regularly and accurately. Good-quality statistics now available in the Third World were developed largely in response to the growth maximisation (and antinatalist) development model of the 1950s and 1960s which did not have much to say about questions of distribution, poverty, unemployment and underemployment. The focus of data collection changed slightly in the 1970s as greater concern was expressed about the failure of previous strategies of development and new models—incorporating basic-needs development ideas, for example—gained some ground. Nevertheless, the poor quality of available data concerning employment and poverty-related indicators is illustrated in this article since most of the estimates made have had to be based on fragmentary evidence concerning employment and good estimates concerning economic and population growth.

Over the period 1960-80 the developing countries' GNP grew at 5.5 per cent per annum; it dropped to 1.0 per cent per annum from 1980 to 1982. Between 1960 and 1980 the importance of agriculture greatly diminished in favour of industry and, in particular, services as a provider of jobs and a source of output. The ratio of women to men in the labour force (as conventionally measured) remained constant and, in the sample countries studied, self-employment decreased and the number of employees increased.

Unemployment in the early 1980s rose in those developing regions more integrated into the world economy, notably in Latin America and the Caribbean (in particular richer Latin America) and the Middle East oil exporters plus Nigeria. The other parts of Africa and Asia, were, in terms of increases in unemployment, hardly affected by the recession.

The change over the period 1960-80 was similar in magnitude for underemployment as for unemployment, with the exception of Africa. This is unsurprising given the methodology used which, as we have seen, was based to a considerable extent on economic growth and population growth rates. With the exception of the poorest countries in Africa, the proportion of people underemployed fell slightly over the period 1974-82, but the total numbers increased from 421 to 448 million. So even with GNP growth outstripping population growth over the period, the problem of poverty and low-productivity underemployment has worsened in absolute terms.

This article has not proposed policies to combat poverty and underemployment; it has merely massed together some basic data to illustrate broad trends in employment in developing countries. Most of the available data have been woefully inadequate even to do that, yet it is hoped that they will at least provoke other people either to do a better job in analysing existing data or to provide the more reliable data required for policy analysis.

What *is* clear from the data presented here is not only that the current recession has, unsurprisingly, exacerbated the poverty and underemployment problem in those countries most closely linked to the world market system, but that this problem would still have been extremely grave in developing countries even if there had been no recession.

Notes

1. Henceforth the expression "developing countries" will be used when referring to these 92 countries even though countries with fewer than 1 million people—and in some cases China—will be excluded.
2. See M. Hopkins and R. Van Der Hoeven: *Basic needs in development planning* (London, Gower, autumn 1983), where this is argued in more detail.
3. Work similar in nature to the contents of this section and consistent with its major conclusion but attempting to analyse causes of changing employment structure in more detail can be found in H. Chenery and M. Syrquin: *Patterns of development, 1950-1970* (London, Oxford University Press, 1975); in N. Gemmell: "Economic development and structural change: The role of the service sector", in *Journal of Development Studies* (London), Oct. 1982; and in A. S. Oberai: *Changes in the structure of employment with economic development* (Geneva, ILO, 2nd ed., 1981).
4. Under the Lewis model agriculture is seen as the motor of development. This may be so, but there is no denying that the major new job-providing sectors are in industry and, in particular, services.
5. This says nothing about worker income distribution *within* each sector. Analysis of the 1960 and 1980 Gini indices of the data in tables 2 and 3 showed worsening worker income distribution between sectors overall and in Asia (middle- and low-income), India, Africa and Middle East (oil exporters) and Africa (low-income) and improving in the other regions. Whether this result can be extended to overall worker income distribution (known as the functional distribution of income) depends on the labour income distribution *within* each sector. This analysis was not done and therefore the results of the distribution exercise are not presented in further detail here.
6. For a discussion on concepts, see G. Standing: *Labour force participation and development* (Geneva, ILO, 1978).
7. R. Berry: "Open unemployment as a social problem in urban Colombia: Myth and reality", in *Economic Development and Cultural Change* (Chicago), Jan. 1975.

For a dissenting view, see G. Standing: "The notion of voluntary unemployment", in *International Labour Review,* Sep.-Oct. 1981.

8. An exercise that we carried out on available unemployment statistics for the years 1975 to 1980 using the ILO *Year Book of Labour Statistics* was worthless to the extent that even comparing census or labour survey data on employment to labour supply gave unemployment rates of as much as 60 per cent in some countries (e.g. Costa Rica, Egypt, Jamaica, Republic of Korea, Peru, Tunisia).
9. How this was done is described in note 2 to table 6. In fact, the measure used is not labour productivity but a proxy for it, namely GDP per person employed in selected countries where this information is available.
10. This is argued further and illustrated in Hopkins and Van Der Hoeven, 1983, op. cit.
11. See resolution concerning statistics of the economically active population, employment, unemployment and underemployment, 13th International Conference of Labour Statisticians, Geneva, 1982, in *Bulletin of Labour Statistics* (Geneva, ILO), 3rd quarter, 1983.
12. O. Altimir: "Poverty in Latin America: A review of concepts and data", in *CEPAL Review* (Santiago, Chile), Apr. 1981.
13. M. J. D. Hopkins: "A global forecast of absolute poverty and employment", in *International Labour Review,* Sep.-Oct. 1980.
14. These include unemployed workers who belong to such families, but there are also some workers who remain in voluntary unemployment awaiting better jobs and who are supported by their families. These latter families may have satisfied their basic needs and hence would not be included under my definition.
15. Estimating levels of underemployment in this way is very much a numbers game. However, the numbers used the assumption made are clearly presented in the notes to table 8 for anyone who wishes to improve on my estimates. Clearly, caution, if not a healthy scepticism, should be used in interpreting these numbers; nevertheless, they give an idea of the orders of magnitude involved and the direction of change of poverty and underemployment in various regions of the world.
16. From table 4 (Hopkins, 1980, op. cit.), 1,110 million were predicted to be in poverty in 1982; this figure, when multiplied by the participation rate of 38.0 per cent, gives 422 million underemployed (see also note 5, table 8).
17. These figures are slightly higher than those suggested in A. Bequele and R. Van Der Hoeven: "Poverty and inequality in tropical Africa", in *International Labour Review,* May-June 1980; this is because the basic-needs poverty line I use is higher than theirs—notably that for minimum housing requirements.

Appendix: Classification of Developing Countries

1. *Latin America and Caribbean (middle-income):* Argentina, Brazil, Chile, Colombia, Costa Rica, Cuba, Ecuador, Guatemala, Jamaica, Mexico, Panama, Paraguay, Trinidad and Tobago, Uruguay, Venezuela.
2. *Latin America and Caribbean (low-income):* Bolivia, Dominican Republic, El Salvador, Haiti, Honduras, Nicaragua, Peru.

3. *Asia (middle-income):* Hong Kong, Democratic People's Republic of Korea, Republic of Korea, Malaysia, Mongolia, Papua New Guinea, Philippines, Singapore, Thailand.
4. *Asia (low-income):* Afghanistan, Bangladesh, Bhutan, Burma, Indonesia, Kampuchea, Lao Republic, Nepal, Pakistan, Sri Lanka, Viet Nam.
5. *Asia (China).*
6. *Asia (India).*
7. *Africa and Middle East (oil exporters):* Iraq, Kuwait, Libyan Arab Jamahiriya, Nigeria, Saudi Arabia.
8. *Africa and Middle East (middle-income):* Albania, Algeria, Angola, United Republic of Cameroon, Congo, Egypt, Ghana, Iran, Ivory Coast, Jordan, Kenya, Lebanon, Liberia, Morocco, Senegal, Syria, Tunisia, Turkey, Yemen Arab Republic, Democratic Yemen, Zambia, Zimbabwe.
9. *Africa (low-income):* Benin, Burundi, Central African Republic, Chad, Ethiopia, Guinea, Lesotho, Madagascar, Malawi, Mali, Mauritania, Mozambique, Niger, Rwanda, Sierra Leone, Somalia, Sudan, Tanzania, Togo, Uganda, Upper Volta, Zaire.

Source: World Bank list of 93 countries with a population of over 1 million in 1979.

II GLOBAL STRATEGY AND POLICY

3. THE RELATIONSHIP BETWEEN THE GLOBAL STRATEGIC PLANNING PROCESS AND THE HUMAN RESOURCE MANAGEMENT FUNCTION

EDWIN L. MILLER, SCHON BEECHLER, BHAL BHATT AND RAGHU NATH

This article discusses the relationship between the Human Resource Management function (HRM) and the global strategic planning processes of five leading U.S. multinational corporations. Data were collected by means of interviewing HRM and strategic planning executives, as well as corporate or strategic business unit senior-level line executive personnel. An HRM presence occurred most frequently in discussion pertaining to the implementation of the global strategy, and management succession and management development activities were the most frequently mentioned areas of involvement. *Edwin L. Miller and Schon Beechler are with the Graduate School of Business Administration, University of Michigan. Bhal Bhatt is with the University of Toledo, and Raghu Nath is with the University of Pittsburgh.*

The rapid increase in U.S. multinational corporations' (MNCs) foreign direct investment has generated a series of intersections between MNCs' human resource management systems and their global strategic planning processes. As the MNCs strive to administer their overseas operations, the control mechanisms developed by the corporate headquarters to regulate the activities of their overseas subsidiaries impact the structure, the human resource management system and the enterprise's internal environment. Structural changes within the parent company or its overseas subsidiaries frequently lead to greater decentralization and increased emphasis on management development. Simultaneously, Human Resource Management (HRM) is placed under increased pressure to solve problems associated with promotion and management succession, measurement of performance, and issues pertaining to the distribution of power between corporate headquarters and overseas subsidiaries.

Because of the increasing importance of human resource issues in the management process of multinational corporations, a longterm research project has been undertaken to examine the nature of the linkages between HRM and the global strategic planning processes of multinational corporations. The first phase of the project has been completed, and this article presents the results of that part of the study. The purpose of this article is to describe the nature of Human Resource Management's participation in the formulation and implementation of global strategic plans of leading American multinational corporations. It also provides information about the role of HR professionals in the planning process.

Edwin L. Miller, Schon Beechler, Bhal Bhatt, and Raghu Nath, "The Relationship between the Global Strategic Planning Process and the Human Resource Management Function," *Human Resource Planning* 9.1 (1986):9–23. Used with permission.

A review of the strategic planning literature indicates that MNCs have adopted a strategic planning perspective as a means for helping them make rational decisions in the face of rapidly changing and complex environments. As the management teams of these corporations begin to develop and implement their firms' global strategic plans, do they concern themselves with human resource issues? Lorange reports that they do, and these issues appear in the context of discussion concerned with such topics as acquisitions or divestitures of overseas production facilities, entering or withdrawing from markets, proposed redesign of corporate structures to accommodate different cultures or nations, the means for controlling relationships between overseas subsidiaries and the parent, and the procedure for effectively managing the fundamental elements of the human resource system, (Lorange and Vancil, 1977).

Bartlett's work on the evolving nature of multinational corporations supports Lorange's conclusion, (Bartlett, 1983). He stresses the importance of human resource issues associated with the structural problems generated by multiple and often conflicting pressures emanating from most host country and global competitors. Bartlett writes:

> *"Human resource issues become critical to the formulation and implementation of the MNC's strategic plan. It is management that must develop the perspective, viable organization structures and systems through which they can interact as well as develop an appropriate decision making apparatus," (Bartlett, 1983).*

When does HRM fit into these strategic concerns of the MNCs? Is the function an active, contributing partner in the global strategic planning activities of MNCs? Or, is it viewed as contributing little of value to the strategic planning process? The strategic planning literature indicates that at least at the corporate level, human resource concerns are a collective top management responsibility rather than that of the HRM function, (Hofer and Schendel, 1981). If this is so, just what is the nature of HRM's involvement? These are important questions because they deal with the future direction and contribution of HRM.

In the HRM literature, it has become fashionable to cast the human resource system into a strategic context. To add legitimacy to their conceptual frameworks, authors and scholars have provided examples of: (1) companies that have successfully linked their human resource management systems to strategic planning, (2) top human resource management executives who have been instrumental in tying the HRM function and its activities to their respective corporations' strategic plan, and (3) procedures for moving a human resource management function into the strategic arena, (Tichy, Fombrun and Devanna, 1984).

K.R. Andrews was one of the earliest advocates for linking business strategy with human resource management, (Andrews, 1957). Although he used different terms, the essence of his argument stressed the value to be achieved by integrating these organizational activities. After almost two decades, HRM scholars and authors have begun to express themselves about the relevance of linking HR activities to the strategic planning process. A plethora of articles and books have appeared, and they have concentrated on strategic human resource management. For example, authors have written about the relationship between staffing and product life cycles,

(Leontiades, 1982; Miller, 1984) performance appraisal and business strategy, (Latham, 1984; Tung, 1984) management succession and stockholder wealth (Reinganum, 1973) and compensation structures and business strategy, (Salter, 1973).

The HRM literature offers a picture of an important and relevant role for the function as well as providing concrete examples of what can be. However, Dyer has written that the interrelationship between HRM and strategic planning represents an uncharted area, (Dyer, 1984). Notwithstanding Dyer's comments, a consensus is emerging among leading HRM scholars and professionals that the function is expanding far beyond the traditionally accepted activities of staffing, training and development, rewards and appraisal.

A distinguishing characteristic of the developing HRM model is its strategic orientation. The HR professional and executive is a central element in the emerging model, and it is noted that the HRM professional is confronted by a twofold challenge: (1) to develop viable processes whereby HRM contributions can and do occur in the strategic planning process, and (2) to adopt and promote strategic thinking within the human resource function itself.

What are the variables that differentiate strategic human resource management from previous definitions of the function? We believe that it is helpful to use Miles and Snow's strategic human resource management dimensions (Miles and Snow, 1984), and the following attributes appear to capture the spirit of the developing model:

1. Top managers of the human resource function should possess at least a conceptual familiarity with all services needed to acquire, allocate and develop managers and employees.
2. The function should have a comprehensive understanding of the language and practices of strategic planning. Appropriate human resource representatives must continually participate in the planning process to assess the probable demand for their unit's services.
3. The human resource function should pursue appropriate strategies of its own to match the organization's business strategy.
4. The function must act as a professional consultant to the line. In addition to their expertise in strictly human resource matters, the human resource specialist should be knowledgeable about organization structure, management processes including communication and control, and organization change and development.

Given these benchmarks, how does one classify the nature of the decisions made by HRM as it goes about discharging its responsibilities? Anthony's classification of management decision making is a useful tool for classifying the nature of HRM participation in the strategic planning process, (Anthony, 1964). According to his classification scheme, there are three levels of decision making: strategic, managerial, and operational. Anthony defined the levels in the following way: (1) Strategic level decisions are concerned with policy formulation and setting of overall goals, (2) Managerial level decisions are more pragmatic in orientation, and these decisions are associated with the development of programs to guarantee the availability of

Table 1

HUMAN RESOURCE MANAGEMENT INVOLVEMENT IN THE ORGANIZATIONAL EMPLOYEE STAFFING PROCESS

STRATEGIC LEVEL	**Strategic Planning Relationship to Human Resource Management System** “What kinds of people will be needed to lead the organization in the years to come?”
MANAGERIAL LEVEL	**Development of Activities to Satisfy Forecasted Organizational Human Resource Requirements** “What programs and activities must be developed to satisfy forecasted human resource requirements?
OPERATIONAL LEVEL	**Implementation and Monitoring of Specific Human Resources Programs and Activities** “What are the specific plans for this year’s college recruiting? What colleges will be visited? How many college recruits must be interviewed? And, what will be the college recruiting budget?”

resources to carry out the strategic plan, and (3) Operational level decisions are concerned with the execution of day-to-day activities, and these decisions are the consequence of programs and issues developed at the managerial level.

Applying Anthony’s framework to HRM’s responsibility for staff, Table 1 provides an example of the three levels of decision making.

Conceptual Framework

Although there are many variables that could be considered as important determinants of HRM’s contribution to the planning process, it is our opinion that three variables are central to a meaningful understanding. Based upon the strategic planning and the HRM research and literature, the following variables comprise the framework that was used in the study: Organizational Level of Strategy, Human Resource Management Functions, and Global Strategic Planning Process.

Organizational Level of Strategy

The nature of a corporation’s business strategy can be viewed in several different ways. In this study, however, strategy was limited to two organizational levels:

corporate and strategic business unit. At the corporate level, strategy is concerned primarily with such issues as long-run organizational survival, domain differentiation, resource allocation and goal formulation. Strategy associated with the strategic business unit is concerned with competition in a particular industry or product market segment. Attention is centered on competencies and competitive advantage and major functional area policy decisions.

Human Resource Management Functions

This variable is divided into the HRM activities of staffing, training and development, rewards and appraisal. In this context the Human Resource system is defined by the breadth and quality of services needed to acquire, allocate, develop and evaluate managerial personnel.

Global Strategic Planning Process

This variable can be divided into four categories: strategy preplanning, strategy formulation, strategy implementation and strategy control and evaluation. For purposes of this research project, only strategy formulation and strategy implementation were used in the analysis. Much of the previous work on strategy has been limited to these two categories, and in the pilot phase of this study, it was found that respondents were familiar and comfortable discussing the formulation and implementation phases of strategy. The respondents found it difficult to describe the involvement in strategy preplanning and evaluation activities because they generally don't view the strategy cycle as being divided into four distinct categories.

The framework for classifying HRM involvement in the global strategic planning process is presented in Figure 1. As one can observe in this framework, HR involvement in the strategic planning process can be divided into four different categories. First, HRM can be involved in the formulation of corporate level global strategic planning. Second, it can participate in the formulation of the SBU's global strategic plan. Third, HRM can be involved in the implementation of the MNC's corporate level global strategic plan. And fourth, HRM can participate in the implementation of the SBU's global strategy.

Methodology

Since very little has been published about HRM linkages with MNC's global strategic planning processes, it was decided to gather data by means of the structured interview technique. The rationale for that decision flowed from the commonly acknowledged fact that structured interviews allow an investigator the freedom and flexibility to explore a wide range of topics as well as the opportunity to collect qualitative data on attitudes, values and opinions. At this stage of the research project, qualitative information was critical for successive phases of the investigation. It was imperative

Figure 1
HUMAN RESOURCE MANAGEMENT FUNCTIONS

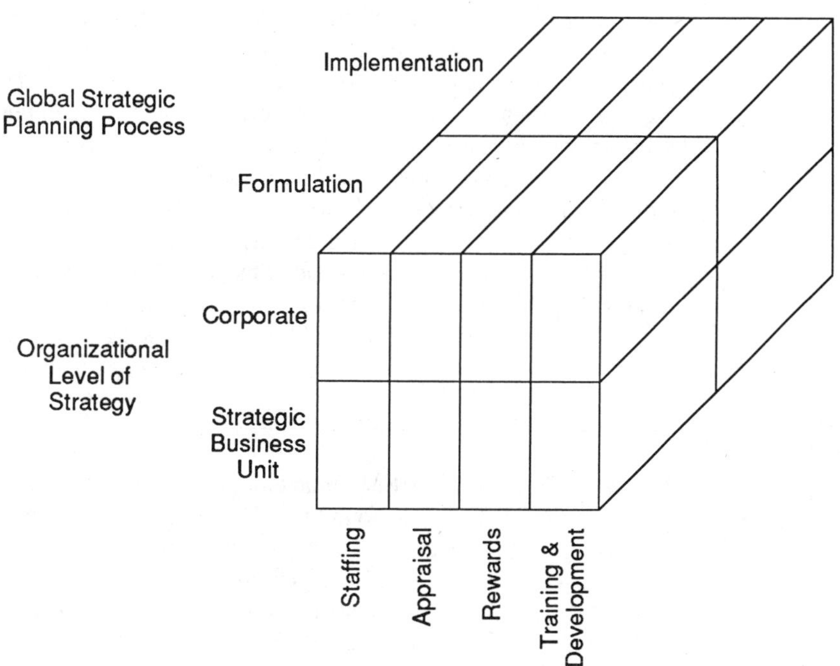

to obtain the subjects' cooperation, and from past experience it was known that more relevant information could be obtained by means of the interview method than by use of the questionnaires. Experience indicated that executives and staff specialists would be much more willing to spend time talking about their participation in the planning process than they would by filling out a survey instrument.

The managers and executives who participated in the study occupied positions in one of the following areas: the strategic planning function, the human resource management system, or as corporate or SBU senior-level line executive. Regardless of their official titles, each participant was involved in the overseas activities of his or her organization. As such, they were able to provide several different and relevant perspectives about the global strategic planning process and HRM involvement in it.

Five U.S. multinational corporations comprised the sample, and they represented several different types of manufacturing industries. The following criteria were used as the basis for choosing the MNC's: (1) The enterprise must have a significant overseas presence i.e., (the firm must have manufacturing, marketing or administrative facilities in at least six different countries), (2) The firm must have been engaged in international business for at least 20 years.

Net annual sales for the corporations ranged from approximately three billion to over twenty billion dollars, and foreign sales represented at least 20% of total sales for each corporation. These were large U.S. firms and their foreign sales represented a significant portion of these firms' total annual sales.

Twenty-two interviews were conducted during the data collection phase of the study. Twelve of the participants were involved in the global strategic planning process at the corporate level. The 10 remaining participants were involved in the global strategic planning process of those SBU's engaged in the production and sale of goods overseas. Consequently, interview data have been obtained on five MNC's global strategic planning processes at corporate and SBU levels.

Among the 12 participants at the corporate level, five were senior HR executives in their respective corporations, four were top-level line executives, and three were responsible for development of their corporations' global strategic plan. At the SBU level, the 10 participants were divided in the following manner: five were in charge of the SBUs' HR systems, four were general managers of the SBUs, and one was responsible for the development of business planning.

Discussion

What was the nature of HRM involvement in the global strategic planning process? In each of the MNCs it was found that HRM was participating in the global planning process. However, the degree of participation did vary across the corporations, which was not surprising. What was interesting was where and how the HR system linked with the MNC's global strategic planning processes and the role the top HR executive played in bringing about those linkages. In this section, we will discuss some of the more interesting findings.

The Nature of Human Resource Management Involvement in the Global Strategic Planning Process at the Corporate Level

Incorporation of a HRM perspective at the corporate level was informal and limited. In two of the MNCs, the senior line executives and strategic planners reported that it wasn't clear how HRM could contribute to the MNC's global strategy. In the words of one of these executives:

> *"Human resource issues are considered when they are pertinent to the topic at hand, but we would never think of asking the HR people to participate in those strategic discussions. Although those guys are nice people, they are soft and they have little to contribute to the broader strategic issues of the corporation."*

When there was HRM involvement in the strategic planning process, the CEO played an instrumental role in that relationship. Three of the top HR executives attributed their effectiveness to their personal relationship with the CEO. As one HR executive said:

> *"I see or talk to the CEO on a daily basis, and we talk about personnel related matters. However, you must understand that he trusts me or else I wouldn't be in this job. We go back a long way together."*

Involvement of HRM was fragile and subject to change given the nature of the personalities involved, and the function's effectiveness was influenced by the executive's ability to develop and maintain personal relationships with the CEO. The presence and participation of HRM at the corporate level required constant revalidation because each time there was a change of CEO or the senior HR executive, a period of testing and critical review occurred. The HR executive had to win acceptance on the basis of value added to strategy matters or else win acceptance on the basis of personal qualifications. However, it was not an either-or situation.

HRM involvement in the formulation and implementation of the MNCs' global strategic planning process varied across organizations and the HR system's four basic activities of staffing, training and development, appraisal of performance, and compensation. It was the area of staffing which represented the major arena in which HR made its presence felt. Management development was another area in which there was a reasonably strong degree of HRM participation in the strategic planning process. Apparently discussions about executive compensation and performance appraisal were considered by these five MNCs to be the responsibility of top management itself, and there was little reason to include an HRM contribution.

Among several of the MNCs, HRM contributions to staffing had moved to the strategic decision-making level, and considerable time and effort were devoted to the process of choosing the very best executives for overseas positions. Many times these assignments were designed to meet three objectives: (1) to assign the very best person to the vacant post, (2) to gather evidence about the expatriate's capabilities to manage in a foreign environment, and (3) to provide the executive with an overseas experience prior to advancing to still higher and more responsible positions within the management hierarchy of the parent organization. The HRM executive was expected to help develop the criteria that an executive must possess in order to successfully perform on the overseas assignment. In two of the MNCs, the senior HR executives indicated that they participated in discussions about the selection of executives to head major geographic regions overseas. In both companies, the HR executive helped develop the slate of candidates and the HR executives offered their opinions about each candidate's qualifications to the CEO and other members of the management committee.

In several of the MNCs, the HRM function was responsible for administering the management succession and career development plans for high potential managerial personnel. These executives and managers were holding key positions within the management hierarchies of their respective firms, and they were judged to possess the potential to rise to senior management positions within the near future. The HR executives who participated in those discussions, reported their opinions were sought out with respect to the following subjects: (1) The managerial qualities required to successfully manage the MNC in the future, (2) The types of domestic as well as foreign assignments that would help the executives build the competencies that would be necessary to lead the corporation in the future, and (3) Which individuals should be considered for overseas assignments as part of their career progression. A particularly helpful insight into HR involvement was provided by the following comments of a senior HR executive:

"I was requested to generate a slate of candidates for the position of president of the Southern Asia region. In my opinion, that geographic region no longer warranted a 'star' just because we had little market share and there were no plans to try and expand it. The job required nothing more than a figurehead, and all we needed to do was to show the flag. An executive close to retirement seemed to be the ideal type of person to assign to the job. I used the BCG framework as the basis for my argument to the management committee because I knew they were familiar with that terminology and approach. Much to my surprise they went along with my argument."

Given the nature of HR involvement in the global strategic planning process at the corporate level, it is somewhat artificial to try to force the function's involvement into formulation or implementation of strategy. It was more meaningful to state there was an HR presence at the corporate level, and the content of the HR decisions was, in Anthony's framework, essentially strategic and managerial in substance. Table 2 summarizes the nature of HRM involvement in the global strategic planning process at the corporate level.

The Nature of HR Involvement at the Strategic Business Unit Level

At the SBU level, HRM participation in the global strategy was well established, valued, and expected by management and planners alike. They reported that an HR perspective added value to the strategic planning process, and there was high regard for the professional competence of the HRM staff and, in particular, the senior HR manager. In general, the HR professionals were considered to be sensitive to the environmental pressures on the SBU, they understood the dynamics of the business and they brought a long-term orientation to the strategic problems facing the business. In the words of one senior SBU HR manager:

"Management and the business planners trust me, and they look for ways to take advantage of my expertise. On technical matters, management will routinely ask me if I see any HR issues. Let me give you an example, as part of our global strategy we began thinking about going into Mexico and opening up a manufacturing facility. As part of the feasibility study, I was asked to provide an HR input. I raised questions and provided information about the reactions of our union if we outsourced part of production, I provided information about the skill level of the potential workforce, its commitment to work and its stance relative to outside management."

Among this sample of companies, HRM was deeply involved in the strategic planning process, and its participation crossed all four HRM functional activities. Perhaps one of the most dramatic statements pertaining to HRM involvement in the planning process was made by one of the HR managers in the following way:

"I have an excellent staff, and it handles the day-to-day HR routine much better than I can. As for me, I'm concerned about the 21st century for this company."

Table 2

HRM INVOLVEMENT IN GLOBAL STRATEGIC PLANNING PROCESS AT THE CORPORATE LEVEL

Formulation Human Resource Management Activities

Decision	Staffing	Development	Appraisal	Rewards
STRATEGIC	Participation in the Development of Qualifications Necessary for Success in an Overseas Position.			
MANAGERIAL	Participation in the Development of Management Succession Program.	Participation in the Development of Management Development Program.		
OPERATIONAL				

Implementation Human Resource Management Activities

Decision	Staffing	Development	Appraisal	Rewards
STRATEGIC				
MANAGERIAL	Administration of Management Succession Program.	Administration of Management Development Program. Integration of Management Development and Management Succession Programs.		
OPERATIONAL	Development of Slate of Candidates for Overseas. Participation in the Selection and Assignment of Executives to Overseas Assignments.	Determination of other type of Development Assignments for Executives and High-Potential Managerial Personnel.		

Management succession and career development again represent two of the main ways in which HRM was involved in the formulation of the SBU's global strategic planning process. In two of the SBUs, the HR executives reported that a key element for tying HRM to the SBU strategic plan occurred by means of the management succession plan, and it was important for the function to play an important role in that relationship. As an example of that, HR executives indicated that they were participants in discussions about the SBU's strategy for a particular market or product and the human resource requirements needed to implement that strategy. Several of the HR officials reported they devoted a large amount of their time to locating managerial and technical professional personnel who could fill vacancies that opened up as a result of the strategic discussions about the future of the SBU's international involvement.

Relatively speaking, HRM was much more involved in the implementation rather than the formulation of the SBU's global strategic plan. One HR executive made a statement that seemed to be a common thread through many of the discussions, "I'm a doer. Give me a direction, and I'm off and running." Examples of such behavior were most evident in the area of staffing. HRM was responsible for the development of managerial and professional technical personnel. In contrast, the performance appraisal and reward programs required HRM to do nothing more than administer them, and it was limited to monitoring the decisions of overseas management to determine if they were in compliance with the corporation's guidelines and stated policies and procedures. In several of the firms, the reward system had been designed by an outside consulting group, and the HRM function did little more than oversee a compensation program that had been developed by a group external to the MNC.

Classifying HRM decisions according the Anthony's classification scheme, the majority of its decision making occurred at the operational level. The HR function was responsible for preparing managerial, professional and technical personnel for impending overseas assignments. For instance, arrangements were made for language training, presentation of indoctrination programs for the soon-to-be expatriates, preparations for moving household goods overseas, making travel arrangements prior to departure from the U.S. and responding as best it could to the personal requirements of the person about to be sent abroad. While the expatriate was away from the United States, the function was in touch with the overseas employee, and it responded to personal requests ranging from seeking college application forms for college-age dependent children, to gathering information about legal issues that sometimes arise between the expatriate and the state and federal government, and finally, locating hard-to-find food and personal products. Prior to repatriation, the function prepared the expatriate and family members for their return to the U.S. This included: (1) locating an assignment within the SBU that would be similar in authority and responsibility to the expatriate's present position, and (2) helping with preparations to move the family back to the U.S. Table 3 summarizes HRM involvement in the global strategic planning process at the strategic business unit level.

Table 3

HRM INVOLVEMENT IN GLOBAL STRATEGIC PLANNING PROCESS AT THE STRATEGIC BUSINESS UNIT LEVEL

FORMULATION
HUMAN RESOURCE MANAGEMENT ACTIVITIES

DECISION	Staffing	Development	Appraisal	Rewards
Strategic	Participation in discussion of qualification necessary for success in an overseas position.			
Managerial				
Operational				

IMPLEMENTATION
HUMAN RESOURCE MANAGEMENT ACTIVITIES

DECISION	Staffing	Development	Appraisal	Rewards
Strategic				
Managerial	Administration of management succession program.	Administration of management development program.	Administration of performance program.	Administration of reward program.
Operational	Identification of potential candidates for overseas assignments. Preparation of personnel for overseas assignment and repatriation to the U.S.	Individual specific development assignments.	Monitor performance appraisals.	Monitor individual compensation decisions.

Conclusion

This article has reported the results of the first phase of a long-term research project designed to examine the interrelationship between HRM and the global strategic planning processes of large multinational firms. It is our opinion that this study has helped to bridge part of the knowledge gap that has existed with respect to the linkages between HRM and the planning processes of MNCs. When considering the findings of this study, one of the most striking results is the potentially influential role that senior HR executives can play in the strategic planning process. That is, among those firms in which there was a high level of HRM involvement in the planning process, the HRM executives were viewed as the functional leaders, and they were judged by senior management as having something of value to contribute to the strategic planning discussions. The professional competence and personal characteristics of the senior HR executive were critical determinants for MNC management willingness to include HRM contributions to the planning process. This finding held true at the corporate as well as the strategic business unit levels.

Professional competence was a necessary but not sufficient condition for inclusion in strategy decisions. In those companies where there were effective HRM inputs, the senior HR executive was described in the following terms: professionally competent, value added, personal confidante, trustworthy and insightful. However, there was not a direct correlation between the power and prestige of the senior HR executives and the involvement of the function, and in some cases the HR executive was involved in the strategic planning process while similar status was not enjoyed by the HRM function.

It is our conclusion that if the senior HR executive and ultimately the function is to be included in the global strategic planning process, several conditions must be met. First, the senior HR executive, as the key legitimate function leader, must be included in the strategic planning process, and legitimacy is the result of professional competence. Although there may be times when HRM contributions to the planning process will be limited, there will be other times when the function's contributions will be critical and participation active. Without inclusion, HRM contributions to the strategic planning process will be minimal and of little consequence.

Second, the senior HR executive must be competent and sensitive to the problems, needs and circumstances confronting the organization. Members of management and strategic planners alike must recognize the value added by the contributions made by the function and its senior executive. As a corollary, HRM must conscientiously strive to understand the language and practice of strategic planning, the nature of the business and a demonstrated sensitivity to the demands and circumstances impacting the manager and his or her job. It is our opinion that such an awareness is just beginning to occur, and the results of this study support such a conclusion.

As firms become more deeply involved in international business, there will be more opportunities for strategic HRM to become active and full participants in the global strategic planning process. The function must seek ways to exploit these opportunities to contribute to the planning process, and the HR professionals must prepare themselves professionally to contribute. The perspective and competence of the HR professionals will be critical for their inclusion in the strategic planning process, and the senior HR executive must provide an important example to management and to lower level HR professionals of how the interface can occur. In this regard the HR executive must be an excellent teacher, and teaching must occur by deeds not words alone. It is our opinion that more HR professionals are becoming aware of the need to prepare themselves and to develop a perspective that will be helpful for building viable and important relationships between HRM and the global strategic planning processes of MNCs.

Third, integrity and the quality of the interpersonal skills possessed by the senior HR executive are critical contextual determinants of his or her participation in the planning process. Several of the HR executives reported that being viewed as trustworthy and the confidante of the CEO were two of the most important elements contributing to the degree of influence they exerted on the MNC's global strategic planning process. However, they were quick to add that without demonstrated professional competence, being trustworthy or a good sounding board to the CEO or other members of management meant very little in terms of the likelihood of being included in the strategic planning process.

If human resource management is to begin moving out of a role of just responding to the global strategic plan, if it is to participate in the strategic arena of the multinational corporation, senior HR executives must begin to recognize and understand at least conceptually the nature of the services needed to acquire, allocate, develop, reward and evaluate managerial personnel. The HR executive must understand how the HRM function relates to other functional activities of the enterprise as well as its contribution and importance for managerial and organizational effectiveness. Finally, the executive must be sensitive to his or her personal image including integrity and interpersonal and communication skills.

It is our conclusion that if senior corporate level HR executives wish to improve upon the degree of participation in the global strategic planning process there are steps that can be taken. Several of these are as follows:

1. Design a Human Resource Management system that meets the needs of management. In part, be concerned with providing the types of services and support that enable management to do its job more efficiently and effectively. Furthermore, strive to guarantee that management consider human resource issues as they plan and implement the global strategic plan.
2. Develop a personal strategy for building a meaningful relationship with his or her CEO. It is our opinion that the strategy must be proactive in its orientation and perspective, and the executive must be committed to it.
3. Assess one's listening and communication skills. These skills are important components for building and maintaining a strong, personal relationship with the CEO. Carl Rogers' work on effective communication and the means for developing nondirective counselling skills should be helpful in this regard, (Rogers and Farson, 1976).
4. Carve out an active, helping and consulting role with top management. The HR executive should be viewed as an individual of high integrity, one who

will be available to listen and talk, and one who provides nonjudgemental but sound advice.

5. Interpret the organizational political signs accurately. Although the HR professional may be politically literate, it should not be construed to mean the successful HR executive is a master politician who relies solely upon political influence to achieve an HR presence in the global strategic planning process.

At the SBU level, HR managers can increase their involvement in the global strategic planning process too. Our recommendations are similar to those that we offer to corporate level HR executives interested in improving relationships with their respective CEOs. For example, SBU level HR managers can develop supportive communication skills, acquire an understanding of the organizational, political and cultural environment, demonstrate professional competence, establish links between HRM and SBU global strategic planning processes. These skills and activities are essentially short-term in their perspective. However, there are activities that will have long-term consequences that should be undertaken too. One such activity is the need to develop strong and meaningful relationships with SBU line management. These managers are the future leaders of their respective MNC's and it is important for the HR manager to establish the relevance of the function's contribution in the eyes of these managerial personnel. The findings of this study indicate that several of the corporate level HR executives indicated their influence could be traced to the strong and trusting relationships they had developed with current top level management while they both served at the SBU level.

Given the findings and our interpretation of them, the second phase of the research project will be developed, with several different dimensions to be explored. For example, one aspect of the new project will be the revalidation of the current findings in a wider sample of MNCs. More firms will be involved in the study, and there will be in-depth investigations occurring in several of those firms. Another dimension of the research project will be to study firms that have successfully integrated HRM into the global strategic planning process in contrast to those companies that have not been as successful in the integration process.

The senior HR executive was a central person in the process of linking HRM and the global strategic planning process of MNCs. As a third facet of the new research project, we are especially interest in studying the senior HR executive role and its occupant closely. Is there something that can be learned from an in-depth study of HR executives who have been successful in bringing about an effective, formal HRM presence in the global strategic planning process? We believe there is.

It is our opinion that we have much to learn about HRM participation in the management process of firms' international business activities. Just what is the scope of HRM involvement in the strategic planning process as well as its responsibilities for maintaining the HR system overseas? Is international HRM different from domestic HRM? This type of research should be of interest and value to the practitioner as well as the academic researcher concerned with the evolving nature of the field.

We would like to express our appreciation for the helpful comments provided by Professors V.K. Narayanan, The University of Kansas; Richard Peterson, the University of Washington; Rosalie Tung, The Wharton School; as well as Noel Tichy and David Ulrich at the University of Michigan.

References

Andrews, Kenneth R., "Is Management Training Effective?", *Harvard Business Review,* March-April 1957, Vol 35.

Anthony, Robert, *Planning and Control Systems: A Framework for Analysis,* Division of Research, Graduate School of Business Administration, Harvard University, 1964.

Bartlett, Christopher, "How Multinational Organizations Evolve," *Journal of Business Strategy,* Summer, 1983 pp. 10–32.

Dyer, Lee, "Studying Human Resource Strategy: An Approach and an Agenda," *Industrial Relations,* Spring, 1985, pp. 156–169.

Hofer, Charles and Dan Schendel, *Strategy Formulation: Analytical Concepts,* (St. Paul, MN, West Publishing Co., 1986.).

Gary Latham, "The Appraisal System as a Strategic Control" in Fombrun et. al. *Strategic Human Resource Management,* (New York: John Wiley & Sons, 1984).

Leontiades, Milton, "Choosing the Right Manager to Fit the Strategy," *Journal of Business Strategy,* Fall, 1982, Vol. 3, pp. 58–69.

Lorange, Peter and R. Vancil, *Strategic Planning Systems,* (Englewood Cliffs, N.J., Prentice Hall Book Co., 1977).

Miles, Raymond E. and Charles C. Snow, "Designing Strategic Human Resource Systems," *Organizational Dynamics,* Summer 1984, pp. 36–52.

Miller, Edwin L., "Strategic Staffing," in Fombrun, Charles, Tichy, Noel and Mary Anne Devanna (editors), *Strategic Human Resource Management,* (New York, John Wiley & Sons, 1984).

Reinganum, Marc R., "The Effect of Executive Succession on Stockholder Wealth," *Administrative Science Quarterly,* 30, 1985, pp. 46–60.

Rogers, Carl and R. Farson, *Active Listening,* (Chicago: Industrial Relations Center, 1976.).

Salter, Malcom S., "Tailor Incentive Compensation Strategy," *Harvard Business Review,* March-April, 1973, pp. 94–102.

Tichy, Noel, Charles, Fombrun and Mary Anne Devanna, "The Organizational Context of Strategic Human Resource Management," in Fombrun, Charles, Tichy, Noel and Mary Anne Devanna (eds.) *Strategic Human Resource Management,* (New York, John Wiley & Sons, Inc., 1984).

Tung, Rosalie, "Strategic Management of Human Resources in the Multinational Enterprise," *Human Resource Management,* Summer, 1984, pp. 129–144.

4. THE CROSS-CULTURAL PUZZLE OF INTERNATIONAL HUMAN RESOURCE MANAGEMENT

ANDRÉ LAURENT

Professor of Organizational Behavior at INSEAD, the European Institute of Business Administration, Fontainebleau, France, André Laurent is a graduate of the Ecole de Psychologues Praticiens de Paris, the University of Paris-Sorbonne (Lisence in Sociology and Doctorate in Psychology) and Harvard University (International Teachers Program). He has been associated for four years with Pechiney as an industrial psychologist in West Africa and for three years with the Institute for Social Research at the University of Michigan as Research Associate and Study Director before joining INSEAD in 1970. Since then he has been a Visiting Scholar at Stanford University, a Visiting Professor at the European Institute for Advanced Studies in Management in Brussels and a consultant to a number of multinational companies.

International Human Resource Management: A Field in Infancy

As noted by Tichy (1983), the human resource field appears to be in a process of gradual and uneven transformation, where different companies may be experiencing different phases of transition: "endings," "inbetween," "new beginning." Against this background, what can be said as to the status of the emerging field of International Human Resource Management which is the topic of this Symposium? Is there such a field?

Interestingly, the international dimension of HRM was apparently not retained among the important themes resulting from the previous HRM Symposium held at the University of Michigan two years ago. While the "importance of cultural phenomena" was selected (Tichy, 1983), this theme was framed more in terms of corporate cultures than in terms of national cultures and international implications.

The organizers of this Fontainebleau Symposium must be credited for creative leadership in launching a symbolic event that calls the attention of both executives and researchers on an emerging reality that is neither systematically managed nor extensively researched.

Recent labels like "Human Resource Management" or newer ones like "International Human Resource Management" obviously do not emerge by accident. Even though they often precede our understanding of what they mean, they are social productions that reflect some shared awareness of something important that has not been given enough attention in the past. When the new label is coined, it has the power of inviting people to wonder what it means and to inquire into the underlying

Audré Laurent "The Cross-Cultural Puzzle of International Human Resource Management," *Human Resource Management* 25, no 1 (Spring 1986): 91–102. Reprinted by permission of John Wiley and Sons, Inc.

reality which the label may be attempting to describe. In the field of organization studies, the concept of organizational culture seems to share a very similar history.

From a more practical point of view, there are some indications suggesting that we are not all caught into some collective illusion. Many organizations are indeed confronted with the issues of managing human resources internationally. "Human Resource Managers" in such organizations are entitled to expect "Professors of HRM" to provide some useful insight on such processes. Yet these new international processes are so complex and so poorly defined and ill-understood at the moment that superficiality remains the mark of most current treatments, including the one attempted during this Symposium. As an illustration of this primitive state of affairs, would it be unfair to suggest that in many cases during this Symposium, participants have made a point of finishing their sentences with the four magic and official words: "within an international context." It remains to be assessed whether the former part of the sentences would have differed in the absence of that ending. If the field of HRM is in a stage of adolescence, International HRM is still at the infancy stage. The intent of this paper is to contribute to the framing of this new domain in building upon the author's inquiry into the cultural diversity of management conceptions across nations.

HRM Practices as Institutionalized Preferences for the Management of People

Managers in organizations hold particular sets of assumptions, ideas, beliefs, preferences, and values on how to manage people toward the attainment of some organizational goals. Over time these various ideas get translated into particular policies, systems, and practices which in turn may reinforce or alter the original ideas. Furthermore, organizational members have sets of expectations related to those practices which may again reinforce or alter the existing policies. Through this complex process of mutual interaction between various actors' ideas and actions, certain preferred ways of managing people tend to emerge in some organized fashion which we may then call Human Resource Management.

As different organizations have developed different ways of managing their human resources that seem to have been more or less successful, this observation has reinforced the intuition that more strategic thinking was required in this area and that some competitive advantage could be acquired through some form of excellence. Future historians of work organizations may well have a hard time understanding why it took so long to realize the strategic importance of the management of human resources.

If HRM policies and practices reflect managers' assumptions about how to manage people, it becomes very critical to understand such assumptions in order to correctly interpret the meaning of particular policies and practices.

National Differences in Management Assumptions: A Research Inquiry

In the past few years, we have been interested in systematically exploring management assumptions in an attempt to enrich our understanding of management and organizational processes. The initial research objective was not to explore national differences but to bring into focus some of the implicit management and organizational theories that managers carry in their heads (Laurent, 1981).

As it is very difficult to inquire into beliefs that individuals take for granted, our research strategy has consisted in writing up a large number of possible assumptions about the management of organizations which we inferred from discussing organizational issues with managers. These assumptions were expressed in the form of statements within a standard questionnaire that would seek from respondents their degree of agreement/disagreement with such statements.

Typical survey statements read as follows:

- The main reason for having a hierarchical structure is so that everyone knows who has authority over whom.
- Most managers seem to be more motivated by obtaining power than by achieving objectives.
- It is important for a manager to have at hand precise answers to most of the questions that his subordinates may raise about their work.
- In order to have efficient work relationships, it is often necessary to bypass the hierarchical line.
- Most managers would achieve better results if their roles were less precisely defined.
- An organizational structure in which certain subordinates have two direct bosses should be avoided at all costs.

Successive groups of managers participating in executive development programs at INSEAD (The European Institute of Business Administration) were surveyed. These managers came from many different companies and many different countries.

When their responses were analyzed, it appeared that the most powerful determinant of their assumptions was by far their nationality. Overall and across 56 different items of inquiry, it was found that nationality had three times more influence on the shaping of managerial assumptions than any of the respondents' other characteristics such as age, education, function, type of company . . . etc.

One of the most illustrative examples of national differences in management assumptions was reflected in the respondents' reaction to the following statement:

> *It is important for a manager to have at hand precise answers to most of the questions that his subordinates may raise about their work.*

As indicated in Figure 1, while only a minority of Northern American and Northern European managers agreed with this statement, a majority of Southern Europeans and South-East Asians did. The research results indicated that managers from different national cultures vary widely as to their basic conception of what management is all about (Laurent, 1983).

Conceptions of organizations were shown to vary as widely across national cultures as conceptions of their management did. Across a sample of 10 Western national cultures, managers from Latin cultures (French and Italians) consistently perceived

Figure 1

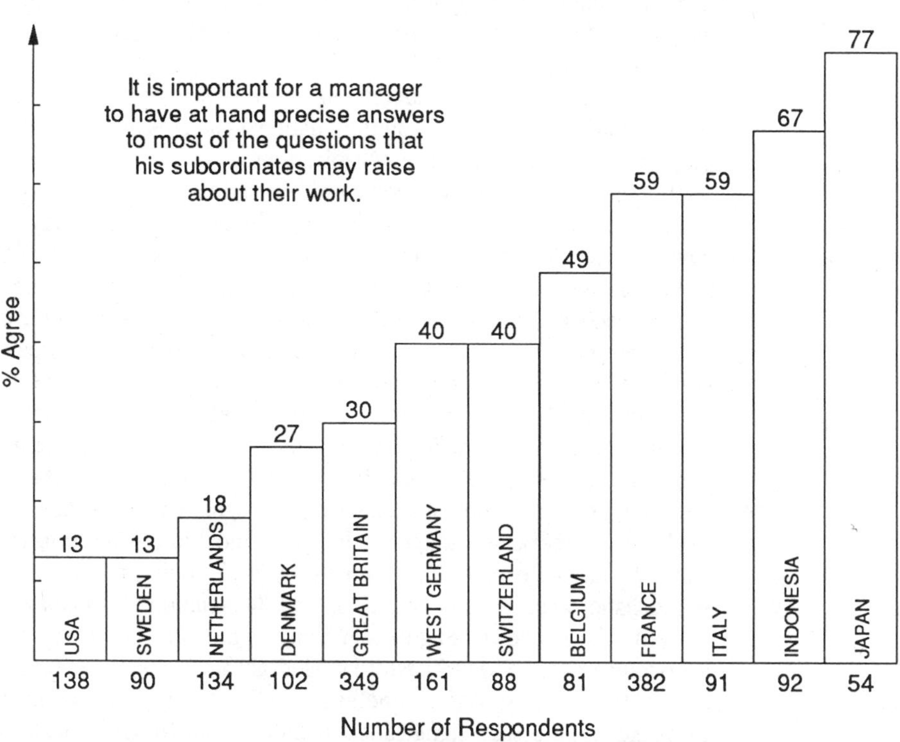

organizations as social systems of relationships monitored by power, authority, and hierarchy to a much greater extent than their Northern counterparts did.

American managers held an "instrumental" view of the organization as a set of tasks to be achieved through a problem-solving hierarchy where positions are defined in terms of tasks and functions and where authority is functionally based. French managers held a "social" view of the organization as a collective of people to be managed through a formal hierarchy, where positions are defined in terms of levels of authority and status and where authority is more attached to individuals than it is to their offices or functions (Inzerilli and Laurent, 1983). Once these results were obtained, the question arose as to whether the corporate culture of multinational organizations would reduce some of the observed national differences and therefore bring some more homogeneity in the picture.

A new research study was designed to test this hypothesis. Carefully matched national groups of managers working in the affiliated companies of a large U.S. multinational firm were surveyed with the same standard questionnaire. The overall results gave no indication of convergence between national groups. Their cultural differences in management assumptions were not reduced as a result of working for the same multinational firm. If anything, there was slightly more divergence between the national groups within this multinational company than originally found in the INSEAD multi-company study. These findings were later replicated with smaller matched national samples of managers in several American and European multinational corporations.

The overall research findings led to the conclusion that deep-seated managerial assumptions are strongly shaped by national cultures and appear quite insensitive to the more transient culture of organizations.

Further exploration was conducted with different methods of inquiry in order to better assess the validity of the findings. In one research study, a large U.S.-based multinational corporation was approached because of its high professional reputation in human resource management. This corporation has implemented for years a standardized worldwide system for the multiple assessment of managerial potential and performance. Open-ended interviews were conducted across a number of affiliated companies in an attempt to identify what managers perceived as being important to be successful in their career. This led to a list of 60 criteria mentioned by managers as being most important for career success. Matched national groups of managers were later asked, in a systematic survey, to select among these 60 criteria those they saw as most important for career success within the firm.

For the American managers, the single most important criterion in order to have a successful career with the company was "Ambition and Drive"—a pragmatic, individualistic, achievement-oriented, and "instrumental" reading of the assessment system. The French managers saw things quite differently. For them the single most important criterion was "Being labelled as having high potential," a more "social" and political reading of the same system. The degree of consensus on what it takes to be successful was significantly higher within the American Affiliate—culturally closer to the designers of the HRM system—than it was in the British, Dutch, German, and French Affiliates.

In spite of the convergence effects that could be expected from a similar and global administrative system of assessment and reward, managed by the U.S. Headquarters on a worldwide basis, a remarkable degree of cultural diversity was observed again across countries in managers' perceptions of the determinants of career success. In a later part of the study, the same national groups of managers were asked to list what they thought were the features of a well-functioning organization, the attributes of effective managers, and the most important things that effective managers should be doing.

The analysis of some of the results can be summarized as follows:

German managers, more than others, believed that creativity is essential for career success. In their mind, the successful manager is the one who has the right individual characteristics. Their outlook is rational: they view the organization as a coordinated network of individuals who make appropriate decisions based on their professional competence and knowledge.

British managers hold a more interpersonal and subjective view of the organizational world. According to them, the ability to create the right image and to get noticed for what they do is essential for career success. They view the organization primarily as a network of relationships between individuals who get things done by influencing each other through communicating and negotiating.

French managers look at the organization as an authority network where the power to organize and control the actors stems from their positioning in the hierarchy. They focus on the organization as a pyramid of differentiated levels of power to be acquired or dealt with. French managers perceive the ability to manage power relationships effectively and to "work the system" as particularly critical to their success.

From the perspective of these various results, international human resource management may only be international in the eyes of the designers.

Discussion

Naive parochialism has plagued the field of Management and Organization Studies for a long time. The societal and cultural context of theories and practices has long been ignored or overlooked by both researchers and practitioners (Hofstede, 1980). Management approaches developed in one particular culture have been deemed valid for any other culture. Models of excellence (Peters and Waterman, 1982) are still being presented with virtues of universality.

A comparative analysis across national cultures brings the startling evidence that there is no such thing as Management with a capital M. The art of managing and organizing has no homeland.

Every culture has developed through its own history some specific and unique insight into the managing of organizations and of their human resources. At the same time, any single cultural model may become pathological when pushed to its extreme, an illustration of the fact that every culture has also developed specific and unique blindspots in the art of managing and organizing. There lie the still largely undiscovered opportunities and threats of international management.

The emerging field of Human Resource Management is not compelled to fall into the trap of universalism. It has the opportunity and the challenge to integrate cultural relativity in its premises. In fact, and given the global context of international business, this field has no choice but to take into full consideration the international dimension of the organizational world.

Comparative research shows that managers from different national cultures hold different assumptions as to the nature of management and organization. These different sets of assumptions shape different value systems and get translated into different management and organizational practices which in turn reinforce the original assumptions. Among such practices, human resource management practices are likely to be most sensitive to cultural diversity as they are designed by culture bearers in order to handle other culture bearers. Thus the assumptions and values of the local designers are likely to be amplified by the expectations of the natives to create a cultural product that may be highly meaningful and potentially effective for the home country but possibly meaningless, confusing, and ineffective for another country.

If we accept the view that HRM approaches are cultural artifacts reflecting the basic assumptions and values of the national culture in which organizations are imbedded, international HRM becomes one of the most challenging corporate tasks in multinational organizations.

With varying degrees of awareness, such organizations are confronted all the time with strategic choices that need to be made in order to optimize the quality and effectiveness of their very diverse human resources around the world. In order to build, maintain, and develop their corporate identity, multinational organizations need to strive for consistency in their ways of managing people on a worldwide basis. Yet, and in order to be effective locally, they also need to adapt those ways to the specific cultural requirements of different societies. While the global nature of the business may call for increased consistency, the variety of cultural environments may be calling for differentiation.

Faced with such a high degree of strategic complexity in managing human resources internationally, corporations have become increasingly seduced by a new and highly attractive dream called corporate culture, that would encapsulate on a worldwide basis their own genuine and unique ways of managing people. What if our corporate culture could act as a "supra-culture" and be expected to supersede some of the annoying specificities of the different national cultures in which we operate?

Indeed different organizations from the same country develop different organizational cultures over time and there is no doubt that the recent recognition of the importance and reality of organizational cultures represents a step forward in our understanding of organizations and of their management. However, and in spite of the interest of the concept, it would probably be illusionary to expect that the recent and short history of modern corporations could shape the basic assumptions of their members to an extent that would even approximate the age-long shaping of civilizations and nations. Indeed the comparative research reported above indicates that the corporate culture of long established large multinationals does not seem to reduce national differences in basic management assumptions across their subsidiaries.

Our tentative interpretation of this finding is that a conceptualization of organizational cultures in terms of basic assumptions (Schein, 1985) may be searching for the reality of organizational culture at a deeper level than it really is. To a certain extent, it may be useful to interpret the current appropriation of the concept of culture in the field of organization studies as a modern attempt at increasing the legitimacy of management in business firms by calling upon a higher order concept of almost indisputable essence. Who can deny the existence of an IBM culture?

Instead of locating the roots of organizational culture at the deepest level of basic assumptions, an alternative and possibly more realistic view would be to restrict the concept of organizational culture to the more superficial layers of implicit and explicit systems of norms, expectations, and historically-based preferences, constantly reinforced by their behavioral manifestations and their assigned meanings. Under this view, organizational members would be seen as adjusting to the behavioral requirements of organizational cultures without necessarily being so deeply immersed into their ideological textures.

Consistent with the previous arguments on the deep impact of national cultures upon organizational theories and practices, our proposed interpretation of the concept of organizational culture probably reflects the Frenchness of the author through his eagerness to differentiate "actors and systems" (Crozier and Friedberg, 1977).

Thus on the international scene, a French manager working in the French subsidiary of an American corporation that insists on an opendoor policy may very well leave his office door open—thus adjusting to the behavioral requirements of the corporate culture—without any modification whatsoever of his basic conception of managerial authority. In the French subsidiary of a Swedish firm, whose corporate values include an almost religious reliance upon informality, French shopfloor employees were recently observed as addressing their managers by their first names and using the intimate "tu" form within the boundaries of the firm. The same individuals immediately reverted to "Monsieur le Directeur" and the more formal "vous" form whenever meeting outside the firm.

Similarly the degree of ingeniosity and creativity that can be observed in order to recreate private space and status out of open space offices probably expresses some of the same dynamics whereby organizational members may very well play the expected game without abdicating their own personal values.

Deep-rooted assumptions could then be better understood as the historical result of broader cultural contexts like civilizations and nations. Organizations would only select from the available repertory of their larger cultural context a limited set of ideas that best fit their own history and modes of implementation. This would be called their organizational culture and would strongly reflect national characteristics of the founders and dominant elite of the organization (Hofstede, 1985).

Steps Toward the International Management of Human Resources

In dealing with other cultures than their home-based culture, international organizations need to recognize more explicitly that they are dealing with different "fabrics of meaning" (Geertz, 1973). Therefore, whatever can be the strength, cohesiveness, or articulated nature of their corporate cultures, the same HRM policy or practice is likely to be attributed quite different meanings by different cultural groups. Behavioral adjustment may occur at a superficial level and provide the designer from Headquarters with an illusory feeling of satisfaction in front of apparent homogeneity across subsidiaries. The dances will appear similar while their actual meaning may be quite different and thus lead to very different outcomes than anticipated. Fortunately, in many other cases, the dances will also be different enough across subsidiaries so as to effectively remind Headquarters that the rest of the world is different from "home."

In the Italian subsidiary, the introduction of a Management-by-Objectives system may be experienced as follows: "We used to be rewarded for our accomplishments and punished for our failures. Why should we now sign our own punishment even before trying?" For the Indonesian affiliate company, the inclusion of negative feedback in performance appraisal interviews may mean "an unhealthy pollution of harmonious hierarchical relationships." The introduction of a matrix-type multiple reporting relationship system may be experienced as a horrible case of divided loyalty in the Mexican subsidiary. Unlike many others, the subsidiaries of Swedish multinational corporations may complain that they do not receive enough "help" from Headquarters. Participative management may mean very different things to Scandinavians and North Americans.

To a large extent, Human Resource Managers who operate internationally know these things and multinational organizations have accumulated wisdom from experience and developed skills to handle cultural diversity. Yet, more often than not, such organizations must have learned by accident or out of necessity how to cope with cultural differences. Only on rare occasions have they explicitly and consciously set out to develop a truly multinational identity by building upon cultural differences in their human resources. How many headquarters genuinely believe that they can learn from their foreign subsidiaries? How many implement such a rare belief by internationalizing headquarters' staff and top management? It may be that recent trends toward multinational cooperative ventures and networks (Lorange, 1985), characterized by a lesser degree of centralized power, will accelerate such development processes.

A truly international conception of human resource management would require a number of critical and painful steps that have not occurred yet in most instances:

- an explicit recognition by the headquarter organization that its own peculiar ways of managing human resources reflect some assumptions and values of its home culture.
- that as such these peculiar ways are neither universally better or worse than others, they are different and they are likely to exhibit strengths and weaknesses particularly when travelling abroad.
- an explicit recognition by the headquarter organization that its foreign subsidiaries may have other preferred ways of managing people that are neither intrinsically better nor worse but that could possibly be more effective locally.
- a willingness from headquarters to not only acknowledge cultural differences but also to take active steps in order to make them discussable and therefore usable.
- the building of a genuine belief by all parties involved that more creative and effective ways of managing people could be developed as a result of cross-cultural learning.

Obviously such steps cannot be dictated or easily engineered. They have more to do with states of mind and mindsets than with behaviors. As such, these processes can only be facilitated and this may represent a primary mission for executives in charge of international human resource management. They may also represent some of the prerequisites and foundations for the development of forward-looking international corporate cultures.

Such cultures could then provide the impetus and the proper framing to address important strategic issues in the area of international HRM such as: how much consistency and which similarity in policies and practices should be developed? How much variety and differentiation and what adaptation should be encouraged? Which policies should be universal and global? Which ones should be local? Which HRM practices should be designed at the center? Locally? By international teams? Which processes can be invented to reach agreement on objectives and allow variable paths to achieve them? Which passports should key managers have in the headquarter organization and in the main subsidiaries? Home office nationals? Country nationals? Third nationals? How much and which expatriation should occur? How to manage the whole expatriation process? How to properly assess management potential when judgment criteria differ from country to country? How to orchestrate the management of careers internationally? All of these issues require strategic choices that cannot be left to an obscure function as they need to be fully integrated in a global vision of the firm and as they feed and shape that vision.

The challenge faced by the infant field of international human resource management is to solve a multi-dimensional puzzle located at the crossroad of national and organizational cultures. Research is needed on the various strategies that international firms are using as their own attempts at solving the puzzle.

References

Crozier, M., and Friedberg, E. *L'Acteur et le Systeme: Les Contraintes de L'Action Collective.* Paris: Editions du Seuil, 1977.

Geertz, C. *The Interpretation of Cultures: Selected Essays.* New York: Basic Books, 1973.

Hofstede, G. Motivation, Leadership and Organization: Do American Theories Apply Abroad? *Organizational Dynamics,* Summer 1980, 42–63.

Hofstede, G. The Interaction between National and Organizational Value Systems. *Journal of Management Studies,* 1985, 22(4), 347–357.

Inzerilli, G., and Laurent, A. Managerial Views of Organization Structure in France and the USA. *International Studies of Management and Organization,* 1983, XIII(½), 97–118.

Laurent, A. Matrix Organizations and Latin Cultures. A Note on the Use of Comparative Research Data in Management Education. *International Studies of Management and Organization,* 1981, X(4), 101–114.

Laurent, A. The Cultural Diversity of Western Conceptions of Management. *International Studies of Management and Organization,* 1983, *XIII*(½), 75–96.

Lorange, P. Human Resource Management in Multinational Cooperative Ventures and Networks. Paper presented at the International Human Resource Management Symposium, Fontainebleau, August 20–23, 1985.

Peters T. J., and Waterman, R. H. *In Search of Excellence.* New York: Harper & Row, 1982.

Schein, E. H. *Organizational Culture and Leadership.* San Francisco: Jossey-Bass Publishers, 1985.

Tichy, N. M. Foreword. *Human Resource Management,* 1983, 22(½), 3–8.

III GLOBAL PRACTICES

5. CRITERIA FOR SELECTING AN INTERNATIONAL MANAGER

JEAN E. HELLER

Jean E. Heller is a special consultant to the director of Career Services, American Graduate School of International Management (Thunderbird), Glendale, Arizona. She received a B.A. from Catholic University in Washington, D.C., an M.A. from the University of Chicago, and an M.I.M. degree from the American Graduate School. Ms. Heller has been a free-lance writer for many years and was also a writer, researcher, and judge for the award-winning G.E. College Bowl TV show.

No one familiar with business and trade statistics can dispute that the international business scene has been the most impressive area of business growth since World War II. World trade went from \$110 billion in 1949 to \$2.3 trillion in 1978, with U.S. exports climbing from \$12.5 billion in 1948 to \$143.4 billion in 1978 and U.S. imports increasing from \$7.2 billion to \$172.0 billion. Then there is the tremendous growth of U.S. direct investment abroad, the impressive increase in the overseas assets of foreign affiliates of U.S. multinationals, and the sales of those U.S. affiliates—not to mention the spectacular jump of foreign investment in the United States.

Largely responsible for this growth were the multinational corporations and at their head, of course, the engine that powered them—modern management, management of resources, management of facilities, management of capital, management of people. Although much has been written about the multinational or international corporation, very little has been written about the multinational manager—this in spite of the fact that the international executive is of great importance in the scheme of things.

What kind of man or woman should this international manager be? What distinguishes international management from management per se? According to the Advisory Committee on Business and International Education of the U.S. National Commission for UNESCO, it is this:

> *Management initiates, organizes, plans, directs, [and] controls the scope and nature of an enterprise in all of its multiple internal and external relationships; international management includes all of this, and, as well, the added complexities of quite different cultures, economics, politics, and the levels of responsibility to fellow humans. In short, it is a management per se—plus!*

It would seem then that an international manager must possess all of the usual managerial skills and then some. One author on the subject wrote:

> *Ideally, it seems, he should have the stamina of an Olympic runner, the mental agility of an Einstein, the conversational skill of a professor of languages, the detachment of a judge, the tact of a diplomat, and the perseverance of an Egyptian pyramid builder. . . And if he is going to measure up to the demands of living and working in a foreign country he should also have a feeling for culture; his moral judgements should not be too rigid; he should be able to merge with the local environment with chameleon-like ease; and he should show no signs of prejudice.*

Another idealized version of a candidate for an international executive post put it this way. He must have:

> *a flexible personality, with broad intellectual horizons, attitudinal values of cultural empathy, general friendliness, patience and prudence, impeccable educational and professional (or technical) credentials—all topped off with immaculate health, creative resourcefulness, and respect of his peers. If his family is equally well endowed, all the better.*

Desirable Traits: From the Ideal to the Real

Well, now that we've gotten that out of the way, let's get down to reality. Almost everyone agrees that foremost among the many traits an international manager must possess is the ability to do the job. This may seem to be stating the obvious, but it cannot be stressed too strongly. As one study put it: "Resident nationals will overlook qualities in an American they believe are abrasive—if he is efficient and knowledgeable and can get results for them."

Cultural Empathy

Ideally, of course, we would hope to eliminate or at any rate soften any "abrasive" qualities such a manager might have. All authorities agree that high on the list of desirable traits is what is called "cultural empathy"—an awareness of and a willingness to probe for the reasons people of another culture behave the way they do. Thomas Aitken has pointed out that while sensitivity is accepted as an essential attribute of the international manager, not everyone has it to the same degree and that, meantime, "awareness is an *attitude* and this can be assumed even when sensitivity comes in short supply."

Adaptability

Closely allied to awareness and sensitivity is adaptability—a key personality trait for the international manager. In a 1970 survey by Business International of 70 companies, adaptability—along with its twin, flexibility—was listed as the second most important criterion for overseas executives. Specific types of adaptability and flexibility are listed in an American Management Associations research study written in 1965, and they are just as valid today. Among them are:

1. A high degree of ability to integrate with other people, with other cultures, and with other types of business operations.
2. Adaptability to change: being able to sense developments in the host country; recognizing differences, being able to evaluate them, and being able to qualitatively and quantitatively express the factors affecting the operations with which he is entrusted.
3. Ability to solve problems within different frameworks and from different perspectives.
4. Sensitivity to the fine print of differences in culture, politics, religion, and ethics, in addition to industrial differences.
5. Flexibility in managing operations on a continuous basis, despite lack of assistance and gaps in information rationale.

All of the above imply a person with great breadth. The international manager must not only know his job, his company, and his business, he must know and understand the history, cultural background, economic achievements, and social and political life of the country he works in, and of other countries as well. He must be "geocentric" in his attitude; he must think in world terms and see differences as opportunities rather than constraints.

> *"[L]ocal criteria for leadership may be quite different from American standards. They may in fact be based on the position of the employee's father in the community, tribal origins, various family connections, and other criteria."*

Language Skills

Language skills or capability are also significant. In fact, Exxon has said of international management candidates that "we have only one test that has proven successful, and that is language aptitude." Many other corporations also put great emphasis on language skills or, at any rate, the ability to acquire them easily. One American expatriate, formerly with Univac, noted that:

> *Language facility is a fundamental prerequisite. As is the case with missionaries, one just cannot sell religion unless he is able to talk the language of the local people. Nor can he sell successfully if he is unable to take the local pulse, if he remains a country boy amid a sophisticated business environment.*

Nevertheless, in the 1970 Business International Survey of 70 companies, language skills/ability was indicated by only 11 percent of the companies that checked off the criteria they considered important in selecting executives for overseas operations. And there are some companies that, although they feel sure language ability is helpful, don't rank it as an important feature to be sought in appraising international management development.

Education

Education—that is, a good academic degree and preferably a graduate degree—is considered of critical importance in an international executive. By far the biggest source of senior management staff is the university graduate. The familiar story of the messenger boy who rises to the president's chair never was very common, but today it is virtually unheard of—although, to be sure, a company may take its future management staff through a number of lowly training steps.

Corporations disagree on type of degree preferred. Companies with highly technical products tend to prefer science degrees. Other firms feel that successful management requires depth, drive, imagination, creativity, and character—and that the type of person exemplified by these traits is more likely to be produced by a liberal arts education. But the overall prize-winning combination seems to be an undergraduate degree combined with a graduate business degree from a recognized business school.

It goes without saying that an overseas manager must possess "managerial qualities"—in particular, such traits as supervisory ability, training ability, and the ability to organize. These traits are always important, but particularly so overseas where the manager must operate more on his own and, as an essential part of the job, build an effective overseas team. This requires a tremendous breadth of understanding of other people, other ways of thinking, other ways of doing things.

Leadership and Other Individual Traits

Picking the right people to head subordinate functions or to train employees to take over top spots is also difficult. The ones who speak English are the ones who stand out in the minds of most Americans, but they may not be the natural leaders. What's more, local criteria for leadership may be quite different from American standards. They may in fact be based on the position of the employee's father in the community, tribal origins, various family connections, and other criteria that would not be immediately apparent to an American.

Many other desirable traits come to mind in connection with an international manager. Besides what we have already discussed, he or she should be mature and creative, show independence and initiative, possess emotional stability, and have a high tolerance for frustration. That such a manager should also possess excellent health goes without saying. Some very effective domestic executives must have access to highly sophisticated medical facilities. This doesn't impair their effectiveness at home, but could be a problem in some overseas locations.

Maturity

What about age? Should younger people be sent because they "make the necessary adjustments better?" Some corporations believe this to be true. But others prefer middle-aged people for overseas assignments. In fact, one New York corporation specified a minimum age of 35 years. Another multinational manufacturer established a prerequisite of at least 16 years business experience, five of them in key supervisory positions, and fixed the minimum age at 40.

Certainly some of the criteria considered necessary for an international manager—such as experience, ability to do the job, breadth, and broad horizons—are most apt to be found in a mature person. Then too, of course, certain cultural factors might enter into the decision. Some foreign cultures might not accept young people in authority; some companies want a more established, "mature" image. On the other hand, some firms might decide they want a young look. So it is a complex question.

Motivation

In the end, much of it boils down to the candidate's interest in international work—vital to his motivation. Does he really want to work overseas? Many Americans (and this phenomenon has greatly increased in the last few years) are very reluctant to go overseas. This is a result, to a large degree, of value reorientation. It used to be "the organization first," but now employees in increasing numbers are putting their children's education, their spouses' careers, their enjoyment of their leisure time, and many other elements ahead of the lure of an international assignment. And unless a strong interest, a strong desire, is there, the risk of failure overseas escalates. As one U.S. executive put it:

> *Many of the failures overseas are of people who were shoved into something, rather than going into it on their own initiative . . . In our company, the casualty list has been extremely large in the group where we said, 'go' as compared [with] the people who said, 'I want to go. I don't give a damn about living conditions or language problems. I'm technically qualified and I want that job.'*

But nevertheless, motivation alone is not enough in a psychological profile. One personnel executive tried to build his cadre of international managers on their willingness and desire to work abroad. But he found after a short time that "a wish to go overseas may not reflect the ability to adapt to a foreign way of life. It may, indeed reflect only an inability to adjust successfully to the social and work structure in one's own country." Since one of the key criteria we have been discussing is the ability to adapt or adjust anywhere, clearly the absence of this trait could be disastrous.

Adaptability of the Candidate's Family

We have so far omitted another critical factor: The adaptability of the executive's family. Family, in this case, almost always refers to wife and children, since women are only just beginning to be given overseas assignments. In a 1978 survey of 25 U.S. firms by Business International, only one cited the assignment of women employees to international overseas positions. In a survey that was recently conducted by the American Graduate School of International Management among 33 companies that regularly come to the school to recruit, we asked if they felt that the international field was opening up for women. Twelve companies replied, "Yes," while five said, "It already has." But it should be noted that those five replies were from banks, which added that they generally didn't have a problem placing women overseas. Eight of the firms pointed out that the response depended on the country. Women were simply not accepted everywhere, especially in the sales and marketing area. Other replies (one each) included: "Opening up," "Firm has no bias," "Actively seeking women," and "I see the E.E.O.C. doing that; more and more women are coming into the international field because of it."

> *"[M]ost multinational companies do not accept the practice of assigning women overseas. The primary reasons given include the one we found (women are simply not always accepted by the host countries) and another that we also encountered (the difficulty of finding a position for the woman's husband)."*

According to the 1978 Business International survey, however, most multinational companies do not accept the practice of assigning women overseas. The primary reasons given include the one we found (women are simply not always accepted by the host countries) and another that we also encountered (the difficulty of finding a position for the woman's husband). In fact, one firm told us that it had to bring back a young woman from her overseas position because she wanted to get married and her fiance had a good position in the United States. So there are problems with such assignments for women. Again according to the Business International survey, however, European firms are using women expatriates to a great degree and they are operating harmoniously and successfully with government officials in such unexpected locations as Brazil and Egypt, where professional women are not so readily accepted.

In general, then, since it is men who are usually offered international assignments, the adaptability of wives and children is of critical importance. Some companies will go to great length in the initial screening process to make sure the attitude of the candidate's family is favorable—even to the point of testing and interviewing them as well as the candidate—but others feel, as most European firms seem to, that the adjustment of the family is the husband's concern.

Methods of Selection

Given such criteria, just how do multinational companies (MNCs) go about finding and selecting these paragons who are to operate as international managers? Most human resources executives agree that the selection of the candidate for an overseas position is *the* deciding factor in the assignments' success or failure. So do the MNC's have some elaborate procedure, some foolproof method of testing potential international executives? Alas, no. In fact, the selection procedure in most firms varies little from that used for domestic manpower posting. However, enlightened companies are aware that in addition to an employee's professional qualifications, it is necessary to examine his psychological and emotional stability, family situation, language skills, and cultural awareness if he is to be considered for an international assignment.

Does this mean that personnel screening can be accomplished through a battery of tests? Some firms believe it can be, at least as a help in screening candidates for overseas assignments. But others do not believe that the tests designed by industrial psychologists provide the predictive measures needed.

> *"[D]o the multinational companies have some elaborate procedure, some fool-proof method of testing potential international executives? Alas, no. In fact, the selection procedure in most firms varies little from that used for domestic manpower posting."*

It is generally agreed that extensive interviews of candidates (and their wives) by senior executives still ultimately provide the best method of selection. And although there is no agreement concerning the positive features that differentiate an international manager from a domestic one, two negative norms appear: (1) The executive who likes to go abroad for short trips but doesn't want to live outside his home country should not be selected, and (2) the executive who says he would love to go to the French or German subsidiary, but not to the Tanzanian or Peruvian one, appears less than truly internationally minded. As Honeywell puts it, "Corporations should be alert to weed out those candidates who feel they are primarily interested in a Cook's tour abroad."

But, at best, this point of view is negative. It indicates what should *not* be done—not what should be done. Why then are corporations so negligent in setting up criteria for the selection of managers to head those critical overseas operations? Why do many use the same selection method for international managers that they use for domestic personnel, even though it is known that the business situation overseas is compounded by an infinite number of variables? Why do some ignore the language factor? Perhaps the answer here is that they subscribe to one American executive's emphatic sentiment: "To hell with the local language. They can understand me in English if I talk loud enough." Various authorities have suggested that use of the same policies arise from a need for expediency and cost effectiveness, and that furthermore, the picture is not likely to change as long as companies feel that their foreign market penetration and their overseas profits are adequate.

Four Kinds of Approaches

Basically there are four approaches to international management development, and a particular company's selection methods depend on which approach it adopts. These four distinct approaches are as follows:

1. Colonialism—parent-company nationals only.
2. Bilateralism—local nationals only.
3. Regionalism—limited use of third-country nationals.
4. Internationalism—unrestricted use of any nationals.

Both colonialism and bilateralism reject the view that the best person for the job should be chosen. The regional approach is a compromise between bilateralism and internationalism, providing a gradual shifting of third-country nationals into executive positions. If carried further, it blends into internationalism, according to which executives are chosen on the basis of their ability, regardless of the country of their origin. They may be posted anywhere in the world, so their management training is aimed not at preparing them for a particular foreign location, but for global assignments.

The Ultimate Goal

Some companies have a cadre of seasoned international executives who have served in a number of foreign operations and attained a high degree of mobility and adaptability. They are often called the "Foreign Legion" of their companies. This appelation is similar to what another authority has dubbed the "Supranational Executive Corps"—a management pool:

> *composed of individuals from many national backgrounds who are thoroughly imbued by cosmopolitan corporate culture, which both balances and expands their national and international normative orientation, and who are available for assignment wherever their skills are required throughout the world.*

No company is known to have reached this stage, but many have set this model as their ultimate goal.

No matter what the philosophy of the company, however, the selection of international managers remains a difficult one, suffering from imperfect testing and screening techniques and complicated by the fact that success in domestic operations is no guarantee of success in foreign assignments. Business International drew up a checklist ten years ago of certain personal qualifications that a candidate should have—such as motivation, independence, resourcefulness, resilience, intelligence, tolerance, and so on—in addition to technical competence and business expertise. The American Graduate School of International Management, which trains future international managers, found in a survey that companies recruiting at the school tend to agree with Business International's checklist. In particular, they cited the motivation, maturity, and adaptability of students.

Of course, recruiting at a graduate business school of international management is one way to find an international manager—though it is by no means the only way. But no matter which route a company takes, one point seems clear: The prosperity if not the very survival of any business depends on the performance of its managers, and this is even more critical when we are talking about that very special person—the international manager.

6. SELECTION AND TRAINING PROCEDURES OF U.S., EUROPEAN, AND JAPANESE MULTINATIONALS

ROSALIE L. TUNG

An earlier version of this article was presented at the International Symposium on Cross-Cultural Management held in Montreal, October 15–18, 1981.

The policies and practices of U.S., West European, and Japanese multinationals differ with respect to the procedures used for selecting personnel to fill positions overseas and the training programs used to prepare candidates.

In light of the increasing demand by both private and governmental agencies for people who can function effectively in a foreign environment and the high incidence of expatriate inability to adapt to foreign countries, it is imperative that researchers and practitioners in the field of selection and training for expatriate assignments understand the means for reducing failure and poor performance in overseas assignments, and how such means can be implemented to improve the company's overall efficiency. In a study of how the policies and practices of U.S., West European, and Japanese multinational corporations differ with respect to selection and training of personnel for overseas assignments, information was gathered in the following areas: the extent to which affiliates of U.S., European, and Japanese MNCs in different regions of the world are staffed by parent country nationals; the criteria and procedures used for selecting personnel for different categories of overseas job assignments; the training programs used to prepare candidates in each of these job categories; and the failure rate and reasons for such failures. These findings are discussed here primarily in terms of their implications for management practices and development of a selection-and-training paradigm for overseas assignments.

Procedure

A questionnaire was developed for studying the characteristics mentioned above. The questionnaire was pretested with a sample of twelve U.S. personnel administrators of MNCs. As a result of the pilot study, certain terminologies and items in the questionnaire were revised to improve readability of the questionnaire and to facilitate responses on the part of the administrators.

The questionnaire was translated from English to German, French, Spanish, Italian, Dutch, and Japanese by bilingual researchers thoroughly fluent in the respective languages. The translated questionnaires were then translated back into English by separate bilingual researchers. Comparison of the original English questionnaire against the retranslated version facilitated the identification of problem phrases and terminologies, which were modified.

The English-language questionnaires were sent to a sample of 300 of the largest U.S. MNCs listed in Angel's *Directory of American Firms Operating Abroad,* and 105 questionnaires were returned; of these 80 were usable. Questionnaires in the respective European languages were sent to 246 West European multinationals located in Belgium, the U.K., Germany, Sweden, Netherlands, Norway, Switzerland, Denmark, France, Italy, and Spain. These companies were identified in Fortune's *Directory of the 500 Largest Industrial Companies Abroad.* None of the questionnaires sent to Denmark, France, Italy and Spain were returned. Of the remaining 196 questionnaires sent to the other European nations, 29 usable questionnaires were returned. The Japanese-language questionnaires were sent to a sample of 110 of the largest Japanese multinationals listed in Fortune's *Directory of the 500 Largest Industrial Companies Abroad.* Thirty-five usable questionnaires were returned. The questionnaires for all three samples were completed by the vice-president of foreign operations (or some similar designation) of each of these firms.

Locations of overseas affiliates were categorized into one of eight regions: Western Europe, Canada, Eastern Europe, Middle and Near East, Latin and South America, Far East, Africa, and the U.S. Respondents were asked to identify the regions in which they had affiliate operations. Table 1 presents a breakdown of the percentage of firms that had affiliate operations in each of these eight regions. As compared to the U.S. and West European samples, few or none of the Japanese MNCs included in this study had affiliate operations in Middle and Near East, Eastern Europe, or Africa. This could reflect the stage of development of Japanese MNCs. Multinationals are still a fairly recent phenomenon to the Japanese industrial scene.

Table 1

PERCENTAGE OF FIRMS IN DIFFERENT PARTS OF THE WORLD

	Western Europe	Canada	Middle/ Near East	Eastern Europe	Latin/ South America	Far East	Africa	United States
U.S. MNCs	95	86	66	19	91	88	71	NR*
West European MNCs	100	62	48	7	66	72	69	79
Japanese MNCs	62	39	29	0	86	81	29	57

*NR = Not relevant.

Staffing Policies

Respondents in the three samples were asked to identify whether management personnel at three different levels (senior, middle, and lower) in each of the eight regions were primarily "parent-country nationals" (citizens of the home country of the MNC), "host-country nationals" (citizens of the country of foreign operation), or "third-country nationals" (neither citizens of the home country of the MNC nor of the country in which the foreign operation is located).

Table 2 presents a breakdown of the responses by regions at the three different management levels for U.S., West European, and Japanese multinationals. Frequency distributions in Table 2 show that for the U.S. and European samples, host-country nationals are used to a much greater extent at all levels of management in developed regions of the world as compared to the less developed regions. This is logical, as one would expect the more developed nations to have a larger pool of personnel that would possess the necessary manpower and technical skills to staff management-level positions. The Japanese MNCs, on the other hand, employ considerably more parent-country nationals in their overseas operations at the senior and middle management levels. The Japanese MNCs do not use third-country nationals at any level of management in their overseas affiliate operations, except Africa.

Respondents were asked to identify the reasons for staffing overseas operations with parent-country nationals, host-country nationals, and third-country nationals. For the U.S. sample, the most important reasons mentioned for staffing with parent-country nationals and the relative frequencies with which the reasons were cited were: foreign enterprise in start-up phase (70 percent); and technical expertise (68 percent). The most important reasons for staffing with host-country nationals and the relative frequencies with which the reasons were cited were: familiarity with culture (83 percent); knowledge of language (79 percent); reduced costs (61 percent); and good public relations (58 percent). The most important reasons for staffing with third-country nationals and the relative frequencies with which the reasons were cited were: technical expertise (55 percent); and third-country national best person for the job (53 percent). For the West European sample, the most important reasons identified for staffing with parent-country nationals and the relative frequencies with which the reasons were cited were: parent firm wishes to develop an internationally oriented management for headquarters, where foreign assignments are seen as management development (69 percent); technical expertise (69 percent); and foreign enterprise in start-up phase (68 percent). The most important reasons for staffing with host-country nationals and the relative frequencies with which the reasons were identified were: familiarity with culture (72 percent); and knowledge of language (69 percent). The most important reason for staffing with third-country nationals and the relative frequency with which the reason was cited was: third-country national best person for the job (53 percent). The respondents were mixed about the other reasons for employing third-country nationals. For the Japanese sample, the most important reason for staffing with parent-country nationals and the relative frequency with which the reason was cited was that the parent-country national was the best person for the job (55 percent). All the other reasons were considered relatively

Table 2

EXTENT (IN %) TO WHICH FOREIGN AFFILIATES ARE STAFFED BY PARENT-COUNTRY NATIONALS (PCN), HOST-COUNTRY NATIONALS (HCN), AND THIRD-COUNTRY NATIONALS (TCN)

	U.S. MNCS	European MNCS	Japanese MNCS
U.S.A.			
Senior Management PCN	NR[1]	29	83
Senior Management HCN	NR	67	17
Senior Management TCN	NR	4	0
Middle Management PCN	NR	18	73
Middle Management HCN	NR	82	27
Middle Management TCN	NR	0	0
Lower Management PCN	NR	4	40
Lower Management HCN	NR	96	60
Lower Management TCN	NR	0	0
Western Europe			
Senior Management PCN	33	38	77
Senior Management HCN	60	62	23
Senior Management TCN	7	0	0
Middle Management PCN	5	7	43
Middle Management HCN	93	93	57
Middle Management TCN	2	0	0
Lower Management PCN	0	4	23
Lower Management HCN	100	96	77
Lower Management TCN	0	0	0
Canada			
Senior Management PCN	25	28	33
Senior Management HCN	74	67	67
Senior Management TCN	1	5	0
Middle Management PCN	1	11	33
Middle Management HCN	99	89	67
Middle Management TCN	0	0	0
Lower Management PCN	3	0	17
Lower Management HCN	96	100	83
Lower Management TCN	1	0	0
Middle/Near East			
Senior Management PCN	42	86	67
Senior Management HCN	34	14	33
Senior Management TCN	24	0	0
Middle Management PCN	27	50	83
Middle Management HCN	63	29	17
Middle Management TCN	10	21	0
Lower Management PCN	9	7	33
Lower Management HCN	82	86	67
Lower Management TCN	9	7	0

Table 2 *(continued)*

	U.S. MNCS	European MNCS	Japanese MNCS
Eastern Europe			
Senior Management PCN	15.5	100	NR[2]
Senior Management HCN	69	0	NR
Senior Management TCN	15.5	0	NR
Middle Management PCN	8	100	NR
Middle Management HCN	92	0	NR
Middle Management TCN	0	0	NR
Lower Management PCN	0	100	NR
Lower Management HCN	100	0	NR
Lower Management TCN	0	0	NR
Latin/South America			
Senior Management PCN	44	79	83
Senior Management HCN	47	16	17
Senior Management TCN	9	5	0
Middle Management PCN	7	37	41
Middle Management HCN	92	58	59
Middle Management TCN	1	5	0
Lower Management PCN	1	0	18
Lower Management HCN	96	100	82
Lower Management TCN	3	0	0
Far East			
Senior Management PCN	55	85	65
Senior Management HCN	38	15	35
Senior Management TCN	7	0	0
Middle Management PCN	19	25	41
Middle Management HCN	81	75	59
Middle Management TCN	0	0	0
Lower Management PCN	2	5	18
Lower Management HCN	96	95	82
Lower Management TCN	2	0	0
Africa			
Senior Management PCN	36	75	50
Senior Management HCN	47	15	33
Senior Management TCN	17	10	17
Middle Management PCN	11	35	0
Middle Management HCN	78	65	100
Middle Management TCN	11	0	0
Lower Management PCN	5	0	0
Lower Management HCN	90	95	100
Lower Management TCN	5	5	0

[1]Data were collected on staffing policies of foreign affiliates only. Hence, no statistic was gathered for home country of MNC.

[2]None of the Japanese MNCs included in this study has affiliate operations in Eastern Europe.

unimportant. The same held true for staffing with host-country nationals. The most important reason given for staffing with host-country nationals and the relative frequency with which the reason was cited was: that the host-country national was the best person for the job (68 percent). Since Japanese MNCs do not use third-country nationals in almost all of their foreign affiliates, no reason was given under this category.

Criteria for Selection

In this study, overseas managerial assignments were classified into four major categories: the chief executive officer whose responsibility is to oversee and direct the entire foreign operation; the functional head, whose job is to establish functional departments in a foreign subsidiary; the trouble-shooter, whose function is to analyze and solve specific operational problems; and the operative. Jobs in each of these categories involve varying degrees of contact with the local culture and varying lengths of stay in a certain country. One would expect a chief executive officer to have more extensive contacts with members of the local community than a trouble-shooter, and the trouble-shooter's job in a certain country to be of shorter duration than the CEO's. Given these differences, it would be interesting to study whether there were variations in criteria used for selecting personnel in each of the job categories.

Analysis of variance showed that for the U.S. sample, the criteria used for selecting candidates in each of the job categories were significantly different at the .005 level. For the U.S. sample, for each job category, certain criteria were considered more important than others. In jobs which require more extensive contacts with the local community (CEO and functional head), attributes like "adaptability, flexibility in new environmental settings," and "communication" were more frequently identified as being very important, compared to jobs that were more technically oriented (trouble-shooter). For the West European and Japanese samples, the pattern was slightly different. The most important criterion for selecting candidates in the CEO category in both samples was "managerial talent," and the most important criterion for selecting candidates in the functional head, trouble-shooter and operative categories was "technical knowledge of business." In the West European sample, adaptability/flexibility was considered a very important criterion in three of the four different job categories: 77 percent of the respondents cited this as a very important criterion for jobs in the CEO category, 81 percent in the functional-head category, and 62 percent in the trouble-shooter category. "Interest in overseas work" was cited as a very important criterion for each of the four job categories by a majority of the firms, although not cited as frequently as the other aforementioned criteria. Besides technical knowledge of business, most of the Japanese firms included in the study considered "experience in company" a very important criterion for jobs in three of the four job categories: 89 percent of the respondents identified this as a very important criterion for jobs in the CEO category, 71 percent cited this as a very important criterion for jobs in the functional-head category, and 53 percent mentioned this as a very important criterion for jobs in the trouble-shooter category.

This, perhaps, reflects the system of employment in Japanese society. Adaptability/flexibility in new environmental settings was also cited as a very important criterion for each of the four job categories by a majority of the firms, although not cited as frequently as the other aforementioned criteria. An interesting finding was that "sex of candidate" was mentioned by over half of the West European and Japanese multinationals as a criterion used in all four job categories. Sex was not mentioned as a criterion by any of the U.S. multinationals. This is probably due to differences among the countries in terms of equal employment opportunities. The West European and Japanese multinationals were perhaps less inhibited in acknowledging that there are problems in assigning women as expatriates because of the attitude towards working women in some societies.

Selection Procedures

The study examined the procedures undertaken by the firms to determine the candidate's suitability for the overseas position. To the question "Are tests administered to determine the candidate's technical competence?" 3 percent, 5 percent, and 14 percent, respectively, in the U.S., Japanese, and West European samples replied in the affirmative. To the question, "Are tests administered to determine the candidate's relational abilities?" 5 percent of the U.S. firms and 21 percent of the West European firms said yes. None of the Japanese firms used any such test. The U.S. firms who do test the candidate's relational abilities described such tests to include judgment by seniors, psychological appraisal, and interviews by a consulting psychologist with both candidate and spouse. In the European sample, the most common screening device to determine the candidates' relational abilities was psychological testing. Psychological testing was used more often by the West European multinationals than their U.S. counterparts.

It is rather surprising that an overwhelming majority of the U.S. firms included in the study failed to assess the candidate's relational abilities when they clearly recognize that relational abilities are important for overseas work, as evidenced by their responses discussed under the "criteria for selection" section, and when research shows relational abilities to be crucial to success in overseas assignments.[1] Given the increasing demand for personnel who can function effectively abroad and the relatively high incidence of failure, there certainly appears to be room for improvement in this area.

For the Japanese sample, it is interesting to note that even though none of the firms administered tests to determine the candidate's relational abilities, the Japanese MNCs clearly recognize the importance of such skills to success in an overseas environment, as evidenced by the fact (discussed later) that 57 percent of the firms had specialized training programs to prepare candidates for overseas work.

The respondents were asked to indicate whether interviews were conducted with the candidate or candidate and spouse in management-type positions and technically oriented positions. In the U.S. sample, for management-type positions, 52 percent of the firms conducted interviews with both candidate and spouse, 47 percent conducted interviews with the candidate only, and 1 percent did not conduct any interviews. For technically oriented positions, 40 percent of the companies conducted interviews with both candidate and spouse, 59 percent of the companies conducted interviews with the candidate only, and 1 percent did not conduct interviews. The profile of West European multinationals is similar to that of the U.S. firms. For management-type positions, a full 41 percent of the companies interviewed both candidate and spouse, while the remaining 59 percent interviewed the candidate only. For technically oriented positions, 38 percent of the companies interviewed both candidate and spouse, while the remaining 62 percent interviewed the candidate only. These figures suggest that in management-type positions which involve more extensive contact with the local community, as compared to technically oriented positions, the adaptability of the spouse to living in a foreign environment was perceived as important for successful performance abroad. However, even for technically oriented positions, a sizable proportion of the firms did conduct interviews with both candidate and spouse. This lends support to the contention of other researchers that MNCs are becoming increasingly cognizant of the importance of this factor to effective performance abroad.[2]

For the Japanese sample, 71 percent of the firms conducted interviews with the candidate only for management-type positions, and 62 percent conducted interviews with the candidate only for technically oriented positions. None of the firms included the spouse in interviews for positions in either category. This is strikingly different from both the U.S. and West European samples, and could be attributed to the fact that Japanese culture has a different view of the spouse's (in this case, the wife's) role and status in the family.

Training Programs

Training programs designed to prepare personnel for cross-cultural encounters were classified into six major categories. Presented in ascending order of rigor with which the program sought to impart knowledge and understanding of a foreign country, the six types of training programs were: environmental briefing (information about the geography, climate, housing, schools); cultural orientation (information about the cultural institutions, value systems of host country); culture assimilator (brief episodes describing intercultural encounters); language training; sensitivity training to develop attitudinal flexibility; and field experience, wherein trainees are actually sent to the country of assignment or a "microculture" nearby where they could undergo some of the emotional stress of living and working with people from a different subculture.

In the U.S. sample, only 32 percent of the respondents indicated that their company had formalized training programs to prepare candidates for overseas work. A full 68 percent of the respondents did not have any type of training program to prepare the candidate for cross-cultural encounters. The reasons, and the relative frequencies with which the reasons were cited, for omitting training programs were: trend toward employment of local nationals (45 percent); temporary nature of such assignments (28 percent); doubt effectiveness of such training programs (20 percent); and lack time (7 percent).

In contrast, 69 percent of the respondents in the West European sample sponsored training programs to prepare the candidates for overseas assignment. The reasons, and the relative frequencies with which the reasons were cited, for omitting training programs were: temporary nature of such assignments (30 percent); lack of time (30 percent); trend toward employment of local nationals (20 percent); and doubt effectiveness of such training programs (20 percent).

Fifty-seven percent of the Japanese MNCs responding had training programs to prepare candidates for overseas work. For those firms that did not have training programs, the reasons, and the relative frequencies with which the reasons were cited, for omitting training programs were: lack time (63 percent); and doubt effectiveness of such training programs (37 percent).

The firms that sponsored training programs were asked to indicate the types of training programs they used for training personnel in each of the four job categories. Table 3 presents the relative frequencies with which a particular program was used for each of the job categories in all three samples. Results indicate that for both the U.S. and West European samples, most of the firms that had training programs recognized the need for more rigorous training for the CEOs and functional heads than for trouble-shooters and operatives. In contrast, the Japanese firms that sponsored training programs appear to provide slightly more rigorous training for operatives. This could arise from the fact that since CEOs have more extensive records of overseas work experience, the need to subject them to the more rigorous programs was perceived as less important.

Table 3

FREQUENCIES OF TRAINING PROGRAMS USED FOR EACH JOB CATEGORY IN U.S., EUROPEAN, AND JAPANESE SAMPLES (IN PERCENT)

Job Category	CEO			Functional Head			Trouble Shooter			Operative		
Training Programs	U.S.	Eur.	Jap.	U.S.	Eur.	Jap.	U.S.	Eur.	Jap.	U.S.	Eur.	Jap.
Environmental Briefing	52	57	67	54	52	57	44	38	52	31	38	67
Cultural Orientation	42	55	14	41	52	14	31	31	19	24	28	24
Culture Assimilator	10	21	14	10	17	14	7	10	14	9	14	19
Language Training	60	76	52	59	72	57	36	41	52	24	48	76
Sensitivity Training	3	3	0	1	3	0	1	3	5	0	3	5
Field Experience	6	28	14	6	24	10	4	3	10	1	7	24

The firms that sponsored training programs were asked whether they evaluated the effectiveness of such training programs and to enumerate the types of evaluation procedures used. Thirty-two percent of the U.S. firms, 26 percent of the West European firms, and 33 percent of the Japanese firms adopted some form of evaluation process. For all three samples, procedures used to evaluate the effectiveness of such training programs included trainees' subjective evaluation and supervisors' subjective evaluation.

Failure Overseas

Respondents were asked to indicate the most important reasons for an expatriate's failure to function effectively in a foreign environment. For the U.S. sample, the reasons given in descending order of importance were: the inability of the manager's spouse to adjust to a different physical or cultural environment; the manager's inability to adapt to a different physical or cultural environment; other family-related problems; manager's personality or emotional maturity; manager's inability to cope with the larger responsibilities posed by the overseas work; manager's lack of technical competence for the job assignment; and lack of motivation to work overseas. These findings are in line with R. D. Hays's assertion that family situation and relational abilities were responsible, in the main, for failure or poor performance abroad.[3] In light of these findings, it appears all the more surprising that while most personnel administrators recognize the importance of these factors, a majority fail to take appropriate actions—few companies actually pursue rigorous methods for assessing and developing the relational abilities of their expatriate personnel.

In the West European sample, responses were fairly mixed. Only one reason was mentioned by most firms as being important for explaining failure or poor performance abroad—the inability of the manager's spouse to adjust to a different cultural or physical environment. Other possible reasons were perceived to have a marginal impact upon the expatriate's performance. This could indicate that either the failure rate for European MNCs was very low (as was the case) or that the European MNCs were not aware of the reasons and potential reasons for failure.

For the Japanese sample, the reasons given in descending order of importance were: inability of the manager to cope with the larger responsibilities posed by the overseas work; manager's inability to adapt to a different physical or cultural environment; manager's personality or emotional maturity; manager's lack of technical competence for the job assignment; inability of the manager's spouse to adjust; lack of motivation to work overseas; and other family-related problems. This ordering of reasons for failure is in contrast to that for the U.S., but does not come as a surprise because of the role and status to which Japanese culture relegates the spouse.

Respondents were asked to indicate the percentage of expatriates that have to be recalled to their home country or dismissed because of inability to function effectively in a foreign country. For the U.S. sample, 7 percent of the respondents indicated that the recall or failure rate was 20–40 percent; 69 percent of the firms had a recall rate of 10–20 percent; and the remaining 24 percent had recall rates of below 10 percent. For the West European and Japanese samples, the failure rates were lower. Fifty-nine percent of the West European firms had recall rates lower than 5 percent; 38 percent had recall rates of 6–10 percent; and only 3 percent had failure rates of 11–15 percent. For the Japanese sample, 76 percent of the firms had failure or recall rates of below 5 percent; 10 percent had failure or recall rates of 6–10 percent; 14 percent had failure rates of 11–19 percent. There are two possible explanations for this finding: West European and Japanese expatriates by nature, selection, and training are more adept at living and working in a foreign environment; or European and Japanese multinationals use different criteria for judging whether a person could work effectively in a foreign country. In the case of Japan, this could arise from the more paternalistic role assumed by the firm and also the practices of lifetime employment and promotion based on seniority rather than merit.

The study sought to analyze the relationships between the types of selection and training procedures used and the failure rate. Given the rather qualitative nature of the responses with respect to selection and training procedures, it was not possible to use sophisticated statistical techniques and the researcher had to settle for less sophisticated assessment devices. Each respondent firm received an overall score on the degree of rigor of its selection and training procedure. The scores ranged from 1 to 5. A low score indicated that the MNC did not use rigorous procedures in its selection and training; a high score indicated very rigorous selection and training procedures. An overall score for each respondent was arrived at through the raters' assessment of the appropriateness of the criteria used in selecting candidates for the different job categories, the procedures (tests, interviews) undertaken by the firm to determine the candidate's suitability for the foreign position, and training programs used (type of programs and evaluation of effectiveness of such programs). A firm which received a high score was one that: used appropriate criteria for selecting candidates in each of the four categories (emphasizing "relational abilities" for management-type positions and "technical competence" for the more technically oriented positions); adopted rigorous procedures for determining the candidate's suitability for the position (tests administered to determine candidate's relational abilities for management-type positions, interviews with both candidate and spouse); sponsored appropriate training programs that would better prepare the candidate for the overseas assignment (for example, for a CEO position, more rigorous techniques, such as sensitivity training and field experience, were used); and evaluated the effectiveness of the training programs used.

Two raters were used. Each rater independently evaluated the procedures and criteria used by each firm and assigned a score accordingly. The two raters' assessments were correlated as an indicator of inter-rater reliability. The r was .78. This showed that in general there was agreement between the raters in their assessments of the degree of rigor in the selection and training procedures used by the firm. These overall scores were then correlated with the failure rates of the respective firms. For the U.S. sample, the r was −0.63. This means that the more rigorous the types of selection and training procedures used, the lower the failure rate. For the European sample, the r was −0.47. For the Japanese sample, the r was −0.34. The lower correlations in the West European and Japanese samples (as compared to the U.S. sample) may be attributed to the fact that the scoring procedure used to determine the rigor of selection and training is more appropriate for the North American sample, which was used to empirically test the validity of the contingency framework for selection and training of personnel for overseas assignment developed by the author.[4]

Cross-tabs showed that for all three samples, the use of rigorous training programs significantly reduced the incidences of expatriates' inability to function effectively in a foreign environment (p less than/equal to .005). For the U.S. sample, cross-tabs showed that the adoption of appropriate criteria for selecting candidates and the use of interviews in management-type positions significantly reduced the incidences of expatriates' inability to function effectively in a foreign environment (p less than/equal to .01). For the West European sample, the relationships between the two were significant at the .05 level. For the Japanese sample, the relationships between the two were not statistically significant.

Conclusion

Implications for Management Practices

In the U.S. and West European samples, there was a definite relationship between the rigor of selection and training procedures used and the expatriates' ability to perform successfully in a foreign environment. In general, the more rigorous the selection and training procedures used, the less the incidences of poor performance or failure to work effectively in a foreign country. In the Japanese sample, it was found that more rigorous training programs could significantly reduce the incidences of expatriates' inability to function effectively in a foreign environment. This points to the need for MNCs to adopt more rigorous procedures in the areas of selection and training for expatriate assignments.

The study highlights the importance of the family situation to successful performance in both the U.S. and West European samples. This points to the need to include an assessment of the candidate's spouse to determine the candidate's suitability for overseas work and the need to include candidates' spouses in training programs to prepare them for living in a different cultural environment. In the U.S. sample, relational abilities were recognized as an important factor that could affect performance. Efforts should be made to assess and develop the candidate's relational abilities.

Given the relatively high failure rate in the U.S. sample, where possible, U.S. MNCs should use host-country nationals. The advantages associated with the use of host-country nationals include greater familiarity with local culture, reduced costs, and good public relations.

Implications for the Training Paradigm

The data on the U.S. sample provide support for the contingency framework for selection and training developed by the author.[5] The model essentially states that given the differences in degrees of contact required with the local culture, varying durations of stay in the foreign country, and the varying degrees of differences between home and other foreign cultures, there is no one selection criterion that could be emphasized and no one training program that should be used regardless of the task and environment. Rather, the contingency framework allows for the systematic analysis of variations in task and environmental factors. The contingency framework provides the selection criteria and training programs that should be used in each of the four job categories and for different countries of foreign assignment and provides for the selection of the right person to fill the position, and the prescription of the best type of training programs after a careful analysis of the task and environment in question.[6]

Preliminary analysis of the data collected on the West European sample provides moderate support for the model, while the data collected on the Japanese sample do not provide support for the contingency framework developed by the author. This highlights the importance of cultural differences in the development and application of paradigms. As compared with Japan, the U.S. and West Europe are more similar, culturally speaking. This may account for the similar practices observed among U.S. and West European MNCs. However, even here we observe that while the two cultures could be similar, there are still differences in practices and outcomes. This finding points to the need to empirically test theories and models which apply and work in one culture before their use and application in other cultures which are substantially different from our own, even where the economic systems may be fairly similar.

References

1. R. D. Hays, "Ascribed Behavioral Determinants of Success-Failure among U.S. Expatriate Managers," *Journal of International Business Studies,* vol. 2 (1971), pp. 40–46; idem, "Expatriate Selection: Insuring Success and Avoiding Failure," *Journal of International Business Studies,* vol. 5 (1974), pp. 25–37; J. M. Ivancevich, "Selection of American Managers for Overseas Assignments," *Personnel Journal,* vol. XVVLLL (1969); E. L. Miller, "The Selection Decision for an International Assignment: A Study of the Decision Maker's Behavior," *Journal of International Business Studies,* vol. 3 (1972), pp. 49–65.
2. Hays, "Expatriate Selection"; W. A. Borrmann, "The Problem of Expatriate Personnel and their Selection in International Business," *Management International Review,* vol. 8, no. 4/5 (1968), pp. 37–48; P. R. Harris and D. L. Harris, "Training for Cultural Understanding," *Training and Development Journal* (May 1972), pp. 8–10.
3. Hays, "Expatriate Selection."
4. R. L. Tung, "A Framework for the Selection and Training of Personnel for Overseas Assignments," paper presented at the International Meetings of the Academy of International Business, Manchester, England, 1978; idem, "Selection and Training of Personnel for Overseas Assignments," *Columbia Journal of World Business* (Spring 1981), pp. 68–78.
5. Ibid.
6. Tung, "Selection and Training."

7. THE MANAGEMENT PRACTICES OF JAPANESE SUBSIDIARIES OVERSEAS

ANANT R. NEGANDHI, GOLPIRA S. ESHGHI, and EDITH C. YUEN

The success story of Japanese firms, both in their home country and in their overseas subsidiaries, has been the focal point of comparative management research in the 1970s and early 1980s. Several scholars attributed the impressive productivity gains in Japanese industries to the basic principles of Japanese management. Further, they advocated the utilization of these principles by American and European businesses in order to solve employee morale and productivity problems.[1]

However, in recent years, the validity of the "happy worker" hypothesis in explaining the effectiveness of Japanese management has been seriously questioned. In fact, the results of several empirical studies indicate that Japanese firms are facing manpower management problems both at home and in their overseas subsidiaries.[2]

The main purpose of this article is to identify and discuss the Japanese management problems of overseas subsidiaries, and it is based on several empirical studies of Japanese overseas subsidiaries undertaken by the authors of this article and their colleagues during the last 16 years (1968 to 1984). These studies are:

- A comparative study of American, Japanese, and local firms in Taiwan. Intensive interviews were conducted during 1968–1969 of top level managers. A total of 27 companies were included in the study.[3]
- A comparative study of 124 American, European, and Japanese multinationals' subsidiaries in Brazil, Peru, India, Malaysia, Singapore, and Thailand. The study was undertaken between 1974–1979 and utilized intensive interviews.[4]
- A comparative study of 151 American, German, and Japanese multinationals (31 headquarters and 120 overseas subsidiaries) in the United States, Western European countries, Australia, and Japan. Data for this study was collected through intensive interviews during 1976–1981.[5]
- A comparative study of 95 upper-level Japanese and American managers of subsidiaries of Japanese firms in the United States. Data was collected during 1981–1982 through a mail survey.[6]
- A comparative study of 20 subsidiaries of American and Japanese multinationals in Singapore in 1984.[7]
- An intensive case study of a Japanese subsidiary in Australia in 1978.[8]

The Japanese Success Story: Facts Mixed Up

For more than a decade, Western admirers have loudly praised the unique features in Japanese management, manufacturing, and labor relations that have made Japan a formidable worldwide competitor. Some of the most important elements of the "Japanese Management System" include: the custom of lifetime employment; the seniority-based, implicit and infrequent performance review process; and consensus-based decision making.[9] In comparing the salient features of Japanese and Western management, Matsusaki perhaps best describes the differences by suggesting that Japanese management has a "generalist orientation," while Western management has a "specialist orientation."[10]

In the United States, several scholars have argued that the principles of Japanese management have been successfully applied to foreign subsidiaries of Japanese MNCs. The natural extension of this line of argument is that these principles can (and should) be applied successfully in American companies.

The results of several studies show that the management style of Japanese expatriate managers falls into two categories: they either try to adopt local management practices or they try to keep the Japanese practices as much as possible. However, in reality, only modified versions of the local or Japanese systems are practiced.

The Modified Local System

Japanese managers who choose to adopt local management practices do so because they are concerned about their lack of familiarity with local culture, practices, and institutions. They may also be wary of the possibility of conflict with local employees. Thus, while Japanese managers retain control over policy formulation and key decisions, administrative duties which involve sensitive and direct contact with locals and local institutions are delegated to a few trusted local managers. In doing so, they want to avoid "sticking out like a sore thumb" or attracting criticism unnecessarily.

Given this context, it is hardly surprising that local managers come to interpret their duties as implementing a management system which is as dogmatically "local" as possible. They follow wage guidelines strictly and adhere to legal regulations regarding recruitment and dismissal. They play it safe by delivering to the Japanese managers a system which follows established rules and policies to the letter.

Legal regulations prescribe only minimal behavior and, in practice, rules are often softened by customs, toleration of minor deviations, and personal considerations. In the case of Japanese overseas subsidiaries, the strict adherence to legal regulations results in a system which, on the one hand, is as dogmatically "local" as possible and, at the same time, is much more bureaucratic, rigid, and insensitive (to the employees' needs) than most other local firms actually are.

In a comparative study of 27 American, Japanese, and local companies in Taiwan, Negandhi found the modified local system to be dominant in Japanese companies.[11] The study revealed that there were many similarities between management practices of Japanese subsidiaries and local firms in Taiwan, while the practices of the American subsidiaries differed markedly. Specifically, the study showed that:

- In contrast to the major U.S. subsidiaries, the Japanese subsidiaries were quite diffused in their functional area policies. Only one out of seven of these companies formally stated its major policies; two subsidiaries outlined only marketing and product-line policies.
- There were more hierarchies and centralization of decision making among Japanese and local firms than American subsidiaries. Regarding the leader's perception of subordinates' abilities, the Japanese and Chinese leaders seemed to have much less confidence and trust in their subordinates than their American counterparts. Both Japanese and Chinese managers felt that subordinates needed close watching and guidance and should not be left to function on their own. Japanese and Chinese managers were autocratic/paternalistic in decision making while Americans utilized consultative/democratic leadership styles.
- Although the Japanese and local firms appeared to stress the importance of their employees' security and socio-psychological needs, there was no specific management practice to satisfy those needs. In fact, contrary to the American firms, the Japanese subsidiaries and the local companies were unable to attract qualified and trained personnel and the majority of the executives and technical personnel in these companies were poorly trained. The higher effectiveness of the U.S. subsidiaries in attracting trained personnel was attributed to such factors as high monetary rewards, opportunity for advancement and individual development, and objective criteria for promotion and rewards.
- Regarding management and organizational effectiveness, executives of seven out of the nine U.S. subsidiaries viewed achieving of the firm's objectives as most crucial. In contrast, only three of the seven Japanese subsidiaries and three of the eleven local companies were able to emphasize the achievement of the firm's overall objectives as most important. In other words, in the Japanese and local companies, departmental goals preoccupied the executives' time and talent.
- Because of the greater cultural differences, it was expected that American subsidiaries would have the most difficult time in understanding and adapting to Taiwan's environmental conditions. However, the data revealed that local companies and Japanese subsidiaries had many more problems in dealing with the environment than the U.S. companies. Table 1 presents some of the important differences between American, Japanese, and local firms regarding their management practices and effectiveness.

A recent study of the management practices of 20 American and Japanese subsidiaries in Singapore also found that the American companies have been able to successfully transfer many features of their management practices to their operations in this country. Meanwhile, the management style of the Japanese companies in Singapore had little resemblance to the "Japanese management system."[12] For example, of the 10 Japanese companies in the study, only one company used the "ringi" system or the consensus approach to decision making. Furthermore, as was the case in the Taiwan study, Japanese companies in Singapore exercised tight control on their operations and decision making was centralized. Several executives of these companies stated that high turnover and the statutory requirements of compulsory contributions to the Central Provident and Skills Development Funds were major factors why Japanese companies were hesitant about extending some of their home management practices to Singapore.

There are examples of tensions and conflicts between management and local employees of Japanese subsidiaries in developed as well as developing countries. In a YKK plant in Italy, workers struck for 18 months complaining about the hard-driving ten-men Japanese management team. Although the Japanese managers, to demonstrate their corporate loyalty, attempted to man the machines themselves, a labor magistrate found the company guilty of "anti-union activity" and ordered the managers to keep away from the production line during the strike.[13]

It seems that the "modified local system" of management is practiced by Japanese management more frequently in their subsidiaries in less-developed countries. In a study of 120 American, European, and Japanese subsidiaries in less-developed countries, Negandhi and Baliga found that the "localized" approach was dominant among the Japanese firms.[14] This resulted in maintenance of status quo, and the employees were often held in low esteem—as was the custom in many local enterprises and government agencies. The outcome of these policies was low morale, low productivity, and high absenteeism and turnover rates. Although the expatriate Japanese managers failed to see the causes of their problems, they did admit that they had serious manpower and personnel problems in their operations. Compared to U.S.- and European-based MNCs, Japanese companies experienced a larger number of operational conflicts in their Latin American and Far-East subsidiaries (see Table 2).

Sim's study of American, British, and Japanese subsidiaries in Malaysia[15] supports Negandhi and Baliga's findings. He found that the extent of participation and information sharing in planning was greatest in the American subsidiaries and lowest in the Japanese subsidiaries. In the Japanese subsidiaries, planning and decision making tended to be confined to Japanese executives.

The Modified Japanese System

The second approach is to adopt a "Japanese" system as far as possible. The problem with this approach is that the Japanese management practices mirror Japanese language, culture, and environment to such an extent that it is almost impossible to adopt the type of management and employment systems practiced at the headquarters in foreign subsidiaries. Given these constraints, the system which ends up being adopted by the local subsidiary is little more than a "Mickey-Mouse" Japanese system, with only symbolic gestures of paternalism.

The "modified Japanese system" in its variations has been practiced in the subsidiaries of Japanese firms in developed countries such as Western European nations and the United States. Several studies of Japanese subsidiaries in the United States

Table 1

PROFILES OF MANAGEMENT PRACTICES AND EFFECTIVENESS OF THE U.S. SUBSIDIARY, JAPANESE SUBSIDIARY, AND THE LOCAL (TAIWAN) FIRM.

Management Practices and Effectiveness	U.S. Subsidiary	Japanese Subsidiary	Local Firm
Planning	Long range (5 to 10 years)	Medium to short range (1 to 2 years)	Medium to short range (1 to 2 years)
Policy-making	Formally stated, utilized as guidelines and control measures	Formally not stated. Not utilized as guidelines and control measures	Formally not stated. Not utilized as guidelines and control measures
Other Control Devices Used	Quality control, cost and budgetary control. Maintenance. Setting of standards.	Quality control maintenance	Some cost control. Some quality control. Some maintenance
Organizational Set-up			
Grouping of activities	On functional-area basis	On functional-area basis	On functional-area basis
Number of departments	5 to 7	5 to 7	5 to 7
Use of specialized staff	Some	None	None
Use of service department	Considerable	Some	Some
Authority definition	Clear	Unclear	Unclear
Degree of Decentralization	High	Low	Low
Leadership Style	Consultative	Autocratic	Paternalistic-autocratic
Trust and confidence in subordinates	High	Low	Low
Managers' attitudes toward leadership style and delegation	Would prefer autocratic style. Authority should be held tight at the top	Not available	Would prefer consultative type

Table 1 *(continued)*

Management Practices and Effectiveness	U.S. Subsidiary	Japanese Subsidiary	Local Firm
Manpower Management Practices			
Manpower policies	Formally Stated	Not Stated	Not Stated
Organization of Personnel Dept.	Not Separate Unit	Not Separate Unit	Not Separate Unit
Job Evaluation	Done	Done	Done by Very Few
Development of Election and Promotion Criteria	Formally Done	Done by Some	Done by Some
Training Programs	Only for the Blue-Collar Employees	Only for the Blue-Collar Employees	Only for the Blue-Collar Employees
Compensation and Motivation	Monetary Only	Monetary Only	Monetary Only
Management Effectiveness			
Employee morale	High	Moderate	Moderate
Absenteeism	Low	Low	Low
Turnover	High	Low	High
Productivity	High	High	High
Ability to attract Trained Personnel	Able to Do So	Somewhat Able to Do So	Somewhat Able to Do So
Inter-Departmental Relationships	Very Cooperative	Somewhat Cooperative	Somewhat Cooperative
Executives' Perception of the Firm's Overall Objectives	Systems Optimization As an Important Goal	Sub-Systems Optimization As an Important Goal	Sub-Systems Optimization As an Important Goal
Utilization of High-Level Manpower	Effectively Utilized	Moderate to Poor Utilization	Moderate to Poor Utilization
Adapting to Environmental Changes	Able to Adapt Without Much Difficulty	Able to Adapt with Some Difficulty	Able to Adapt with Considerable Difficulty
Growth in Sales	Phenomenal	Considerable	Considerable to Modest

Source: Anant R. Negandhi, *Management and Economic Development in Taiwan* (The Hague, Martinus Nijhoff, 1973), pp. 125–127.

Table 2

CONFLICT VERSUS CONTROLLING OWNERSHIP OF MNC (BY REGION)

	Latin America			Far East		
	U.S.	**European**	**Japanese**	**U.S.**	**European**	**Japanese**
Negotiational	4/40	1/9.0	0/0.0	13/39.4	12/52.2	5/29.4
Policy	3/30	6/54.5	0/0.0	13/39.4	9/39.2	4/23.5
Operational	3/30	4/36.3	6/100	7/21.1	2/8.6	8/47.1
	10/100	11/100	6/100	33/100	23/100	17/100
	N = 27 CHI SQUARE = 12.0 4 DF.; P = 0.0173			N = 27 CHI SQUARE = 8.4 4 DF.; P = 0.0757		

Source: Anant R. Negandhi and B. R. Baliga, *Quest for Survival and Growth* (New York: NY: Praeger Publishers, 1979), p. 119.

have identified common elements in the management of these companies.[16] These commonalities include some form of job security and, compared to similar American companies, more concern for the welfare of the employees (including both blue-collar workers and management). Overall, it seems that Japanese subsidiaries in the developed countries are more successful and encounter fewer management problems than their counterparts in the less-developed countries. Regardless of whether the "modified local system" or the "modified Japanese system" is utilized by the management of Japanese subsidiaries, there are several important problem areas. These problem areas include:

- **Centralization of decision making**—In general, research on management of Japanese overseas subsidiaries has found that the prevalent style of decision making is the autocratic style and there is no evidence of the practice of the consensus style.

As stated earlier, in the comparative study of MNCs in Taiwan, Negandhi found that in Japanese subsidiaries, all major decisions were made by Japanese expatriates or by the headquarters.[17] In a study of top- and middle-level expatriate and local managers in Japanese firms in the United States, Negandhi and Baliga found that a collegial approach had been substituted for the consensus approach.

Eshghi provided the American and Japanese managers in her study[18] with definitions of four different approaches to decision making, ranging from an authoritarian to a consensus-seeking style. They were asked to identify the style which they used more often. Only 17.1 percent of the Japanese managers indicated they sought consensus in decision making. In fact, the dominant mode of decision making among Japanese was directive (45.7 percent), followed by consultative (34.3 percent). In contrast, the majority of American managers in the study (73.2 percent) stated that they practiced a consultative style of decision making. When probed about why they did not practice the consensus-seeking approach, one Japanese expatriate manager said, "Our company is multinational and America's approach to decision making is rather different from our family-concern approach." Several other Japanese managers said that selection of a decision-making style depends on the people and the subject of the decision and that the consensus style was generated in Japan and could not be applied in the United States.

Other studies on management of foreign subsidiaries of Japanese MNCs have found little evidence of a "bottom-up" decision-making process. In a study of twelve Japanese companies with major manufacturing operations in the United States, Johnson found no evidence of the consensus-approach to decision making.[19] Similarly, Hatvany and Pucik, regarding decision making in U.S.-based Japanese companies, state:

> *Although the level of face-to-face communication in Japanese organizations is relatively high, it should not be confused with participation in decision making. Most communication concerns routine tasks. . . . Moreover, consultation with lower-ranking employees does not automatically imply that the decision process is "bottom-up," as suggested by Peter Drucker and others. Especially in the case of long-term planning and strategy, the initiative comes mostly from the top.*[20]

As stated earlier, centralized decision making in its extreme is prevalent in Japanese subsidiaries in the less-developed countires. In the developed countries, market conditions and the existence of industrial democracy have forced Japanese subsidiaries to make some modifications in their approach to decision making. However, as the evidence suggests, decision making in these firms is not what the "consensus-seeking" should be. At best, Japanese managers simply "inform" the lower-level employees of issues and the management's decisions.

■ **Low level of confidence in subordinates' abilities**—This issue surfaced in two separate studies by the present authors. In the comparative study of American, Japanese, and local Chinese companies operating in Taiwan, it was found that in comparison with American managers, both Japanese and Chinese managers had much less confidence in their subordinates. Chinese and Japanese managers in the study felt that subordinates needed close watching and guidance and should not be left to function on their own. And in a recent study of expatriate and local upper- and middle-level managers of U.S.-based Japanese firms, both groups were asked to evaluate performance of their subordinates and identify the subordinates' nationalities. The study found a strong case of nationality bias among Japanese managers; they rated the Japanese subordinates more favorably than American subordinates.[21]

These findings are supported by Sim's study of Japanese MNCs in Malaysia and Putti and Chang's study of American and Japanese subsidiaries in Singapore.[22]

■ **Low level of trust for local managers**—Trustworthiness for the Japanese is a much more demanding quality than is commonly perceived in the West. DeMente[23] states that in the West, if a businessman fulfills his contractual agreements, he can be called trustworthy. To the Japanese, a man in whom they can have *Shinyo* (trust) is a man of honor who will do what is expected of him whatever the cost and whatever the situation. Trust is the result of a long-term, successful relationship in which both parties find fulfillment of mutual expectations. It is a relationship which takes years to develop.

In this context, it is easy to understand why Japanese managers are hesitant to extend trust to local managers whom they do not know on a personal basis. However, over a period of months and years, a few local managers may succeed in gaining the trust of the top Japanese officials in the overseas subsidiary. There is, then, a tendency for the Japanese to rely heavily on few local managers, effectively treating them as key local officials. This situation was observed in the case of a Japanese firm in Australia. Several other scholars found a similar problem in their studies. Thurley and his associates also observed this tendency of Japanese managers to restrict their trust to a few key officials in the U.K.-based Japanese companies.[24] Johnson proposes that this "trusted" local manager, who occupies a delicate position at the interface between the American and Japanese nationals, suffers from the problems of having to maintain a balance between two cultures and is in the middle of organizational conflict and miscommunication.[25]

- **Ceiling on promotion for locally employed managers**—It has been well documented that among multinationals of all countries, Japanese companies are the most ethnocentric in their staffing policies. This phenomenon has been observed in Japanese subsidiares in both developed and developing countries.[26] Kobayashi, summarizing the results of a study of 89 Japanese multinationals, states that among areas of management process, the area of hiring and promotion of locally recruited employees is the least multinationalized.[27] Since senior positions in most Japanese overseas subsidiaries are filled by Japanese nationals, it is not surprising that an unofficial ceiling on promotion exists for the locally employed managers. The exact level at which this ceiling on promotion is pegged appears to be something which is determined ultimately by head office control. With the promotion ceiling for local managers, Japanese and local managers enjoy two basically different employment systems. They pursue different career paths, enjoy different levels of job security, and receive different types of training (or no training) and different fringe benefits. In addition, Japanese managers have exclusive access to headquarter personnel—which is the locus of power, influence, and information. This problem is aggravated by the fact that, particularly in Japanese subsidiaries based in the less-developed countires, there is not a formulated set of human resource management policies.

As noted in the Taiwan study, Japanese subsidiaries were the most diffuse about their policies on human resources, with only one out of seven having specific, established policies regarding manpower. In contrast, 5 of the 9 U.S. subsidiaries and 5 of the 11 local firms documented their manpower policies.[28] This lack of concern for preserving and developing the subsidiary's human resources is further highlighted by the fact that in none of the Japanese subsidiaries in the sample was there a separately organized personnel department.

- **Problems with unions and equal employment regulation**—The major union structure in Japan is the "enterprise union," which caters to workers employed in a particular enterprise. Over 90% of the Japanese unions belong to the enterprise category. The union in Japan, unlike its counterpart (the "local") in the United States, has a very detached affiliation with the national labor centers. Structurally, the essential characteristic of the enterprise union is that its very existence depends upon the survival and growth of the firm.

The union structure in Japan has two important implications for the management of Japanese firms. First, Japanese unions are unable to standardize wages either by industry or by occupation. This has kept labor costs in Japan relatively lower than those in other developed countries, particularly the United States. Second, having been stripped of any real source of power, the enterprise unions in Japan have usually maintained a cooperative relationship with the management.

In their foreign operations, Japanese firms face two different situations. In the less-developed countries, because of high unemployment rates or a lack of a democratic government, labor unions either do not exist or have very little bargaining power. Despite the weak position of labor unions in the less-developed countries, claims of anti-union activities by Japanese firms have been reported in Thailand, Malaysia, Korea, and the Philippines.[29] On the other hand, Japanese subsidiaries in the developed countries, particularly the United States, are well aware of the potential problems that may be created by the labor unions. To keep their labor costs down and to avoid conflicts, the common strategy of many Japanese firms has been to avoid labor unions as much as they can.

According to a report by the government of Japan, out of 14 manufacturing companies surveyed in the United States whose majority capital was owned by a Japanese parent company, only 5 were organized by American labor unions.[30] But several instances of hostility and conflict between unions and Japanese firms have been reported in the American media.[31]

Similarly, several Japanese firms in the U.S. have been accused of discriminating against women and minorities. Having been accustomed to the utilization of women as lower-level, part-time, and temporary workers in Japan, U.S.-based Japanese firms find it difficult to comply with U.S. laws and promote women to management positions. For example, in 1981, three Japanese subsidiaries—Sumitomo, C. Itoh & Co., and Hitachi—faced court cases regarding job bias.[32]

Concluding Notes

The review of our empirical studies and other published research has pinpointed several important problems that Japanese are facing in the management of their subsidiaries. Problems include centralized decision making, low confidence in employees' abilities, low level of trust in employees, lack of a clearly formulated human resource policy, and problems with labor unions and equal-employment regulations. Most of these problems are more serious in the less-developed countries, while a few occur more in the developed nations.

However, there is no doubt that Japanese companies, both at home and abroad, have been relatively more effective than their American and European counterparts. Competence in both production management and engineering and smooth relationship with local governments are two important areas where Japanese MNCs have shown superiority over other MNCs and over local companies. For example, a recent major study of managerial practice in Europe (undertaken by the International Center for Economic and Related Disciplines (ICERD) at the London School of Economics) emphasize that Japanese-based companies' attention to detail, work discipline, and superior interdepartmental coordination are reasons for superior performance levels in their TV manufacturing plants. In another electronics study in the U.K., Takayama found that while the Japanese companies provided much poorer incentives than those traditionally used in the West, there was one case where a Japanese factory in the U.K. produced lower rejection rates than a comparable British company with more sophisticated testing equipment.[33]

The apparent contradictions between the findings of recent studies as to the effectiveness of Japanese overseas subsidiaries indicate that we must seriously question the validity of recent proposals for the application of the basic principles of Japanese management to other societies. These proposals were based on studies of the limited number of Japanese companies in the United States in the early and mid 1970s. While the survey method of data collection characteristic of most of these studies has provided some insight into the effectiveness of Japanese management in overseas subsidiaries, it has failed to pinpoint the underlying causes of the observed phenomenon. Future research needs to be supplemented with other methods such as case studies, in-depth personal interviews, and observations. Before we try to adopt the "successful" aspects of Japanese management practices, we must develop a better understanding of Japan's own problems in applying these practices in their overseas subsidiaries.

References

1. R. T. Johnson and W. Ouchi, "Made in America, Under Japanese Management," *Harvard Business Review,* 52, No. 1 (1974):61–69; W. Ouchi, *Theory Z: How American Business Can Meet the Japanese Challenge* (Reading, MA: Addison-Wesley, 1981).
2. S. P. Sethi, N. Namiki, and C. L. Swanson, "The Decline of the Japanese System of Management," *California Management Review,* 26, No. 4 (Summer 1984): 35–45; see also, K. Koshiro, "Foreign Direct Investment and Industrial Relations: Japanese Experience After the Oil Crisis," in S. Takamiya and K. Thurley, eds., *Japan's Emerging Multinationals* (Tokyo: University of Tokyo Press, 1985), pp. 205–228.
3. A. R. Negandhi, *Management and Economic Development: The Case of Taiwan* (The Hague: Martinus Nijhoff, 1973).
4. A. R. Negandhi and B. R. Baliga, *Quest for Survival and Growth* (New York, NY: Praeger Publishers, 1979).
5. A. R. Negandhi and B. R. Baliga, *Tables are Turning: German and Japanese Multinational Companies in the United States* (Cambridge, MA: Oelgeschlager, Gunn, and Hain Publishers, 1981).
6. G. S. Eshghi, "Values and Organizational Behavior: A Comparative Study of American and Japanese Managers of Japanese-owned Firms in the United States," unpublished Ph.D. dissertation, University of Illinois, Champaign-Urbana, IL (1984).
7. J. M. Putti and M. Chong, "American and Japanese Management Practices in Their Singapore Subsidiaries," faculty working paper, National University of Singapore, (1984).

8. E. C. Yuen, "The Management Porblems of a Japanese Subsidiary in Australia," paper presented in the Annual Conference of the Australian Society of Asian Studies (1978).
9. M. Y. Yoshino, *Japan's Managerial System* (Cambridge, MA: MIT Press, 1968).
10. H. Matsusaki, "Japanese Managers and Management in the Western World: A Canadian Experience," in A. R. Negandhi, ed., *Functioning of the Multinational Corporation: A Global Comparative Study* (New York, NY: Pergamon Press, 1980), pp. 226–254.
11. Negandhi (1973), op. cit., pp. 124–127.
12. Putti and Chong, op. cit.
13. J. S. McClenanhen, "Cultural Hybrids: Japanese Plants in the U.S.," *Industry Week,* February 19, 1979, pp. 73–75.
14. Negandhi and Baliga (1979), op. cit.
15. A. B. Sim, "Decentralized Management of Subsidiaries and Their Performance," *Management International Review,* 2 (1977): 45–50.
16. R. T. Johnson, "Success and Failure of Japanese Subsidiaries in America," *Columbia Journal of World Business,* 12, No. 1 (Spring 1977): 30–37; N. Hatvany and V. Pucik, "Japanese Management Practices and Productivity," *Organizational Dynamics* (Spring 1981), pp. 5–21.
17. Negandhi (1973), op. cit.
18. Eshghi, op. cit.
19. Johnson, op. cit.
20. Hatvany and Pucik, op. cit., p. 17.
21. G. S. Eshghi, "Nationality Bias and Performance Evaluation in Multinational Corporations," *1985 Proceedings of the Academy of Management,* (forthcoming).
22. Sim, op. cit.; Putti and Chong, op. cit.
23. B. DeMente, *Japanese Manners and Ethics in Business* (Tokyo: Simpson-Doyle and Co., 1975).
24. K. E. Thurley, M. Nangaku, and K. Uragami, "Employment Relations of Japanese Companies in the U.K.: A Report on an Exploratory Study," paper given to the British Association for Japanese Studies (1977).
25. Johnson, op. cit.
26. S. Van der Merwe and A. Van der Merwe, "The Man Who Manages Multinationals: A Comparative Study of the Profiles, Backgrounds, and Attitudes of Chief Executives of American, European, and Japanese MNCs," in A. R. Negandhi, ed., *Functioning of the Multinational Corporation: A Global Comparative Study* (New York, NY: Pergamon Press, 1980), pp. 209–225; and Negandhi and Baliga (1979), op. cit.
27. N. Kobayashi, "The Patterns of Management Style Developing in Japanese Multinationals in the 1980s," in S. Takamiya and K. Thurley, eds., *Japan's Emerging Multinationals* (Tokyo: University of Tokyo Press, 1985), p. 249.
28. Negandhi (1973), op. cit.
29. *The Report of the 1st International Trade Union Seminar between Japan and Malaysia* (Tokyo: TCM, 1975); *The Report of the International Trade Union Seminar between Taiwan, Korea, and Japan in Tokyo* (Tokyo: TCM, 1976); *The Report of the 4th International Trade Union Seminar between Japan and the*

Philippines in Manila (Tokyo: TCM, 1977); *The Report of the 5th International Trade Union Seminar between Japan and Thailand in Bangkok* (Tokyo: TCM, 1978); *The Report of the 6th International Trade Union Seminar between Japan and Indonesia in Jakarta* (Tokyo: TCM, 1979).

30. Ministry of Labor, "Summary Report of Case Studies on Personnel Policies and Industrial Relations of the Japanese Companies in the USA," *TCW News,* June 25, 1979.
31. "Supreme Court to Hear Japanese Job Bias Suit," *Iron Age,* December 16, 1981.
32. "Business Feels the Heat of U.S. Antibias Laws," *Business Week,* November 23, 1981, pp. 57–58.
33. M. Takayama, "Japanese Multinationals in Europe: Internal Operations and Their Policy Implications" (Berlin: International Institute of Management, 1979).

8. EMPLOYER-EMPLOYEE BASED QUALITY CIRCLES IN JAPAN: HUMAN RESOURCE POLICY IMPLICATIONS FOR AMERICAN FIRMS

GEORGE MUNCHUS, III

George Munchus, III, is Associate Professor of Management in the Department of Management, University of Alabama, Birmingham.

This paper traces the development of the quality circle in Japan with reference to such traditions as permanent employment, nenko (seniority-based compensation), enterprise unionism, and management paternalism. Quality circles are examined as tools for motivating employees, reducing labor turnover, effecting employee "career expansion," and allowing employee participation in job redesign.

Quality circles typically are small groups of volunteers from the same work areas who meet regularly to identify, analyze, and solve quality and related problems in their area of responsibility. During the first circle meetings, members are trained in quality control, communication skills, and problem solving techniques. Members of a group choose a particular problem to study, gather data, and use such methods as brainstorming, Pareto analysis, histograms, and control charts to form a recommendation that can be presented to management.

Although quality circles are a Japanese invention, the idea of quality circles has its basis in motivational theory, which advocates increased responsibility by employees for their own quality of work. The circle often is permitted to select its own projects. However, members generally are restricted to problems concerning quality or productivity in their area of expertise, not other areas such as compensation or product planning. Circles are used primarily in manufacturing areas, but they have been successfully applied in some white collar areas.

The purpose of this paper is (a) to provide a short summary of quality circles and (b) to review Japanese labor laws and labor relations as they impact human resource policies. The paper will utilize published studies as a basis for the quality circle summary and labor relations review.

Quality Circles in Japan

Early History of the Quality Circle Concept

Cole (1980), in reviewing the development of the quality circle idea from the post-WWII period, noted that American quality control experts were first working with

George Munchus, III, "Employer-Employee Based Quality Circles in Japan: Human Resource Policy Implications for American Firms," *Academy of Management Review* 8.2 (1983): 255–61. Reprinted by permission.

the Occupation authorities in an effort to rebuild the Japanese economy. Immediately after this, William Deming lectured on quality control methods, and to honor his contribution the Deming Prize was established in 1950 as part of an annual nationwide competition in the area of quality control. In 1954 J. Juran began another series of lectures that emphasized the participation of middle and top management in the implementation of quality control systems. The Japanese studied these lecturers' recommendations and put them into practice on a large scale basis from 1955 to 1960, with an important modification: instead of allowing quality control to remain the province of quality control engineers, management made it the responsibility of all rank and file employees as well. Blue-collar workers were taught quality control techniques and allowed to participate in quality control groups. A survey conducted by the Union of Japanese Scientists and Engineers (UJSE) of the 360 companies in 1976 showed that 52 percent of the quality circle meetings were held both during and outside regular working hours. Another survey, made in 1971, showed that, of workers meeting outside regular working hours, 24 percent were not paid and 60 percent received their regular overtime pay.

Cole (1980) stated that this innovation to include blue-collar participation implied a fundamental difference between the Japanese managers' belief in the perfectibility of man and the opposing ideas of American managers. For example, unlike Japan, where workers are granted the opportunity to redesign their work, in the United States many managers do not permit employees to inspect their own work. Cole stated that many U.S. managers believe that "workers know how to raise productivity and improve quality, but are holding back for no justifiable reason" (1980, p. 142). Cole related this attitude to the influence of the Taylor school, which he stated was partially responsible for the separation of the functions of planning, which are performed by engineers, and execution, which is performed by production supervisors. However, Vough (1975), an IBM executive, illustrates how production employees at IBM inspect their own work, leading to improved quality.

The idea behind the quality circle is that, armed with the proper training, the worker can discover previously unrecognized quality problems. However, the Japanese system does not rely on worker initiative in the absence of strong management control of the group program. Also, according to Cole (1980) quality circles have succeeded in Japan partially because most high school students have been introduced to the mathematical and statistical skills needed in quality circle analysis. It was the labor shortage of the 1970s, as well, that forced Japanese companies to recruit more actively the better educated high school graduates, as well as middle school graduates, and to adopt programs involving increased worker responsibility. Cole (1980) emphasized that the ability of circle participants to follow up their own suggestions is one feature that makes circles such a "people-building" device.

The UJSE, a nonprofit research and training institute, was organized in 1948 to involve foremen in the quality circle idea and to bring foremen together from different companies. UJSE was composed of engineering and science professors and industrial engineers. Its magazine, *Genba to QC,* later renamed *FQCC,* disseminated information to company foremen with case studies of circles already in operation. The involvement for foremen as representatives of the workers was considered crucial to the success of quality circles. Foremen generally received 30 to 40 hours of training.

Although the exact number of quality circles in Japan is unknown, 87,540 circles were registered with UJSE in 1978, up from 1,000 registered in 1964 (Cole, 1980). Most of these were hourly employees in manufacturing. Assuming there were 10 members per circle, Cole estimated a membership of 840,000 employees nationwide. This meant that of the total labor force of 37 million in 1978, 1 in 8 belonged to quality circles. Yeager (1980) estimated that nearly one-fourth of all Japanese hourly employees belong to quality circles. He also stated that there are not many white-collar participants.

Characteristics of Japanese Quality Circles

According to Cole (1980), although membership varies from 3 to 20 members, circles generally are of from 5 to 10 members. Membership is voluntary and, varying with the company, circle members meet either during regular working hours or after hours or both. At Toyota Auto Body, which Cole (1980) made the subject of a case study, a foreman described the procedure followed by the company, one that typifies circle activities:

> *We think that the first step of analysis is to see whether or not the work is being implemented in accordance with the job standard. Usually, we grasp this phenomenon by plotting the cause-and-effect diagram with the relevant factors contributing to production being reviewed one by one. This is a time-consuming but effective method which involves extensive data gathering by each member of the circle (1980, p. 133).*

Toyota began its circle program in 1964 and by 1976 had 760 circles, involving over 4,000 workers, almost all of whom were blue-collar. The company won the Deming Prize in 1970. Employees could join more than one circle. The initial circle leaders had been foremen, but by 1969 ordinary workers were taking the place of the foremen. The size of the circles gradually decreased from the original size of 20.

According to Ishikawa (1968), who was a founding member of UJSE and who often has been called the father of quality control circles, 50 percent of circle activities focus on quality control, 40 percent on productivity and cost considerations, and 10 percent on safety and other affairs. At each meeting members are given assignments to complete before the group meets again. In the meetings circle leaders encourage the participants to present their opinions and analysis freely, regardless of how unimportant, irrelevant, or incorrect they may seem. Circles operate independently of other circles in the organization, but the circles may meet to discuss a common problem. Visits between circles in different companies are arranged through UJSE.

The techniques (Cole, 1980) most commonly used by circles are Pareto diagrams, cause-and-effect diagrams, and graphs. Ishikawa (1968) described the eight major problem solving techniques:

1. Brainstorming is used to identify all problems, even those beyond the control of the circle members.
2. A check sheet is used to log problems within the circle's sphere of influence within a certain time frame.

3. A Pareto chart graphically demonstrates check sheet data to identify the most serious problem, i.e., those 20 percent of the problems that cause 80 percent of the major mistakes.
4. A cause-and-effect diagram graphically demonstrates the cause of a particular problem.
5. Histograms or bar charts are graphed showing the frequency and magnitude of specific problems.
6. Scatter diagrams or "measle charts" identify major defect locations by having dots on the pictures of products, thus identifying dense dot clusters.
7. Graph and control charts monitor a production process and are compared with production samples.
8. Stratification, generally accomplished by inspecting the same products from differing production areas, randomizes the sampling process.

Results of Circle Implementation at Toyota

The estimated yearly per capita cost of implementing employee suggestions at Toyota Body increased from $1,245 in 1967 to $3,382 in 1973. The cost of such implementation at best is only a rough proxy for the value of the innovation (Cole, 1980). This was a 126 percent increase, but there was a 1,086 percent increase in per capita employee suggestions. Although management sets suggestion quotas for each work section, 25 percent of the suggestions received annually are from individuals who are not working with circles or other worker groups. This suggests that Toyota is effective, indeed, in mobilizing worker peer pressure and competition. The company pays a maximum of $272 to groups; $227 to individuals. Annually, the company president recognizes the recipient of the highest award at a public ceremony. The winner also earns a study-tour trip. The company pays $2.27 for individual suggestions that are not accepted; $2.75 for group suggestions. The per capita suggestion rate increased from 0.29 to 3.44 from 1967 to 1973.

Cole (1980) compared these results with those of the GM suggestion box program, which showed a decline in per capita suggestion rate from 1969 to 1976 of 2.40 to 0.80. This was despite the increase from $62 to $133 in the average award per accepted employee suggestion over this period.

Compensation in Other Circles

Compensation is relatively low for suggestions made by circle members that are successfully implemented by the company at cost savings. It ranges from less than $10 to over $600 for good suggestions, such as those leading to a patent (Cole, 1980).

There often is little monetary reward for circle involvement in Japan. Although American firms would be required to pay overtime rates for circle attendance, Cole said, sometimes the Japanese production worker will receive only nominal payments. Such is the nature of the practice of permanent employment in Japan, which may have created a long term commitment on the worker's part and thus makes uncompensated circle work acceptable.

Industry Week ("Talking in Circles," 1977) reported that $2.5 million had been awarded to Toyota Motor Co. employees involved in both quality circle and suggestion programs the previous year. Of the 527,718 suggestions submitted, 86 percent had been accepted. The financial rewards offered to participants whose ideas are accepted by management often are small, it was stated, and not as important to the employees as being cited by top management and being allowed to participate in the National QC Conference. Another incentive to join circles is the education and training received by employees.

Worker Dissatisfaction with Quality Circles

Cole (1979) feels that as quality circles mature in an organization, they tend to become viewed more as an instrument of management than as an opportunity for employees to initiate improvements. Toyota Auto Body recognized the declining employee interest a few years after the system's inception, but the company successfully renewed the system by making quality circles responsible for a new area, customer complaints.

On the other hand, a 1975 morale survey at Toyota Auto Body (Cole, 1979) showed that 30 percent of the workers found quality circles to be a "burden"—up from 20 percent in 1972. Union-sponsored surveys of employees have demonstrated that participation in circles increases the worker's physical and mental strain. At Toyota these burdens took the form of increased competition between groups and pressure to submit suggestions, because there were mandatory suggestion rates. Also, circle leaders at Toyota constantly struggled with a certain amount of worker apathy.

Labor-Relations in Japan

Management Paternalism

The quality circle is part of a Japanese tradition that has molded Japanese employees in general and union members in particular according to the recommendations of both the government and business. At the same time, quality circles and other employee participative schemes can be regarded as motivational tools to increase productivity at a time when the traditional system of management paternalism is, in fact, weakening. In particular, wage differentials between employees of large and small firms, to the disadvantage of the latter, and the growing age of the total population, in combination with a declining economic growth and a surplus of labor, are changing the nature of labor-management.

Bullson (1969) described the features of the traditional system of management paternalism in large firms. He identified two areas in which Japanese labor practices were distinctive from those in the West: (1) In Japan occupational pride was not as important to the worker as the place of work; the worker was more conscious of his industrial "family" than he was of his occupation. The percentage of union members in enterprise or firm-based unions in Japan was 91.4 percent, compared to 4.9 percent union members in enterprise or firm-based unions and .7 percent in occupation-wide unions in the West. Thus, Bullson (1969) feels that the employees themselves and the unions were organized according to the work place. (2) There was little labor mobility in Japan compared to other countries. Lifelong employment tenure meant that employees were seldom fired and usually remained with their employer from the time they graduated from school until they retired. Middle-aged employees considered it immoral to seek a "better" place of work. However, not all workers were satisfied with the prospect of job tenure. Where job mobility existed, it usually was in the form of large firm to small firm to even smaller firm. Abegglen (1973) explained this pattern of job mobility by relating it to the tendency of the largest firms to recruit employees directly from school only, not from affiliated companies or the outside labor market. Individuals were not hired for particular positions. They were hired because they had a good educational record or attractive personal qualities, and also because they promised to be loyal employees whose talents could be shaped to the singular needs of the organization without prior prejudicial work experience. The system of nenko, or seniority-based compensation, provided that compensation was to be based on length of service, not occupation or skill.

Labor Unions in Japan

Labor unions in Japan traditionally were under the shadow of stronger institutions. The Peace Policy Law of 1900 had prohibited strikes and unions and was not repealed until 1925, although there actually were 273 unions in Japan in 1920 (Cole, 1980). The beginning of cooperative relations between unions and government and management after WW II has been described by Tsuda (1979). The Red Purge period of the Occupation until the 1960s saw the rapid rise of subcontracting to meet some of the economic crises of industrial development aggravated at the time of labor shortages. Subcontracting grew from a level of 20 percent of working hours in 1957 to 65 percent in 1962. To meet the labor problems of the time, the Occupation authorities took certain steps to bring the labor movement more in line with government objectives (Bullson, 1969). At the time, militant unions at individual firms were protesting the economic hard times by supporting a socialist state. To counter the unions' efforts, business was encouraged: (1) to adopt American technology and management practices; (2) to bring union members over to management's side, especially through the training and cooperation of foremen; and (3) to convert radical unions by including white collar workers and foremen in their membership. Management counteroffensives were started by public corporations and government enterprises and subsequently were adopted in the automobile, power, steel, electrical machinery, and coal industries. In 1955 the spring labor offensive became established as the primary coordinated instrument for wage increases, involving the federations of the enterprise unions.

Japanese Union Reaction to Quality Circles

Cole (1980) stated that unions in the private sector, although generally cooperative with management in its efforts to increase productivity, carefully monitor management's attempts to induce employees to volunteer for circle participation. His case study of Toyota Auto Body showed that the company was careful to consult the union on personnel changes and also that union officials generally supported management attempts in job enlargement and the introduction of improvement groups. However, although union leaders find increased job rotation at Toyota to relieve job monotony, they have no voice in controlling job transfers or job rotations. These remain under the purview of the foremen, the supervisor, and the section chief.

Toyota Auto Body has a more passive union leadership than does Nissan, the second largest auto maker. Whereas Nissan union members participate somewhat in defining company production goals, the preoccupation of the Toyota unions is with wage administration. The Toyota unions do not appear to use the grievance procedure often, and when questioned as to their policy regarding production speedups and labor intensification, union officials said that they had no such policy because it was difficult for them to receive information on the actual number of people needed for certain tasks (Cole, 1980).

A problem for quality circles from the point of view of management in Japan is that in Japanese enterprise unions foremen and subsection chiefs frequently are members of the company union (Koike, 1978). (In the United States foremen are excluded by law from joining unions.) Full-time union officials, once promoted, often resign as active workshop representatives (Koike, 1978)—a hamper to effective union participation in management affairs.

Criticisms of Unions and Management

Yamamoto (1980) described the powerlessness of Japanese unions in the face of employment adjustments such as layoffs, subcontracting, reduction of overtime and paid vacations, and the maintenance of the retirement age at 55. In the 1970s a surplus of labor in Japan caused management to embrace more severe employment adjustments than had been used in the past, and a recession was putting pressure on businesses to concentrate on maintaining their level of profits, often at the expense of the firms' "social responsibilities" to their employees. Although Yamamoto acknowledged that the spring labor offensive was becoming more powerful, he criticized the unions for the continued lack of resistance to corporate discrimination toward older workers, female workers, and temporary workers. Also, because past recessions had been of a temporary nature, the unions were not prepared to defend even the regular worker against anything more severe than a temporary furlough. He also criticized the unions for not being willing to submit to the companies' policies of voluntary retirement at age 55. The population is undergoing a significant aging process, however, and there are other Japanese scholars who oppose supporting a mandatory retirement age at 55. The inadequate social security system does not permit a standard of living for retired workers comparable to the nationwide growth levels of the GNP.

Employment adjustments were being directed largely at older workers because during the recession firms found it advantageous to dismiss those older workers who, according to the nenko system, had higher labor costs (Yamamoto, 1980). Also, small firms—the traditional employers of older jobseekers—had hired many of them during the previous period of labor shortages when there was an increased incidence of middle school graduates going on to high school. Later these smaller companies also discharged older employees on a large scale.

As for the corporations, Yamamoto (1980) criticized them for their treatment of temporary and part time workers, who are not protected by the laws regarding dismissals because their contracts are not for an indefinite period but for a term generally between three and six months. The Employment Standards Law requires that rights and obligations of workers be clearly specified in individual worker's labor contracts. Although many work rules and labor agreements obligate employees to abide by employment adjustments such as temporary furloughs and subcontracting, the Supreme Court of Japan has held that these changes are not binding on the workers if the contract is silent on the issue of such adjustments. However, the workers have little legal defense against mass discharges, except in cases in which the courts have decided that the criteria for dismissal are not fair, objective, and rational and, according to the labor Union and the Employment Standard laws, except in cases in which workers are discharged unlawfully because of union activism or personal creed or belief. Other scholars critical of the Japanese labor relations system are Koike (1978) and Maruo (1978). Maruo (1978) criticized management paternalism in Japan for not observing the 5-day work week (although 23 percent of employers did so in 1978), for not permitting workers to take their paid holidays in full, and for not emulating Sweden, Norway, and Denmark in the area of workers' education. In Sweden there is no tuition charge for education through graduate school, he wrote, and at least 2.7 million of the population of 8.2 million voluntarily participate in work study groups, the largest of which are, in fact, sponsored by labor unions. Maruo (1978) feels that in Japan there is insufficient encouragement to workers to resume their education. He quoted one worker attitude survey as revealing that the greatest concern of present-day Japanese workers is that the course of one's life is determined by academic credentials.

Koike (1978) also criticized the lifetime employment and nenko systems because of the wage and promotion discrimination practiced according to level of education. Koike (1978) thinks that although lifetime employment was practiced on a somewhat wider basis in Japan than in the United States, the seniority system of compensation was not more widespread in Japan than in the United States. For both countries, Koike (1978) found that it was only for regular workers and white-collar males of large corporations that wages actually increased with years of service, with wages rising most dramatically by age for higher educated employees.

Hazama (1980) inferred that the nenko system of compensation was in fact not being utilized by smaller Japanese companies. Most employees in Japan, he said, are employed by small firms that are not unionized. In 1974, of all of the nonagricultural employees, 38 percent belonged to public enterprises or to large firms with 500 or more workers, and 62 percent belonged to medium or small firms. Hazama (1980) compared wage levels for Japanese and American firms by company size, and it was only when the firm size exceeded 100 employees that the level of Japanese wages exceeded the American level. Hazama (1980) feels that labor-management relations in Japan are deteriorating for three reasons: (1) Employment adjustments have weakened the practice of lifetime employment and thereby have bred worker resentment. (2) The fastest growing employee sectors include white-collar workers and other nonunion employees who might oppose a strengthened union position. This could be because the small companies are beginning to hire the highly educated workers, who previously had been attracted largely to positions in the largest companies. He associated this trend with the results of a public opinion survey that showed that 90 percent of the population consider themselves middle class. (3) Although, traditionally, women in Japan have been considered secondary workers who quit work when they marry or have a child, Hazama (1980) predicted a disruption in the male-oriented labor relations system as more and more women begin to prolong their careers, partly because of the declining family income occasioned by the weakening of the seniority wage system. Therefore, a decline in labor union loyalty is possible (Hazama, 1980).

Summary

Results of the literature review that forms the basis for this paper suggest that U.S. management should monitor Japanese quality circles and labor closely. One cannot argue with the success in Japan. The question remains open regarding the application and success of such programs in the United States' cultural setting. Perhaps successful U.S. companies already utilize such concepts. Will quality circles lead to improved quality and productivity in U.S. firms? One is reminded of the conclusions reached by Wood and LaForge (1979) regarding the relationship between strategic *planning* and *performance* in the U.S. banking industry—clearly, high performing banks plan strategically. But these banks *also* do a lot of other things very well, strategic planning being but one component of overall good management practice. Perhaps a close look at attributes of the Japanese experience will lead to a better understanding of the *participation* and *performance* relationship in U.S. firms.

There may be potential gains in both productivity and quality through the use of the quality circle program. This is especially true because the white-collar area is growing so rapidly and yet has not really applied in depth the quality circle approach. The method's capacity to stimulate communication, innovation, and an increased sense of worker responsibility has coincided, in some cases, with the employee's rejecting the available financial rewards for such activities. Also, the program has succeeded in widely divergent cultures, which creates a need for empirical research on what motivates workers to join circles—an area difficult to measure. Matsushita Electric, a leader in quality circles in Japan, does not have circles in its Chicago (U.S.) plant because it does not consider the American worker suited to circle activities (Cole, 1979). Many Japanese scholars see for their country significant changes in the practices of permanent employment and seniority-based compensation that might impact greatly on the future growth of quality circles. American based firms and management scholars should review the human resource policy implications that such changes may have.

References

Abegglen, J. *Management and worker: The Japanese solution.* Tokyo, Japan: Sopkia University, 1973.

Bullson, R. J. (Ed.). *The Japanese employee.* Tokyo, Japan: Sopkia University, 1969.

Cole, R. E. Made in Japan—Quality control circles. *Across the Board,* 1979, 16 (11), 72–78.

Cole, R. E. *Work, mobility, and participation: A comparative study of American and Japanese industry.* Berkeley, Cal.: University of California Press, 1980.

Hazama, H. The motivation of society and labor-management relations. *Japanese Econ. Studies,* Spring 1980, 48–77.

Ishikawa, K. *Q C Circle Activities.* Tokyo, Japan: Union of Japanese Scientist and Engineers, 1968.

Koike, K. Japan's industrial relations: Characteristics and problems. *Japanese Econ. Studies,* Fall 1978, 42–48.

Maruo, N. The levels of living and welfare in Japan reexamined. *Japanese Econ. Studies,* Fall 1978, 12–15.

Talking in Circles Improves Quality. *Industry Week,* February 1977, 62–64.

Tsuda, M. Japanese-style management: Principle and system. *Japanese Econ. Studies,* Summer 1979, 1–12.

Vough, C. C. *Tapping the human resource: A strategy for productivity.* New York: AMACOM, 1975.

Wood, D. R., & LaForge, R. L. The impact of comprehensive planning on financial performance. *Academy of Management Journal,* 1979, 22, 516–526.

Yeager, E. Quality circles—A tool for the 80's. *Training and Development Journal,* 1980, 134, 60–62.

Yamamoto, Y. Employment adjustments from the perspective of labor law and labor-management relations. *Japanese Econ. Studies,* Spring 1980, 28–62.

IV SPECIAL TOPICS

9. WOMEN DO NOT WANT INTERNATIONAL CAREERS: AND OTHER MYTHS ABOUT INTERNATIONAL MANAGEMENT

NANCY J. ADLER

Nancy J. Adler is an associate professor of organizational behavior and cross-cultural management at McGill University, Montreal, Canada. She has been on the faculty of the American Graduate School of International Management in Arizona and the Institut Européen d'Administration des Affaires (INSEAD) in Fontainbleau, France. As an international management consultant she has worked with multinational corporations and government organizations for projects in North and South America, Europe, and the Middle East. She has published papers on cultural synergy, re-entry, women in international business, cross-cultural research methodology, domestic multiculturalism, and is currently writing a book, International Dimensions of Organizational Behavior *(Kent Publishing, 1985).*

This research is supported by a grant from the Social Sciences and Humanities Research Council of the Canadian Government. The author would like to thank B. Shaffer for the creative ideas and research assistance that went into the formulation and conducting of the study.

In view of the increasing participation of North American businesses in the international market, multinational companies ought to examine whether their current reluctance to send women managers overseas is valid.

North American business is no longer domestic. By 1978, foreigners had bought United States properties with sales in excess of $150 billion—an amount equivalent to 7% of the U.S. gross national product. In less than 25 years (1958–1981), the percent of gross national product (GNP) exported per year has more than doubled (4.0% to 8.1%). United States, foreign direct investment abroad has continued to grow at 10% per year on a base of $164 billion dollars. Canada, with an economy only one-tenth that of the United States, has attracted more foreign investment than even the United States has—that is, nearly $50 billion Canadian dollars' worth compared with $40 billion U.S. dollars' worth. Thus neither Canada nor the United States can enjoy the luxury of pretending that the rest of the world does not exist. International business has perforce become a major component of their business operations.

Given international business' growing importance, many observers are predicting that the next generation of executives will have to have experience in a foreign assignment to reach the upper echelons of management. This has not been true in the past. A 1975 *Dun's* survey, for example, found that only a handful of the 87 chairmen and presidents of the 50 largest multinational corporations could be con-

*Reprinted, by permission of the publisher, from *Organizational Dynamics* (Autumn 1984).

sidered career internationalists. Sixty-nine of the 87 top executives had had, with the exception of inspection tours, no overseas experience at all.

Who are today's expatriates? Generally, they are managers and technical professionals selected primarily for their technical expertise and their records of success within domestic organizations. Depending on the company, they can be junior-, midcareer-, or senior-level personnel. In a major survey of 1,161 U.S. expatriates in 40 countries, the U.S. executive overseas was found to be a relatively young male who was born in a large city and had an educated, high-social-status father. Such an executive belongs to a social and economic elite from birth and is highly educated—often in the liberal arts—as is his wife. His career has been marked by a rapid rise within one or two companies. The expatriate executive tends to consider foreign and domestic experience as a continuum leading to top-level responsibility in the company.

One notable characteristic of expatriate managers is that they are overwhelmingly male. Of the 13,388 expatriates identified in a survey of 686 U.S. and Canadian corporations with overseas subsidiaries, only 3% were women. Most female expatriates in Europe have been sent by Eastern block countries, not by the United States or Canada. The majority of female U.S international managers have had only travel assignments lasting less than a month; one 1975 study found only one women in an expatriate position.

When the domestic workforce is compared with the international workforce in terms of the patterns of women's participation over the last decade, very different pictures emerge. On the domestic front, women have become increasingly involved in all managerial levels. By 1979, one quarter of all U.S. managers were women, but the percentage of female managers is still smaller than that of men—15% of the male labor force compared with only 6% of females. The women are definitely not equally distributed through all levels of management: By the end of the 1970s, 20% of current M.B.A.s were women; 15% of managerial trainees were women; 5% of middle-level managers were women; and barely 1% of top managers were women. In the highest-ranking executive jobs, women are almost nonexistent. A recent *Fortune* survey of the 1,300 largest companies in the United States found only ten women among the 6,400 corporate officers. Although the percentage of boards having at least one female director had increased from 10.7% in 1973 to 36.4% by 1979, there are still only 300 to 400 women on corporate boards compared with an estimated 15,000 men. Although the participation of women in domestic management is clearly lowest at the top-executive levels, such participation at all levels is higher than that of women at any level of international management.

What's in store for international managers—particularly women—in the future? This study focuses on the international career plans of male and female M.B.A.s graduating from top universities. It also looks at why these future managers think there are currently so few women in international management.

The Study

Is it true that women do not want to be international managers or that they are less interested than their male colleagues in careers that include expatriate assignments?

Are women's reasons for accepting or rejecting assignments similar to or different from those of their male counterparts? Do M.B.A.s believe these three traditional explanations for the scarcity of women in management? (1) Home-country managers responsible for selecting employees for expatriate assignments hesitate or resist sending women overseas. (2) If sent abroad, the women would not be effective because of foreigners' prejudice against them. (3) Women themselves do not want to prepare for, seek, or accept expatriate assignments. This study cannot explain the causes of the current distribution of male and female expatriate managers, but it does attempt to predict future patterns and trends on the basis of the career plans and beliefs of a representative sample of today's graduating M.B.A.s.

The Questions and the Questionnaire

Is women's alleged disinterest in international management myth or reality? To find out, the study asked the following questions:

1. Is the desire to pursue international careers and assignments greater in male M.B.A.s than in female M.B.A.s?
2. Would female M.B.A.s turn down international assignments for different reasons than their male counterparts would? Overall, would women feel more strongly than men about turning down an international assignment?
3. Do M.B.A.s believe that men and women have equal opportunities to be selected, effective, and advanced in an international career?
4. What do M.B.A.s believe to be the biggest barriers to women's becoming international managers? Do men and women perceive the situation similarly?

Structured around these four questions, the questionnaire asked M.B.A.s to indicate the extent to which they agreed or disagreed with each statement. This format allowed the participants to respond to each item—each potential barrier or benefit—individually. To assure that no important opinions were lost, the questionnaire included three open-ended questions that asked participants to simply list their opinions of the major advantages and disadvantages to international work and their perceptions of the major barriers (if any) to women's pursuing international careers. Responses to all items are reported here.

Participants

Because the study was designed to explain future trends in international management, it focused on M.B.A. students who were within six months of graduation and therefore in the process of planning their careers. Seven top management schools were surveyed: two traditional Canadian schools (McGill University and the University of Western Ontario), three traditional U.S. schools (The Tuck School at Dartmouth, University of California at Los Angeles (UCLA), and a large Midwestern school that requested anonymity and will therefore be referred to as Midwestern), and two international schools (the American Graduate School of International Management

(AGSIM) in Arizona and the Institut Européen d'Administration des Affaires (INSEAD) in France. Thus two schools are in Eastern North America (McGill and Tuck); two in the Midwest (Western Ontario and Midwestern), two in the West (UCLA and AGSIM), and one in Europe (INSEAD).

Questionnaires, accompanied by a letter explaining the survey, were distributed and collected in class or through student mailboxes. The response rate was high, averaging more than 80% across the surveyed students at the seven schools. Of the 1,129 M.B.A.s responding, 118 were from McGill, 76 from Western Ontario, 144 from UCLA, 67 from Midwestern, 56 from Dartmouth, 591 from AGSIM, and 77 from INSEAD. In total, 194 were attending Canadian schools, 267 were attending U.S. schools, and 688 were from international schools. The respondents were quite representative of each graduating class as a whole.

The backgrounds of the full-time M.B.A.s from the seven schools were more similar than they were different. They were young (average age 26.5 years), two-thirds were single (68.2%), a third were women (32%), and most were currently studying for their M.B.A. in the country in which they were born, held citizenship, and had received their undergraduate education. Their most common undergraduate degrees were in business and economics (33.8%) or engineering (10.8%), and their most common M.B.A. concentrations were finance (43.5%) or marketing (28.5%). Forty-one percent had in international focus in their studies. While 38% had no work experience at all, the majority had worked for a short time (approximately two years) before entering the M.B.A. program.

The respondents did not have extensive international experience. While most had travelled in foreign countries (84.2%), almost two-thirds (63.9%) had never lived abroad. Similarly, only a third (33.1%) of their parents had worked internationally. Few of their friends were foreign nationals. As might be expected, those attending the international schools (AGSIM and INSEAD) had more overseas experience than those at domestic schools, and they represented a broader range of nationalities. The Canadian M.B.A.s tended to have more international experience than their U.S. counterparts.

Interest in International Careers

To get a fix on M.B.A.s' perceptions about international assignments, we focused on three questions. Participants' responses are summarized below.

1. *Are male and female M.B.A.s equally interested in international careers?* Overall, the M.B.A.s indicated that they are very interested in pursuing the international aspects of their careers. Eighty-four percent indicated that they would like to have at least one foreign assignment during their career. Slightly less than a half seriously wanted an international career (46.9%) with a series of foreign assignments (43.7%). More than a third wanted to travel extensively as a part of their job (38.1%). One-third wanted their first job after graduation to be in a foreign country (33.1%). Clearly, many of the responding M.B.A.s are interested in international management, but fewer are interested in a foreign assignment "right now." Responses from men

Exhibit 1

THE MOST FREQUENTLY CITED REASONS FOR RESPONDING M.B.A.S TO REJECT INTERNATIONAL ASSIGNMENTS*

Respondents		
Percent of Total	**Number**	**Reason for Rejecting an International Assignment**
58.5%	660	*Location.* The assignment would be turned down if the country was seen as too politically unstable, too "uncivilized," too dangerous, too hostile toward expatriates, or if it had extreme poverty, or a high potential for war or violence.
34.6%	391	*Job and career.* The assignment would be turned down if the job itself was boring, unchallenging, or otherwise professionally uninteresting. Beyond the job itself, respondents did not see the foreign assignment as a good long-term career strategy. Respondents saw a higher risk of job failure overseas. They feared the negative impact on their careers of being isolated from the domestic company, displaced from the company hierarchy, and therefore forgotten at times of domestic job promotion and "lost" at reentry.
33.4%	377	*Spouse and family.* The assignment would be turned down if there were inadequate medical or educational facilities, if the children were at the wrong age to move (especially if they were teenagers), or if it would lead to too much strain on the marriage or to potential family breakdown. Dual-career marriages were seen as a major problem. The foreign assignment would be turned down if the spouse was unwilling to move or if it was impossible for the spouse to find a position that would further his or her career.
22.9%	258	*Money.* Respondents would turn down a foreign assignment if the salary and benefits package was not adequate to compensate them for the disruption and additional problems caused by moving and living overseas. Expatriate salary and benefits packages were usually seen as adequate only if they were substantially more generous than the equivalent domestic package.

*1,129 graduating M.B.A.s cited 2,308 reasons for turning down foreign assignments, approximately two reasons per person.

and women showed no difference based on sex in their interest in pursuing international assignments and careers.

In comparing international and domestic careers, most of the M.B.A.s saw themselves gaining more job satisfaction from an international career (including more interesting work and a higher salary) while gaining more organizational recognition (for example, faster promotions) and more personal-life satisfaction from a domestic career. Compared with the women, the men saw greater organizational rewards for pursuing an international career—including more recognition, more status, a higher salary, and faster career progress.

2. *Do male and female M.B.A.s reject international assignments for the same reasons?* Exhibit 1 lists the major reasons given by the respondents for turning down international assignments. There was no difference between the responses of men

Exhibit 1 *(continued)*

Respondents Percent of Total	Respondents Number	Reason for Rejecting an International Assignment
19.4%	219	*Unpleasant life overseas.* Respondents stated that they did not want too much change in their way of life. They didn't want to learn a new language or to adjust to a new culture. Some rejected the isolation, loneliness, fear, and uncertainty that they saw as a part of the overseas living experience. Others stated that they would turn down a foreign assignment if there were too many restrictions on their personal life, such as a lack of physical and intellectual freedom, a lack of recreational facilities, or a lack of access to other people.
13.8%	156	*Disruption of home-country life.* Respondents stated that they would miss their roots and that they therefore had no interest in leaving their home country. The respondents did not want to disrupt their personal and social life or to renege on personal commitments to parents, family, and friends.
5.8%	65	*Contract too long.* Some respondents said that they would accept a short assignment, but not a long assignment.
		Other reasons. Other reasons given for rejecting a foreign assignment included: the country did not accept women (45 M.B.A.s), the person presently had a good domestic position (33 M.B.A.s), the person was against the company's international policies or its product or marketing strategy (28 M.B.A.s), or the foreign position involved too much travel (22 M.B.A.s).

and women on any of the major reasons. A review of a list of 24 individual reasons indicates that male and female responses differed on only two. In both cases, the women rejected foreign assignments less strongly than men did. It was of less concern to female respondents that they or their children might lose their national identity or that they might have to adapt to a foreign culture (including learning a foreign language). (It is interesting to note that while the major reasons cited were unrestricted, written-in responses, the 24 individual responses were questionnaire items measured on a seven-point scale, from *strongly disagree* (1) to *strongly agree* (7). In the two cases in which men agreed with the reason more strongly than women did (significant difference at the .001 level) the means were: fear of losing national identity (male = 2.0 and female = 1.6) and lack of desire to adapt cross-culturally (male = 2.1 and female = 1.6). It should also be noted that neither of these reasons was held particularly strongly by either male or female respondents.)

3. *How do women's chances for success compare with those of men?* Men were seen as having significantly more opportunities than women in every aspect of international careers. Eighty-three percent of all responding M.B.A.s felt that men's chances of being selected for an international assignment were better than those of women; 63.3% felt that men's chances of being successfully advanced in an inter-

national career were better; and 47.7% believed that men's chances of being effective were better. This compares with less than 3% of all respondents who saw women's chances of being selected, advanced, or effective as being better than those of men.

As highlighted in Exhibit 2, both male and female respondents see fewer opportunities for women in international management than for men. Nonetheless, the pattern of opportunities for women in international management does not look the same to men and women. Male respondents saw women's chances of being selected and successfully advanced in an international career as slightly greater than did the women themselves. Female respondents, on the other hand, saw women's chances of being effective internationally to be greater than their male colleagues did.

This pattern of perceived preference for men over women in international management was not found to be a mere replication of the domestic pattern. In every comparison, women's chances for success were seen to be greater in domestic than in international careers. Whereas 12.1% of all respondents saw men's chances to be effective in domestic careers as better than women's, four times as many (47.7%) saw men's chances as better in international careers. Similarly, while 31.8% of all respondents saw men's chances to be successfully advanced in domestic careers as better than women's, twice as many (63.3%) saw men's chances of advancement in international careers as better. Clearly, the opportunities for women are perceived to be fewer in international management than they are in domestic management.

Why Are There So Few Women in International Management?

Although there has been very little research on the role of women in international management, managers, researchers, and journalists attribute the scarcity of women to three principal causes; female managers' disinterest, corporate resistance, and foreigners' prejudice. To put the beliefs held by the M.B.A.s (and therefore the next generation's managers) into context, we need to explore the historic basis for each.

Belief 1: Women neither seek nor accept international management positions. The belief that women are not interested in international assignments has been prevalent among managers. In 1980 *Business Week* reported that, until 1975, "even women's warmest supporters conceded that most women managers resisted geographical transfer." Others believe that women do not want to relocate, that women are just not interested, and that women do not want to move their families. Increasingly people believe that husbands of married women will not be willing or able to transfer overseas and that, consequently, women will turn down expatriate assignments. In addition, some women may avoid careers, such as international management, that have been stereotyped as male professions or for which there are few female role models.

Belief 2: North American managers are reluctant to send women overseas. U.S. and Canadian managers have expressed an unwillingness to take the risk of sending women overseas. Sixty percent of the managers working for multinational corporations (MNC) in Europe said that even though *they* believed women could be successful overseas, they would be apprehensive about assigning a woman to head a MNC subsidiary, because of resistance from superiors, subordinates, colleagues,

Exhibit 2

M.B.A.s' PERCEPTIONS OF THEIR CHANCES FOR SUCCESSFUL INTERNATIONAL CAREERS BY SEX (N = 1,129)

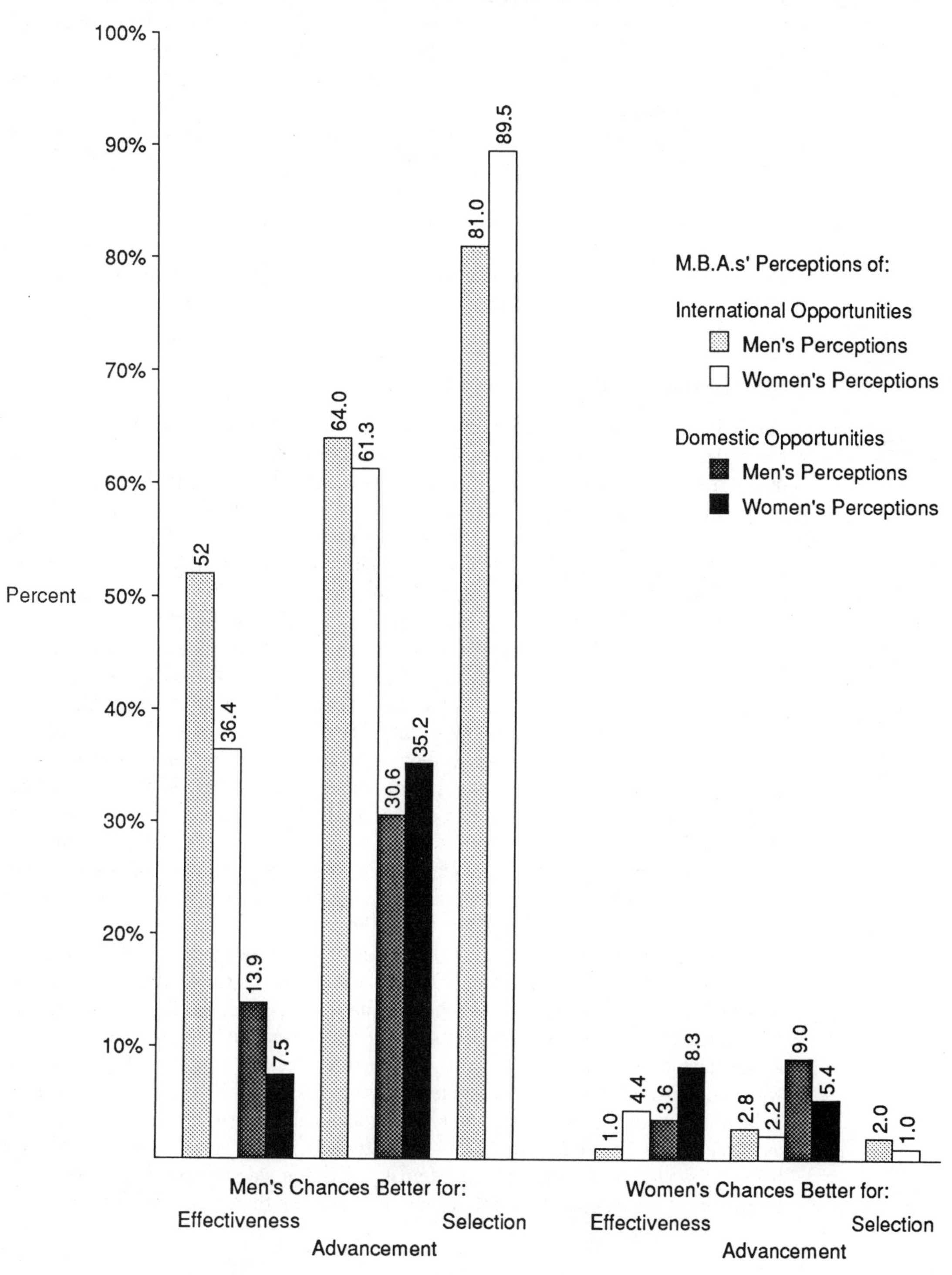

and clients. Other corporate executives whose organizations have not selected women for international positions believe that women would find the international "game" too difficult to master. As the deputy manager of human resources development for Mobil Oil Corporation noted, "The real problem exists in the minds of those who make decisions regarding who shall make business trips abroad and who shall be offered overseas assignments."

Belief 3: Women would not be effective because foreigners are prejudiced against female managers. According to this belief, North Americans are more egalitarian than foreigners: "We" are less prejudiced than "they"; "we" fear that the strong bias against women by foreign executives, staff, colleagues, and clients will render women ineffective in international work. Some managers believe that sending a women overseas would offend foreigners because foreign women do not have equal status with men. But others consider the sex barrier abroad more apparent than real.

M.B.A.s' Views on the Barriers to Women

Foreigners' prejudice against women was the most frequent explanation given by respondents for the scarcity of female international managers. More than 80% (83.6%) of the responding M.B.A.s said that foreigners' attitudes were the biggest obstacle facing women moving into expatriate positions. Seventy-eight percent saw North American companies as reluctant to select women for international positions. The potentially negative impact on the spouse and family was the third most frequently cited reason for the scarcity of female expatriates. Over 70% (72.8%) of the respondents saw dual-career couples as a particularly difficult problem.

Just over 20% of them (21.4%) saw women's own hesitance as an explanation. These described the women as lacking confidence, interest, and willingness to travel or to accept expatriate positions, as well as being less adventurous, less able to take care of themselves overseas, less mentally prepared for a foreign assignment, and more fearful than men. They saw women neither as identifying with the male image of the international manager nor as having female role models. Women, therefore, were not seen as planning their careers to include foreign assignments. Just under 20% (19.1%) saw women as incapable of being effective overseas. A few respondents (5.6%) saw women as basically unqualified for overseas positions. Others described the problem as the increased personal danger that women would face overseas (4.8%) and the absence of experienced candidates (2.1%).

As shown in Exhibit 3, male and female M.B.A.s' perceptions of the barriers facing women were not identical. Although both groups agreed that a major barrier was foreigners' prejudice against women, the female M.B.A.s saw the company's reluctance to select women as an equally major deterrent while the men saw selection as the number two deterrent (behind foreigners' lack of respect). In comparison with the views of the women themselves, male respondents saw women's inability to be effective overseas as twice a great a problem and women's lack of qualifications as three times as great a problem—even though neither was viewed as a major barrier. In all cases, both male and female M.B.A.s saw the barrier to women in international management to be considerably greater than those for women in domestic management.

Exhibit 3

M.B.A.s' PERCEPTIONS OF BARRIERS TO WOMEN IN INTERNATIONAL AND DOMESTIC MANAGEMENT

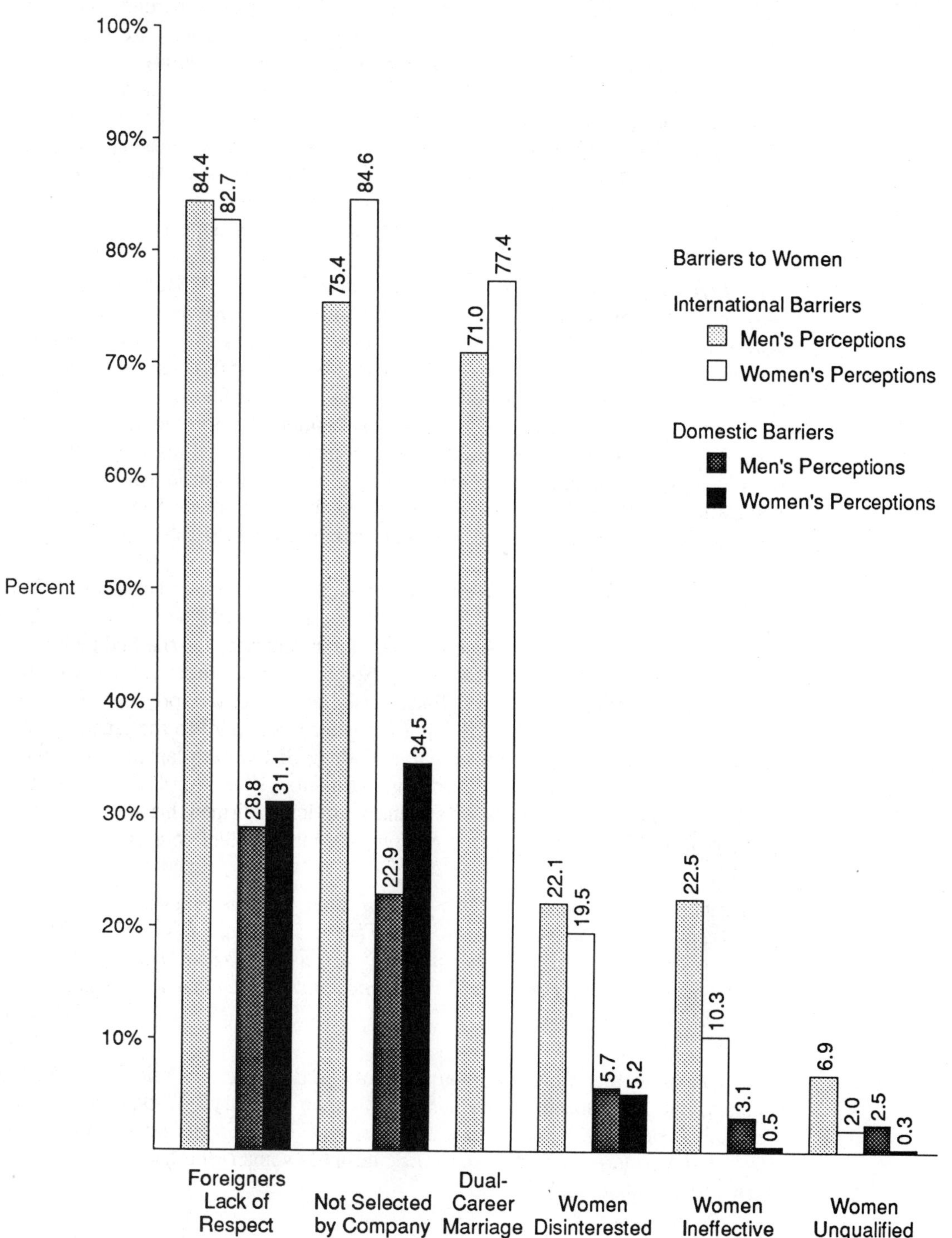

What Assumptions Should We Make?

Are women interested in international careers? The answer, apparently, is "Yes." Judging from responses to the survey, these female M.B.A.s who are graduating from top U.S., Canadian, and international management schools are definitely interested in pursuing international careers. In fact, they are slightly more interested than their male counterparts. Nevertheless, today's graduating M.B.A.s (and tomorrow's managers) apparently still believe that the number of female international managers will be limited because of foreigners' prejudice against women, companies' reluctance to select women, and women's own hesitance to accept overseas assignments. How likely is it that these beliefs are or will remain correct? Let's look at these points in detail.

1. *Foreigners are not as prejudiced as we think.* From the M.B.A. respondents' perspective, the major obstacles facing women in international management is foreigners' prejudice. Is it true that foreigners are prejudiced against female expatriate managers in a way that limits their effectiveness overseas? At this point, on a scientific basis, we do not know. Journalists strongly argue that female expatriate managers are doing extremely well. They give two explanations for the women's success. First, many cultures that have had traditionally male-dominated management have, over the past few years, markedly increased the number of female managers within their own countries. Although progress in Europe has been slower than that in North America, female executives have thus far at least penetrated virtually every European industry and type of management.

Second, both from my own interviews with expatriate women and from journalistic reports, I have ascertained that even in countries in which the local women are not readily accepted as managers—such as Japan, Latin America, and the Middle East—women sent as international managers by North American organizations are succeeding. For example, as a female, Tokyo-based personnel vice-president for Bank of America's Asia Division said: "Being a foreigner is so weird to the Japanese that the managerial impact of being a woman is nothing. If I were a Japanese woman, I know I couldn't be doing what I'm doing." (*Business Week,* April 20, 1980). The female director of Xerox Corporation's China operation confirmed this view. Referring to her year in Africa as a McKinsey & Company management consultant:

> *If you are capable and you're in a position where you can demonstrate results quickly, being a women is not an issue. They know you are different and they accept you as different. They may not want their women to do it, but they know that the culture and customs of Britain and America are different. (*Business Week, *April 20, 1980).*

According to another American woman who was Rank Xerox's sales manager for Hungary, she had "absolutely no difficulty . . . [in Hungary]. Working in Eastern Europe is easier for a woman than it is in the West" (*Wall Street Journal,* March 16, 1978). Furthermore, according to a U.S. businesswoman who had worked in the Ivory Coast, Gabon, and Cameroon:

> *Some places unaccustomed to native businesswomen are willing to accept foreign ones. . . . Those African countries are really quite pleasant and straightforward in accepting Western businesswomen (Eric Morgenthaler,* Wall Street Journal, *March 16, 1978).*

Even in the Middle East, where the perception of discrimination against women is at its highest, a female assistant vice-president with Amex Bank Ltd. found that she was able to manage successfully in Saudi Arabia:

> *Once in the country, I had no problems whatsoever. . . . I suppose that if your company has sent you there and you act in a competent manner . . . [the Saudis will] accept you (Eric Morgenthaler,* Wall Street Journal, *March 16, 1978).*

Although there are fewer local women than men in management around the world, the strongly held belief that foreigners are prejudiced against female expatriate managers and that that prejudice will render women ineffective in international assignments should be seriously questioned.

2. *Companies may be reluctant to select women.* In addition to foreigners' prejudice, over three-quarters of the M.B.A.s surveyed saw the company's reluctance to select women as a major problem. Why might companies hesitate to select women? Perhaps international personnel managers believe that women do not want to go abroad or that they would not be effective if sent. Perhaps they believe that there are no qualified female candidates available. The personnel managers' perspective is currently being investigated in a follow-up to this study to determine whether organizations are inappropriately choosing not to select women for international assignments and whether their policies need to change.

3. *Women are not as uninterested as we think.* The third explanation, given by over 20% of the M.B.A.s, was that women are less willing than men to pursue international careers. Although it may have been true ten, fifteen, or even five years ago, this perception was not substantiated by the results of this study: Male and female respondents were equally willing to work overseas. Furthermore, men were more adamant about a number of the reasons for rejecting a foreign assignment than were their female colleagues. It is no longer true that women are less interested than men in pursuing international careers.

4. *Caveat: "Truth" may lie only in the eye of the beholder.* As mentioned earlier, over 80% of the male and female M.B.A.s believed that the major problem is foreigners prejudice against women and not anything that they themselves, either as individuals or as representatives of companies, are doing. This common tendency to see others rather than oneself or one's group as the cause of a problem can easily cloud our understanding of a situation's dynamics. The view of foreigners as more prejudiced against women than we are may be a false perception. Acting on such a perception, we are likely to try to reduce foreigners' prejudice (or to accept it as unchangeable) before sending more women overseas. This attitude itself may be impeding progress more than the prejudice that it attributes to foreigners.

Since men and women have different beliefs about a number of the reasons for the scarcity of women, the solutions proposed by men are likely to differ from those proposed by women. More male respondents believe the reasons for the scarcity of women overseas rests with the women themselves ("women are not as interested as men in international assignments, nor would they be as effective"); on the other hand, more female respondents believe that the system's intransigence is a primary cause ("organizations are unwilling to select and send women overseas"). Men are therefore more likely to see a need to change the women's attitudes while women are more likely to see a need to change the organization's selection system. Because this study shows that women's interest in international management is equal to (or slightly greater than) that of men, I question the need to change women's attitudes. Only future studies will show whether organizations' selection systems need to be altered.

5. *Dual-career couples: Is this a solvable problem?* Are dual-career couples a problem in transferring expatriates overseas? Is the dual-career "problem" particularly acute for female managers? In the past, most spouses have been the non-working wives of male international managers. The wives' dissatisfaction has been the most important reason for male managers' early return from foreign assignments. Today, the situation is changing for both male and female managers. While most of today's male managers continue to be married, many are married to career-oriented women. Unlike their male colleagues, more than half of the female expatriate managers are single. The vast majority of the married women have career-oriented husbands. The net result is that companies are increasingly becoming involved in securing suitable employment for the spouses of both male and female expatriates.

The results of this study show that the married M.B.A. respondents are slightly less interested in international careers than are the single ones, but married women are no less interested than married men. However, as shown in Exhibit 3, the female M.B.A.s reported that they are more likely than their male colleagues to turn down a foreign assignment if suitable employment cannot be found for their spouse. The concern may be focused more on the husbands of female expatriates than on the wives of male expatriates, because society has traditionally expected men to have continuous careers and to give women the option of working outside of the home, having a career, or working at home. Although the issue seems more apparent for female managers than for male managers, it must be resolved for both men and women if companies want to retain the freedom to select their top candidates for overseas assignments without regard to marital status or gender.

Recommendations

This study was designed primarily to test the belief that women are less interested in international management than are men. The results show that there is no difference between the interest and willingness of male and female M.B.A.s to work overseas. Each of the primary areas of employers' concerns about sending women managers overseas warrants recommendations, which are spelled out below.

- *Women's interest.* Companies should be aware of women's interest in international careers and consider them as well as men as candidates for expatriate assignments.
- *Foreigners' prejudice.* Companies should be aware that M.B.A.s believe that the biggest obstacle for female expatriate managers is the prejudice of foreigners, but that such a belief has not been tested. Companies should realize that foreigners do not treat expatriate women in the same ways that they treat their local women. It may therefore be possible to send expatriate women to countries in which there are very few, if any, local female managers.
- *Organizational rewards.* Companies should be aware that men perceive that international work leads to greater organizational rewards (job recognition and career advancement) than women do. Companies should therefore be careful to make sure that the rewards for equivalent work are equivalent and that they are so perceived by female candidates for international assignments.

The corporate community has yet to have much experience in sending women overseas on expatriate assignments. Because both the companies and the women are experimenting and learning, it is important that both be particularly careful to distinguish between assumptions and realities, to differentiate the past from a possibly different future. Only by carefully examining our own assumptions can we avoid the cycle of prejudice that we are currently blaming on foreigners and that we are explicitly trying to avoid.

Selected Bibliography

While there have been many reviews of women in domestic management (for an excellent review see Linda Keller-Brown's *The Woman Manager in the United States: A Research Analysis and Bibliography,* Business and Professional Women's Foundation, 1981), there have been very few articles on North American women working as expatriate managers.

Some excellent journalistic descriptions of the experience of individual women include the *Business Week* articles, "Corporate Woman: Now Eager to Accept Transfers" (May 26, 1980); and "Corporate Woman: A Rush of Recruits for Overseas Duty" (April 20, 1980); David Cudaback's article in the *Institutional Investor,* "Can a Woman Succeed in International Banking?" (March 1979); Nancy Carter's "Womanpower Development: A New Personnel Goal in International Firms" (*Business International,* June 23, 1978); E. M. Fowler's article in *The New York Times,* "Careers: Job Prospects for Women in Overseas Posts Rise" (July 19, 1978); Eric Morgenthaler's article in *The Wall Street Journal,* "Women of the World: More U.S. Firms Put Females in Key Posts in Foreign Countries" (March 16, 1978); and Marian Houk's "An American Woman Doing Business in the Arab World" (*Working Woman,* November 1979).

There have been a few research studies on women in international management. Suggested reading includes Dafna Izraeli, Moshe Banai, and Yoram Zeira's "Women Executives in MNC Subsidiaries" (*California Management Review,* Fall 1980); Marilyn

Taylor, Marianne Odjogov, and Eileen Morley's "Experienced American Professional Women in Overseas Business Assignments" (*Academy of Management Proceedings,* 1975); L. Ionnou's "Businesswomen Win Positions Abroad: Finding Success on Foreign Soil" (*Journal of Commerce,* August 2, 1978); and Nancy Thal and Philip Cateora's "Opportunities for Women in International Business (*Business Horizons,* December 1979).

The study reported in this article is part of a major four-part study on women in international management. The ideas for the study were originally presented in "Women As Androgynous Managers: A Conceptualization of the Potential for American Women in International Management" (*International Journal of Intercultural Relations,* Fall 1979). The first part of the study, a survey of American and Canadian firms determining the number of male and female expatriates, appears in the *California Management Review* as "Women in International Management: Where Are They?" (Fall 1984). The second part is reported in this article. The third part, a survey of international personnel directors to determine corporate policy toward sending women overseas, will appear as "Expecting International Success: Female Managers Overseas" (*Columbia Journal of World Business,* 1984, in press). The fourth part of the study, interviews with the female expatriate managers themselves, will be published in 1985.

Acknowledgments

The author would like to extend her special thanks to the following people for their support and assistance in data collection: Mariann Jelinek (Dartmouth, now at Case Western Reserve), Robert Moran (AGSIM), Anne Marie Spataru and David Eiteman (UCLA), Joseph DiStefano (Western Ontario), and Danielle Nees (INSEAD).

10. HUMAN RESOURCES AND INDUSTRIAL RELATIONS IN CHINA: A TIME OF FERMENT

I. B. HELBURN and JOHN C. SHEARER

I. B. Helburn is Professor of Industrial Relations and the Bobbie and Coulter R. Sublett Centennial Professor at the Graduate School of Business, University of Texas at Austin; and John Shearer is Professor of Economics at the College of Business Administration, Oklahoma State University. *The authors wish to thank Alan Carsrud, King Chow, Yun Guanping, Charles M. Rehmus, Edward J. M. Rhoads, and Robert C. Rodgers for their comments on an earlier draft of this paper.*

This study of current industrial relations practices in mainland China draws on the relevant literature and particularly on the authors' discussions with managers and government and union officials in the steel industry during a visit to China in March 1983. The authors describe the recruitment, selection, placement, and training of blue-collar and managerial employees; the increasing use of financial incentives; and the "iron rice bowl" approach to discipline, which generally excludes discharge. They also discuss employee participation in management through workers' councils and trade unions and the sometimes conflicting functions of unions as both "arm of the state" and workers' representatives.

One of the most important but least understood parts of the economic system of mainland China is that of the management of human resources. Although there is an English-language literature on some aspects of this subject,[1] we still know little about the extent of worker participation in decision making and even less about the nature of union-management relations and dispute resolution in Chinese industry.

This paper presents some first-hand information on these subjects that we gathered as participants in a study visit to China in March 1983 by a group of ten U.S. labor arbitrators.[2] This visit was the first of its kind by foreigners concerned with exchanging information on the management of human resources and industrial dispute resolution. Some of the information we received was conflicting or ambiguous, a fact we attribute, in part, to the uncertainties resulting from the major changes now taking place in that vast and complex nation. Moreover, because discussions were possible only through interpreters, it is likely that detail was lost in translation or omitted in summarized answers to our questions. Finally, there were times we were convinced that the responses of our Chinese hosts represented the party line rather than more accurate information.[3]

In spite of these qualifications, we believe our information is correct in suggesting that Chinese concerns about human resource management often parallel those com-

I. B. Helburn and John C. Shearer, *Industrial and Labor Relations Review,* 38. 1 (October 1984): 3–15.

mon in our own country. In fact, Chinese responses to human resource problems are often surprisingly similar to those in the United States. We must warn the reader, however, that this paper does not attempt a comprehensive review of all aspects, past and present, of Chinese human resource management or industrial relations; we concentrate instead on the knowledge of recent developments that we gained primarily through discussions with key management and union officials in the steel industry.

Human Resources Management

Recruitment, Selection, and Placement

Until recently, it has been common for even the largest and most modern enterprises in China to use a closed-shop approach to the recruitment of new personnel. Upon their retirement, which was often early by our standards, parents would bequeath their jobs to their offspring. The usual situation now, however, is similar in many respects to that with which Westerners are familiar.

In accordance with government-approved labor plans for each major enterprise, employers recruit and select unskilled workers from those who apply for jobs. Applicants who meet appropriate health and physical standards are tested for basic knowledge in relevant subjects, including mathematics, physics, and chemistry in the case of the steel industry. Selection for placement in particular jobs is based on applicants' physical and intellectual qualifications, usually with little regard to their preferences and with considerably less regard to their "redness," or ideological fitness, than heretofore. Similarly, enterprises recruit skilled workers directly from specialized schools, often operated by the enterprise itself, or train and promote personnel from within the establishment.

Unemployment, especially among youth,[4] and underemployment are pervasive problems in China. An estimated 5 million people have entered the labor force annually since 1977, with 11 million of the recent entrants unemployed at the start of the 1980s.[5] The societal need to create jobs often results in labor plans designed by the central government that require enterprises to employ more people than they can use efficiently. Although it was only occasionally evident or acknowledged to our study group, overstaffing and low labor efficiency are considered, even in official statements, as widespread phenomena.[6]

Upward mobility, or promotion, is carried through by means similar to those in the West. Demotions are rare, however, because industry is generally expanding and therefore not subject to cyclical fluctuations;[7] individuals may use political influence to avoid demotion; and there is an overall tolerance of substandard performance. The few demotions that do occur usually constitute harsh disciplinary action taken only after prolonged rehabilitation efforts have failed.

The means by which workers are promoted to supervisory positions contrast sharply with Western practices. Instead of such promotions being the sole prerogative of management, it is increasingly common for the slogan "the workers control the enterprise" to have operational significance as well as propaganda value. Chinese workers often have considerable influence over the selection and retention of their supervisors. In some enterprises, aspirants to supervisory or managerial positions are given a "people's willingness test," according to which members of the work group are consulted regarding the potential supervisor's acceptability. Usually, workers, through their work groups, or *danwei,* will nominate other workers for consideration, with the *danwei* having considerable consultative influence over promotion decisions about lower-echelon supervisory positions. More and more often, workers choose their supervisors up to the level of department superintendent.

The lateral transfer of Chinese workers is an interesting subject. Workers' ability to change their places of employment is often sharply curtailed by institutional and practical barriers. Because desirable jobs are scarce, it is difficult to secure a position with a different employer, especially if both the present and prospective employers must conform to centrally determined labor plans. A worker cannot simply quit a job in hopes of securing other employment: even if he finds a new employer willing to hire him, that employer cannot sign him on without a release from the previous employer. Centrally planned and egalitarian societies are no different from other societies in their employers' reluctance to release, and desire to secure, the more productive worker. Accordingly, the worker is in a Catch-22 position of not knowing if he will enhance his horizontal mobility by loafing or by superhuman efforts.[8]

In contrast to unskilled workers, graduates of colleges and technical institutes are in very short supply, and their educational specializations already reflect centrally planned labor-supply priorities. A manager of one large steel mill observed, "We get additional college-trained people from the state." Educational institutions cooperate with the appropriate industrial and agricultural ministries in placing each class of graduates. Although authorities contend that allocations of job applicants reflect both state requirements and individual choice (graduates list as many as ten job preferences), practice varies greatly. At one extreme, graduates are assigned as the state sees fit, with little concern for individual preference. Assignees have no knowledge of the selection criteria used and no formal right of appeal. This practice reflects Mao Tse-tung's conviction that the allocation of high-level resources by command worked well for the People's Liberation Army and would also work well in the civilian sector. At the other extreme, educational authorities try to accommodate the preferences of graduates to the extent that state requirements permit.

Beyond these general practices, however, there is a powerful shadow mechanism at work that better serves individual preferences, but at the expense of the state system: allocation by the "side door," or, in the extreme case, by the "back door." Students with appropriately placed friends or relatives (the "side door") or students who risk bribery (the "back door") can, by extraordinary bureaucratic manipulation, obtain assignments more congenial to their preferences. Although it is impossible to quantify the extent of this phenomenon, the side and back doors are clearly active ports of entry to the labor market for high-level personnel.

Moreover, side and back doors often provide for discontented high-level employees an escape from onerous work to more preferred employment elsewhere. The experience of one Chinese we met exemplifies the process. His graduation assignment was to a modest professional position that required a weekly shift rotation that proved intolerable to him as time went on. After two years of fruitless efforts to change jobs through official channels and through the side door, he was finally able, through the back door, to obtain a responsible daytime job in another ministry that was more compatible with his education and preferences.

Often, the priorities of the state have caused the geographic separation of high-level workers married to each other. Although a new national policy is supposedly designed to reunite couples, its implementation has been hindered by the difficulties of securing adequate housing. The Chinese bureaucracy's inability, or unwillingness, to resolve such complex problems is somewhat offset by an active housing exchange system via bulletin boards—a system whose successes are endorsed by officialdom.

Training

Labor-force training is an important activity in the Chinese economic system, especially at the larger enterprises that must train not only for their own needs but also for those of new facilities in their industries. Training offers workers the usual advantages of promotion to higher-skilled and better-paid positions, as well as potential geographic mobility, which is otherwise very hard to come by. Some large enterprises have established their own quasi-colleges to train personnel for technical, engineering, administrative, and managerial positions. The administrative and managerial training seems particularly necessary since traditional colleges and universities in China do not offer degrees equivalent to the bachelor's or master's of business degrees in the United States. Some institutes of higher education do offer courses in industrial management and industrial economics, however, including courses in economics, finance, and marketing. Organizational behavior, personnel management, and industrial relations are still apparently ignored.

As in all societies, training in China is a passport to a better life. But especially because of stringent constraints on individual decision making, the selection of who is to be trained is of special importance to Chinese workers. Selection practices vary widely among enterprises. In some, selections are made by an education committee comprising representatives of unions and workers, department managers, professional employees, and the plant manager. In others, full work-group discussions lead to nominations, and management makes the final decision. In one mill, of 70 workers nominated, management selected 50 for training. Often all workers have a theoretical chance for training, but typically management decides on the basis of past and potential performance, age, intelligence, "professionalism," and test results (less often), rather than "redness."

In large enterprises, foreman training is usually the responsibility of the internal "college," to which the enterprise's best prospects, as selected by management, are sent each year. Nascent disputes over the selection of people for training are usually nipped in the bud by the prior consultation of all interested parties.

Motivation and Compensation

Since the formation of the People's Republic in 1949, many changes in motivational policies and practices have taken place. Revolutionary and developmental zeal, as well as more tangible incentives, has been used in attempts to attain workers' cooperation in achieving the rapid increases in productivity necessary for the national crusade for modernization. Throughout the tortured recent history of wage policy, and continuing today, the Chinese have witnessed a fundamental conceptual conflict between the egalitarian ideal of a "communist" state and the practical reasons for using wages and bonuses as incentives to productivity.

According to Charles Hoffman, one of the few U.S. experts on human resources management in China, the "wage reform of 1956 rationalized wage schedules and differentials in conformity with the specific aims of the FFYP [First Five Year Plan] and the new more heavily socialized nature of Chinese industry."[9] Hoffman also states elsewhere:

> *The basic structure of wage scales was put forth by the State Council (cabinet) in 1956, and remains the standard for workers in China today [1981], though scales for technicians, professional staff, and managerial personnel, also established in 1956, have been telescoped since the Cultural Revolution. Scales vary throughout the country by industry (for instance, scales in steel are higher than in textiles) and geographic location since living costs may vary.*[10]

During the Cultural Revolution, and especially since the death of Mao in 1976 and the demise of the "Gang of Four" (Mao's successors, who were later imprisoned), the basic national wage structure of eight pay grades, with widely varying emphasis over time on bonuses based on industry and geography, has been undergoing fundamental scrutiny. The use of bonuses has increased considerably since the 1980 observations of Chu-yuan Cheng that "egalitarianism still tends to dominate the remuneration system" and that in many enterprises bonuses are universal or are issued on a rotating basis to all workers regardless of the quality of their work.[11] Although the future of a truly discriminating bonus system remains to be seen, a discussion of some of the major recent changes can help in making predictions.

The entire system of eight pay grades plus bonuses is now under review. The present government has already effected some sharp breaks from the post-1956 system, which through most of its duration maintained a basic wage differential of approximately 3:1 between the highest- and lowest-paid workers in an establishment. In early 1983, the lowest basic wage in the steel industry, one of the highest paying industries, was 35 yuan per month.[12] With average bonuses and allowances added, that figure rose to approximately 50 yuan per month for a standard workweek of six eight-hour days.[13]

Average monthly compensation throughout all industries is approximately 100 yuan, including bonuses ranging from a low of six yuan per month to recent highs of one-third, or even occasionally one-half, of base wages. A few top-grade engineers receive up to 340 yuan monthly, only slightly below the 400 yuan rate of the Secretary General of the Communist Party, although he and other top leaders receive perquisites that raise the economic value of their total compensation. In addition to wages, Chinese workers having permanent employment status—the 20 percent of the labor force employed in state-owned industry—receive many more fringe benefits than do workers in the United States.[14]

> *State enterprises provide almost total security for their employees: virtually guaranteed life-time employment, complete disability compensation, paid sick*

> *leave, fully paid medical care for employees and subsidized service for dependents, generous retirement pensions, death benefits for surviving family members, loans for employees in financial trouble, and payment of funeral costs.*[15]

Additional benefits include easy access to hospitals, meal halls, kindergartens, and day-care centers.[16]

Although the importance of incentive bonuses has varied considerably since liberation, bonuses have increased since 1978 when the Chinese government embarked on its "Four Modernizations" program.[17] The acknowledged economic and social catastrophes caused by Mao's Great Lap Forward and Cultural Revolution, both of which generally downplayed the use of bonuses, and the renewed and pragmatic intense drive in recent years for productivity improvements and modernization have increased the status of bonuses as essential parts of the new, universal "responsibility system." The underlying philosophy of the responsibility system is that every enterprise, manager, and worker must be held directly accountable, under increasingly decentralized decision making, for contributing to the national welfare. Thus, each worker is to be rewarded, through bonuses, commensurate with the quality and quantity of his or her production.

Enterprises that exceed their production goals retain a proportion of the additional earnings (the term "profits" is universally used). By decision of the top managers of the enterprise, these profits are then divided among the improvement and expansion of capital facilities and employee bonuses and benefits. Although employee bonuses are most often group bonuses, based at least in part on the "profitability" of production units, there seems to be increasing use of bonuses based on individual performance. The general use of consultative mechanisms for determining bonuses should not be confused with the Western system of mechanical formulae for determining incentive bonuses, since enterprises and work groups can consider "redness" and other nonproduction criteria in setting them. Enterprises that have made the greatest use of incentive bonuses invariably report commensurate increases in productivity, although some ideologues and some workers oppose the expanded reliance on such forms of compensation.[18] The emerging "responsibility system" may serve the dual purpose of providing added motivation for employees while diverting pressures for continuation of the pre-1980 goals of equal pay for all work.

Retention

Although layoffs of permanent employees are almost unknown in China, persistent unemployment, especially among youth, has long plagued the country.[19] Regular (noncontract) Chinese workers enjoy almost absolute job protection, known as the "iron rice bowl," which symbolizes an indestructible employment bond. Under this system, now only gradually changing, a worker can be discharged only for criminal conviction.

Officials and managers assured us that industry is moving away from such guaranteed protection against discharge. But close questioning revealed that a discharge is still only possible among employees who are guilty of the most serious industrial infractions and who have not been rehabilitated through the repeated "educational" efforts of their *danwei* comrades, management, and their trade union, each reinforcing the other in their strenuous efforts to redeem the recalcitrant. In most instances, management even then cannot discharge an employee without approval from appropriate Communist Party officials. There may be a crack or two in the "iron rice bowl," but it still appears to be intact. Instead of resorting to discharge and layoffs, Chinese industry increasingly is using contract (temporary) labor, at low wages and without fringe benefits, as the means for enterprises to adjust their employment levels.[20] (We were unable to determine the extent of this practice in the steel industry itself.)

Workers' Safety

The Chinese acknowledge the need for environmental and plant safety, yet this is not an important priority. "Safety First" signs were prominently displayed in the plants we visited, and we were always provided hard hats, although the workers did not use them. Obviously lacking were guard rails, protective screens, safety shoes, and other protective clothing and equipment. The plant manager has final responsibility for plant safety and may be punished for safety infractions that lead to serious injury. Plant managers apparently had been fined and removed for "serious incidents" resulting from safety violations. Bear in mind, however, that a "serious incident" was defined as one in which "the number of workers killed is as many as ten or a dozen"![21]

Industrial Relations

In the United States, the term "industrial relations" usually refers to relationships between employees or their organizations and their employer or management. The phrase has a similar meaning in China, although there more emphasis is placed on employee participation in industrial affairs than on confrontation between labor and management.

There are two vehicles through which Chinese workers participate in enterprise management: the workers' congress and the trade union. Workers' congresses exist at the level of each enterprise, and they are supposed to conform to regulations issued in June 1981 by the Chinese Communist Party (CCP) Central Committee and State Council.[22] Trade unions exist at national, regional, and enterprise levels. Where both institutions co-exist, it is not always clear how participatory management functions are apportioned. A small number of enterprises have an experimental management system with the workers' congress as the main policymaking body; but in most instances, the "enterprise trade union committee looks after the organisational work before and after a congress is convened, and is its 'working organ'."[23] An organizational chart would show the union as the intermediary between the Party committee and the workers' congress within the enterprise.[24] The unions are thereby assigned the sometimes contradictory tasks of seeing that CCP policy is carried out and representing the workers' interests. Nonetheless, as noted below, it is difficult to separate the precise functions of the workers' congress and the trade union, because of some overlap between the two institutions, a lack of complete information, the current developmental and experimental situation, and the possibility of inaccurate information received during the study tour.

The Workers' Congress

Workers' congresses are elected by enterprise workers and managers, with a typical ratio of one congress representative for each 10 to 15 workers.[25] These bodies, which have existed in various forms since at least the 1950s, are now in a developmental and experimental stage. Chen has provided the most recent information about them,[26] writing that the workers' congress is found at the interindustry and city levels, as well as at the workshop, management, and factory levels within an enterprise. The workers' congress "is considered by China to be an organisation with the authority to implement political democracy, economic democracy, technological democracy and daily-life democracy in a plant."[27] According to Lockett, Article 5 of the Provisional Regulations Concerning Congresses of Workers and Staff Members in State-owned Industrial Enterprises provides that the main functions of the workers' congresses are to:

> *(a) "discuss and examine" the factory director's report, enterprise plans and budgets, major technical innovations and management issues; (b) "discuss and decide" on the use of labour protection, welfare, including housing allocation and bonus funds; (in addition, in "trial" enterprises it has to approve the division of retained profits); (c) "discuss and adopt" changes in organization, wages, training and "important rules and regulations"; (d) "supervise" cadres and managers in the enterprise; (e) "elect" leading cadres in line with "the arrangements of the higher organ of the enterprise" and subject to its approval.*[28]

Chen further notes that among the specific functions of the congress are the examination and approval of union-management "collective contracts"[29] and the examination and approval of proposals for trade union fees. An example of a specific grant of authority to a local workers' congress is that to the Shanghai No. 12 Cotton Mill. In October 1981, its congress was empowered to:

> *(1) prepare and implement the annual budget and production plan; (2) make plans for plant expansion, increased efficiency, and environmental controls; (3) supervise research and development; (4) make decisions on wages, benefits, and working conditions; (5) establish, abolish, or revise work rules; (6) change administrative systems; (7) administer the disciplinary system; (8) plan the use of welfare and bonus funds; (9) publish a manual of administrative procedure; and (10) take such other actions as may benefit the workers.*[30]

This was not a mill in which a union existed.

The role of the workers' congress appears to vary from mill to mill within the steel industry, but according to ministry officials in Beijing, every steel mill in China does have a congress. In the large Beijing steel complex, the annual production and operating plan is developed by the mill's Planning and Production Department. The draft plan is then submitted to the mill's workers' congress for discussion and suggestions, after which the Planning and Production Department makes revisions. In contract to the model presented by Chen, however, the Beijing mill management clearly does not feel bound to accept all of the suggestions of the congress but only those management views as meritorious. The revised plan is then resubmitted to the workers' congress for approval. The impression we received was that approval was expected at that stage of the process.

A somewhat different picture was painted in Nanjing, where the workers' congress itself was to decide the overall operating plan for the steel mill. The possibility of disagreement between the congress and mill officials over regulations and labor rules was acknowledged; and such disagreements were to be resolved through internal mediation.

Although none of the steel industry managers we interviewed specifically charged their workers' congress with responsibility for increased productivity, the congresses and the trade unions may indeed have such a role, as noted below in the section on unions. The congress does seem to be involved in productivity improvement in the Shanghai No. 12 Cotton Mill, and responsibility for efficiency seems implicit in the congress's activities.

Finally, the workers' congress or the trade union, or both, may be involved in the election of supervisory personnel. This practice, although not consistent, "may have begun to be applied in a fairly comprehensive way" in order "to improve the efficiency and legitimacy of management."[31] This move toward greater industrial democracy is not without its limitations, however, The party structure within enterprises, which includes union and top-management representatives, gives the CCP and top management the right to veto elected managers and the ability to influence the nominations.[32]

Leaders are not elected by the workers in Beijing, but they can be in Nanjing, where selection takes place in one of three ways. There they may be assigned by higher management, be drafted by the workers, or volunteer and be selected based on the passage of a "people's willingness test." Selection by the workers was said to be the preferred method, but this was applied primarily to group leaders, with the group being the basic work unit in the mill. Employees do not select office workers or higher levels of management.

In the Ma'anshan steel mill, workshop (group) managers and section chiefs are elected on a trial basis. The group averaged 10 to 30 employees, while a section averaged 200 but could be as many as 600. Managers in both Nanjing and Ma'anshan noted that workers' representatives were elected, with the representatives apparently constituting the workers' congress and participatory groups below the millwide level.

Although the mills we visited and the discussions we had are not necessarily representative of the entire steel industry in China, it seems safe to conclude that participatory management has not reached its potential. The extent of worker participation varies from mill to mill, and none of the workers' congresses in the mills we visited seemed to have functions as extensive as those reported for the Shanghai No. 12 Cotton Mill.

Chinese Trade Unions

Trade unions are supervised and coordinated by the All-China Federation of Trade Unions (ACFTU). Organized in about 1925, the ACFTU was dormant from the beginning of the Cultural Revolution in 1966 until 1978, after the fall of the Gang of Four and when the Ninth All-China Congress of Trade Unions was held. According to Hoffman,[33]

> *Operating unions function on an industrial basis, drawing membership from blue and white collar groups, and on a local and regional basis, paralleling the organization and control of industry. National unions operate vertically along industrial lines, while local, provincial, and regional units operate horizontally to represent the varied unions in the geographic area. . . . Trade union functions in China follow the pattern of other Communist countries. The unions transmit the party line, encourage production in a variety of organized ways, engage in political and ideological education, oversee safety and sanitation, handle grievances (though not exclusively), and execute numerous welfare and cultural responsibilities (social insurance, spare time education, recreation and so forth).*

The most specific recital of union functions we received came from the head of the trade union department (comparable to the chief official in a local U.S. union) at the Ma'anshan steel complex. The union was said to be responsible for the education of workers, the organization of workers' competition, and the ensuring of workers' welfare and fringe benefits. In Nanjing, officials noted that the union represents the interests of the masses and is responsible for educating workers to the tasks of production. Additionally, the union is to unite the workers and to deal with daily matters of production and worker welfare within the mill. Similar assessments surfaced in Shanghai, where the union had regular meetings with management and was expected to work for the employees' benefit.

Locally, unions are financed from dues and from money received by the enterprise. Although membership is reportedly voluntary, approximately 95 percent of those eligible join, with newer employees being more hesitant. This reluctance may be because newer employees have not seen the benefits of union membership or have not yet accepted the "education" about the role of trade unions in the enterprise.

Members pay dues equivalent to one-half of one percent of their wages, while an additional sum equal to 2 percent of the enterprise wage bill is used to fund union activities, including wages for the union staff, welfare programs, spare-time education, and physical training.

The head of the trade union department may be elected by the workers, with the approval of the local CCP, but may also be appointed by the Party. The candidate selected by the workers in Ma'anshan apparently had not been rejected by the Party in recent years. We cannot accurately speculate, however, on how free the choice of union leadership really is.

Our delegation was particularly interested in the role of Chinese trade unions in the dispute resolution process, especially in disciplinary cases. As noted above, discharge is rare and the "iron rice bowl" prevails. Since 1949, self-criticism and criticism by others have been used as means of correcting behavioral problems at the workplace. Criticism might come from the *danwei,* the workers' congress, or even the trade union, depending upon the perceived seriousness of the problem. Such criticism is considered appropriate, for example, in cases of sleeping on the job. Managers were said to be responsible both for production and for criticism of employees and themselves, although it is not clear that the two are distinct from one another. Training is viewed as the best response to inefficiency, with fines possible for accidents and lowered wages likely in the face of persistent inefficiency. But again, discharge is not used unless there is a violation of law.

Answers to questions concerning the extent of employee-employer differences or "contradictions," seemed among the least consistent of those we received.[34] Yet even their inconsistencies provide some insight into the Chinese view of workplace relationships. In Nanjing, it was noted that contradictions in China are within management rather than between union and management. The employee's *danwei,* and presumably larger groups as well, will help him to better understand his "wrong ideas," as investigation and discussion generally resolve disagreements. In case of a disagreement with management, the worker may be able to go to the (Party) leadership in the city or even the province, but this course of action was said to be rare. Asked if insubordination was ever a problem, one group of Chinese managers responded that insubordination and other workplace problems seldom occur because workers are educated in "the three loves": love of socialism, love of the enterprise, and love of their own job. Any contradictions that did occur could be solved by education, the existing system of regulations, demotion, or reduction in wages.

We often inquired about the role of the trade union in resolving disputes between employee and employer, particularly when the employer had accused a worker of wrongdoing (theft was often the example used) and the accusation was denied. There is no grievance procedure in China as we know it in the United States, and certainly no arbitration. Yet the union may sometimes play a role independent of management in resolving such contradictions.

We state the above possibility very tentatively because of varying responses to the question how a dispute over an alleged theft would be resolved. In Nanjing, we were told that the union would indeed "represent" the employee in presenting his or her side of the conflict. "Representation" was thereafter defined by the following statement: "We would educate the worker until he saw the error of his ways and confessed his crime." This approach is most consistent with the often-held view of the union as an arm of the state in communist countries.

On the other hand, when we posed the same hypothetical situation to the head of the trade union department in Shanghai, he replied that union and management would conduct independent investigations. If the union investigation showed the employee's innocence, the union would obviously prevail. There is no doubt that the union serves an educational function, aimed primarily at improving productivity. And not incidentally, this role is consistent with the needs of the state, particularly during a time when the Chinese hope to compete more fully in the world economy.

Our discussions with the Chinese did not clearly reveal whether the union also exercises an independent role on behalf of its members and as a countervailing influence on management, rather than simply as an arm of the state. The Shanghai case raises this possibility, but we simply do not know whether different responses were due to legitimately different ways of doing business in two unlike settings or due to dissimilar perceptions of what we should be told. It may be that differences in Shanghai and Nanjing stem from differences in Western influence in the two cities; Western influence in the business community has been comparatively profound in Shanghai, which also has the largest labor force and the longest history of labor activism of any city in China.

Workers' participation in management takes various forms in different regions of the country, for a number of possible reasons. There may simply have been too little time to implement one model in a country as vast and populous as China. Even given sufficient time, the distance between the central government in Beijing and various mills, regional differences, and differences in the operating systems and personalities within the mills may combine to produce a variety of approaches to workers' influence on enterprise management.

There is also a third possible explanation. Chinese executives and managers may have the same entrepreneurial spirit, the same drive, that has characterized managers in the United States.[35] One manifestation of such spirit is the desire to be left alone to exercise maximum managerial authority and ingenuity to produce the required product. Members of the Ministry of Metallurgy in Beijing gave the impression that workers' participation in management was not high on their list of priorities, that they simply wanted to be left alone to control the steel industry. Occasionally, this feeling of unnecessary constraint was echoed by managers in the field. The desire was most expressively voiced by the Chinese manager who told our delegation leader that although socialism had alleviated much suffering in China, "We could do so much more if it weren't for the bureaucrats." Chinese and American managers may have more in common than is commonly imagined.

The Balance Sheet

Among the reasons for the burgeoning world interest in China is the immense industrial potential of the country. The current State emphasis on the Four Modernizations represents an attempt by the communist leadership to accelerate the fulfillment of that potential. Yet the promise is mixed and there are significant hurdles to leap. Some of those hurdles are part and parcel of managing human resources.

Problems

One problem facing the Chinese economy is that of work schedules. The standard eight-hour day and six-day workweek are coupled with a spartan and arduous way of life in China. There is little time for relaxation and rejuvenation. One silk factory in Hangzhou (Hangchou) uses rotating shifts for continuous-process operation. Unlike the schedules for rotating shifts in the United States, the Hangzhou factory schedules require that workers, most of whom are women, work two days on each of the three shifts, followed by two days off, after which the cycle begins anew. The long workweek, stringent off-work demands, and such onerous conditions as the shift-rotation pattern in Hangzhou are likely to have an adverse impact on productivity.

Individual incentives are more and more common in the steel industry, but the nature of steel production would make group incentives generally more appropriate. And although the Chinese determination to break some of the egalitarian molds of the past should encourage greater productivity and efficiency, the use of bonus incentives for greater production may fall short of potential because the bonus system is not always tailored to the system of production in use.

Another problem for the Chinese economic system is the "iron rice bowl." Chinese managers suggest that serious discipline problems on the shop floor are a rarity, given the "three loves," but we believe that they underestimated the problem. It seems that managers must live with employees who do not respond well to others' attempts to "educate" them to the needs of the workplace and therefore must live with more inefficiency than necessary. Of course, given the problems of unemployment and underemployment that continue to plague China, a policy that makes discharge difficult is understandable, even though it may close doors for more efficient workers.

Finally, although we cannot judge from our own experience, others have commented that industrial growth in China will be hampered by the lack of managerial skills, as much a lack of human resource management skills as of technical skills.[36] Even though Chinese students are attending foreign schools in record numbers for managerial and technical training, it appears that this lack will continue to be a critical one in the foreseeable future.

Prospects

On the other hand, there are obvious moves toward industrialization that go beyond the mere lifting of the "bamboo curtain." The country is a storehouse of resources, and the human resource potential is almost unlimited. The population of China is approximately one billion. Roughly 75 percent of the labor force is employed in agriculture,[37] still often using the most primitive farming methods.[38] Particularly with more efficient farming methods, there will be more than enough people to fill the needs of industry, though it may be difficult to achieve appropriate levels and distribution of skills. Moreover, Chinese tradition places the will of society above individual needs, thus making for a generally disciplined and hardworking labor force.

Particularly where the less skilled and less educated are concerned, there are some elements of systematic personnel management. Industry may actively recruit local workers, screening them through physical and written examinations. These workers may realize opportunities for internal mobility based on their own ability and performance and may also receive training to enhance promotional opportunities. Employees are evaluated periodically, though the criteria for evaluation are unclear, and evaluations seem to influence decisions on internal mobility and wage increases. Thus, we can conclude that some components of a formal personnel or human resource management system are now in place in China.

Workers' participation in management may be another strength of the Chinese system. In many instances, employee ideas are solicited, considered, and adopted.

Although the various forms of *danwei* are not directly comparable to the quality circles of Japan and Western nations, it is likely that improvements in productivity and employee morale have resulted from employee participation in management.

Finally, although the extent to which the responsibility system is being implemented may be questioned, the present government strongly backs that system and the idea that employees must be motivated to be more efficient. Of particular interest in this regard is an opinion article that appeared in a 1983 edition of *China Daily,* the English-language Chinese newspaper:

> *China needs to change its wage system. . . . Its main problem is egalitarianism, which is an obstinate concept that harms the country's socialist construction under the pretense of advancing communism. All serious economic frustrations have had much to do with the egalitarian system.*[39]

The author went on to suggest a wage system that conceptually is compatible with those common in the United States, although, of course, he viewed it as consistent with socialism.

If China is to succeed in its desire to become a major economic and military force by the year 2000, substantial improvements in the management of its human resources will be necessary. Constraints imposed by culture and tradition may hinder achievement of those improvements; but significant changes are taking place in employer-employee relations, and there is a distinct possibility that these changes will help to bring about the increases China seeks in efficiency and productivity.

Notes

1. See, for example, John Philip Emerson, "The Labor Force of China, 1957–1980," in U.S. Congress, Joint Economic Committee, *China Under the Four Modernizations,* Part I (Washington, D.C.: GPO, August 13, 1982), pp. 224–67.
2. The study visit was initiated by the National Academy of Arbitrators, arranged by People-to-People International, and sponsored by the Chinese Ministry of Metallurgy. Over the 16-day visit, we engaged in discussions with government officials, managers, specialists, and trade union officials and visited steel mills and other enterprises in Beijing, Nanjing, Ma'anshan, and Baoshan (Shanghai).
3. During a break from one of the meetings, one Chinese volunteered the information that we were hearing "propaganda" in response to some of our questions during discussion sessions. In context, there was no doubt that "propaganda" meant misinformation or the party line.
4. John Philip Emerson, "Urban School-Leavers and Unemployment in China," *China Quarterly,* No. 93 (March 1983), pp. 1–16.
5. Andrew G. Walder, "The Remaking of the Chinese Working Class, 1949–1981," *Modern China,* Vol. 10 (January 1984), p. 20.
6. See, for example, Zhao Lukuan, "Several Problems of Labor and Employment in Our Country," *People's Daily,* August 19, 1980, p. 5, in *Foreign Broadcast Information Service,* September 4, 1980, p. L-24.

7. In the Ma'anshan steel complex, for example, where railroad wheels and tires are made for export to General Motors among other customers, management said that the introduction of more efficient equipment would not pose a threat to workers' job security because the plant was at that time unable to meet the demand for its products.
8. During the previous year in Ma'anshan, 370 transfers had been approved in a work force for the complex of approximately 50,000, including those who worked in the mines supporting the steel complex. We were unable to learn how many employees had requested transfers. The Baoshan steel complex on the outskirts of Shanghai was being built with close to 40,000 employees who had been transferred from elsewhere in China. Those transferred had to rank within at least a grade 3 on the wage scale of 8.
9. Charles Hoffman, *The Chinese Worker* (Albany: State University of New York Press, 1974), p. 65.
10. Charles Hoffman, "People's Republic of China," in Albert A. Blum, ed., *International Handbook of Industrial Relations* (Westport, Conn.: Greenwood Press, 1981), p. 120.
11. Chu-yuan Cheng, "The Modernization of Chinese Industry," in Richard Baum, ed., *China's Four Modernizations: The New Technological Revolution* (Boulder, Colo.: Westview Press, 1980), p. 39.
12. One U.S. dollar was worth slightly less than two yuan in March 1983. As a standard of comparison, adult one-speed bicycles sold for 191 and 175 yuan at that time, while smaller models sold for 141 yuan.
13. A monthly survey in 1982 of bonuses in the Peking Steel Enterprise showed no bonus for 10.45 percent of the work force, up to 10 yuan for 29.1 percent of the work force, 10 to 20 yuan for 50.87 percent, 20 to 35 yuan for 9.44 percent, and above 35 yuan for 0.14 percent. The monthly average was 11.91 yuan, with the highest bonus being 45.9 yuan. See National Technical Information Services, *China Report: Economic Affairs, No. 289,* microfiche, U.S. Joint Publications Research Service, No. 82364 (Washington, D.C.: GPO, December 2, 1982), p. 50.
14. We were told that workers' compensation payments and pensions were each the equivalent of about 60 percent of wages. It should be noted that fringe benefits are paid only to employees in state-owned industry, who numbered about 75 million in 1978. In the same year, there were about 280 million agricultural employees (75 percent of the entire labor force) and about 20 million (5 percent of the labor force) who worked under collective or cooperative ownership. See James A. Kilpatrick, "Agriculture," in Frederica M. Burge and Rinn-Sup Shinn, eds., *China: A Country Study* (Washington, D.C.: Government Printing Office, 1981), p. 210; and Craig Littler, "Japan and China," in Stephan Feuchtwang and Athar Hussain, eds., *The Chinese Economic Reforms* (London: Croom Helm, 1983), p. 138.
15. Walder, "The Remaking of the Chinese Working Class," pp. 24–25.
16. Ibid.
17. "This program is geared to the primary objective of turning China into a major economic and military power by the year 2000." Baum, *China's Four Modernizations,* p. iii.

18. In discussions, the Chinese claimed that work groups did not set informal labor standards as a means of forestalling higher incentive standards. The reactions of the Chinese whenever we asked about this subject—such as their "body language" and facial expressions—nevertheless provided a strong suggestion that informal standards are a problem.
19. Interestingly, one palliative to youth unemployment now promulgated by the Chinese government is to encourage the jobless to set up cooperatives to engage in service, retail, or production activities for their own profit. We could not help but note that although job creation for youth is also a severe problem in the United States, this capitalist country has made no similar effort to alleviate it by promoting entrepreneurship among its unemployed youth.
20. Emerson, "Urban School-Leavers," p. 9.
21. For more details, see Charles M. Rehmus, "The Academy in China," *The Chronicle* (Journal of the National Academy of Arbitrators), (September 1983), p. 7. The paragraphs here on in-plant safety are reformulations of material in that article.
22. Martin Lockett, "Enterprise Management—Moves Toward Democracy?" in Feuchtwang and Hussain, *The Chinese Economic Reforms,* p. 240.
23. Ibid., p. 240.
24. Ibid., p. 234.
25. Ibid., 240.
26. Peter Kar-nin Chen, "The Practice of Industrial Relations in China: A New Approach to the Four Modernizations," *Proceedings of the International Industrial Relations Research Association, Sixth World Congress, Kyoto, Japan, March 28–31, 1983,* Vol. III, pp. 145–147.
27. Ibid., p. 147.
28. Lockett, "Enterprise Management," p. 241.
29. These are not collectively bargained agreements as they are in the United States, but may be more accurately characterized as documents that set forth the functions that the trade union is to perform.
30. You Yuwen, "Democratic Management: A New Way," *China Reconstructs* (publication of the China Welfare Institute, Beijing), Vol. 30, No. 5 (May 1981), p. 18.
31. Lockett, "Enterprise Management," p. 239.
32. Ibid., p. 239.
33. Hoffman, "The People's Republic of China," pp. 120–21.
34. While Americans would use such words as "disagreement" or "conflict," the Chinese use the equivalent of our "contradiction." Since they had a very difficult time grasping our system of arbitration and the terms associated with it, we readily adopted the more comfortable "contradictions" in our discussions in the hope of encouraging a more candid exchange of ideas.
35. This observation was first voiced by Charles M. Rehmus, delegation leader and Dean, New York State School of Industrial and Labor Relations, Cornell University.
36. See, for example, Lockett, "Enterprise Management," pp. 254–56.
37. Kilpatrick, "Agriculture."
38. We observed many more oxen plowing fields than tractors, which were a rarity.
39. Zhao Lukuan, "Wage Distribution Should Be Based on Productivity," *China Daily,* March 19, 1983, p. 4.

11. JAPANESE-OWNED FIRMS IN THE UNITED STATES: DO THEY RESIST UNIONISM?

PAMELA C. MARETT
Visiting Assistant Professor, Department of Economics and Business, North Carolina State University, Raleigh, North Carolina

The presence of Japanese-owned companies in the United States is a relatively new phenomenon. The increasing rate of this investment, at first welcomed and even encouraged by organized labor, is now questioned. Unions are currently alleging that Japanese-owned firms are antiunion. As evidence they cite fierce resistance to organization efforts to the point of violating United States labor laws.

Is the Japanese presence in the United States accompanied by a systematic bias and resolve to remain union free, or is it no different from the case of United States-owned manufacturing firms? As unions are accepted in Japan, why would Japanese behavior regarding recognition in this country differ? In what follows, it is hoped that some clues will be provided to answer these questions.

The article will begin with a brief survey of the legal and institutional setting of industrial relations in the United States and Japan, with emphasis on union recognition and resulting structures. There are two complementary reasons for this. One is to acquaint the uninitiated with the labor relations environment in Japan. The other is to permit a comparison of the two systems. Most notably it will be seen that, although an antiunion management position in the United States is not only legal but common, it is neither legal nor the typical case in Japan. Thus, although the Japanese may legally and socially choose to avoid unionization in the United States they may not in their own country.

Data and information will then be presented on Japanese-owned manufacturing firms in the United States. This information is developed to determine whether a clear pattern of union avoidance is present or developing. Finally, inferences and conclusions will be drawn from this information.

The data presented and analyzed come from two analyses of Japanese-owned firms in the United States. One is a study done by the Japanese External Trade Organization (JETRO). The other was conducted by the Japan Economic Institute.

An additional, valuable input to this study is a series of six field interviews and four telephone interviews. These interviewees were two officials from the AFL-CIO national office, three union organizers, one official in a union's international department, one state commerce department official, one Japanese government official, one management consultant, and one researcher from an independent institute.

All of these people were most helpful and informative and certainly were credits to their respective positions. The informal format of the interviews in the main encouraged candor. Some comments were given "off the record." Although these comments are not necessarily included it was decided to preserve the anonymity of all interviewees.

United States

Labor relations in the United States is governed by a body of federal and state laws and the interpretations of these laws by the appropriate judicial and administrative bodies. The basic labor relations law for the private sector is the 1935 National Labor Relations Act as amended in 1947 by the Labor-Management Relations Act and in 1959 by the Labor-Management Reporting and Disclosure Act.[1] This legislation establishes workers' rights to join and be active in unions and bargain collectively and protects their right to refrain from these activities.

To guarantee these rights, specified types of employer and union behavior believed to be incompatible with the objectives of the law were banned. These types of behavior are listed in the law and termed unfair labor practices. The law also provides a procedure to determine employee representation preferences. The National Labor Relations Board is the agency established to administer, enforce, and interpret the law.

The result is that the United States has a complex system of laws and regulations governing union-management relations. This becomes especially obvious in the procedures involved for union recognition.

For the union to be the bargaining agent for a group of employees it must first be determined which employees the union should represent and if the majority of those employees desire representation. The first factor involves determining the appropriate bargaining unit. This task, when there is a question, falls to the National Labor Relations Board, which is restricted in its determination by certain statutory provisions. Beyond these the NLRB has established guidelines to aid it in bargaining unit determinations.

The second factor mentioned involves ascertaining the representation desires of the majority of the employees within the appropriate bargaining unit. A union is legally entitled to be recognized as the exclusive bargaining representative for all employees within the appropriate bargaining unit if a majority of employees in the unit desires it to represent them.

The law does not require the use of one particular procedure for the selection of the bargaining representative. It requires only that the representative be the choice of a majority of the employees in the bargaining unit.

The United States has what is generally considered to be a decentralized bargaining structure. In 1978 there were estimated to be 177,715 collective bargaining agreements in effect.[2] Unfortunately, there are no breakdowns of these contracts by size and scope of bargaining unit. A Conference Board survey found, however, that 64 percent of the companies surveyed conducted negotiations at the single plant level.[3] Despite the prevalence of this arrangement, it has been estimated that approximately 250 collective bargaining agreements cover 20 percent of all workers subject to union contracts.[4]

Perhaps diversity is the appropriate way to characterize bargaining structure in the United States. The size and composition of bargaining units tend to reflect the various competitive, organizational, and historical influences operative in each instance.

The organizational structure of the unions reflects efforts to adapt pursuit of goals to the environment. The main components are the local union, the national union, and the federation. The local union is the building block of organized labor. It is the component in which individual workers are members and the element that handles daily problems. Local unions are typically chartered by national unions, which are the central body and core of power in most cases. The nationals exercise considerable control and influence over their locals primarily through the services provided, including organizing, and assistance in negotiating and administering contracts.

The dominant labor federation is the AFL-CIO. Although member national unions remain autonomous, the AFL-CIO offers many services and exerts its influence to promote political and social objectives on behalf of the labor movement.

United States union membership was estimated to be 20.5 million in 1978, for a penetration rate of 20 percent of the total labor force and about 23.6 percent of the employees in nonagricultural establishments.[5] The degree of unionization varied by occupation, industry, and geographic location. In 1978, these organized workers constituted approximately 50 percent of U.S. blue-collar workers and less than 15 percent of white-collar workers. Within the blue-collar classification the semiskilled were most organized followed by the skilled crafts. Within industries at least 75 percent of transportation, construction, and mining workers were organized, and 50–74 percent were organized in transportation equipment and manufacturing.

The five states with the lowest degree of unionization were reported to be North Carolina, South Carolina, South Dakota, Texas, and Florida. Degree of unionization was highest in New York, West Virginia, Michigan, Pennsylvania, and Washington.

There were, in 1978, 174 national unions. Membership was concentrated in a small number of large unions. Sixteen unions represented 61 percent of total union membership and more than 50 percent of all locals were chartered by 14 national unions. Seventy-eight percent of all union members were represented by the 108 national unions affiliated with the AFL-CIO.

Japan

The Japanese system of laws and regulations governing labor relations is less complex than that of the United States. Union representation and collective bargaining are promised in the Japanese constitution of 1949. Article 28 of Chapter III states simply that "The right of workers to organize and bargain and act collectively is guaranteed."[6] The Trade Union Law, originally enacted in 1946 and substantially revised in 1949, provides double assurance of these constitutional guarantees. It gives workers the right to form free and autonomous unions, to engage in collective bargaining resulting in written signed agreements, and when necessary to engage in collective action, including the right to strike.

The law lists four employer unfair labor practices. In brief, the employer may not: discharge or give discriminatory treatment to a worker for union activities or membership; refuse to bargain collectively with the representative of the workers; control or interfere with union formation or management or contribute financially to the union; or discharge or show discriminatory treatment to a worker for having filed a complaint or given testimony against the employer as provided by the law.[7]

For administration and enforcement the Trade Union Law established the Central Labor Relations Commission and Prefectural Labor Relations Commission. The Central Labor Relations Commission assumes "jurisdiction in conciliation, mediation, arbitration, and adjudication in cases which cover two or more prefectures or which present issues of national import," while the Prefectural Labor Relations Commission assumes jurisdiction at the local level.[8] The law provides for penalties for noncompliance of a Commission order when the order is sustained by fixed judgment of the court.

The enterprise union in Japan is the foundation of union structure. It is an independent organization of workers within a given enterprise or company that includes all regular employees of the enterprise regardless of job. Over 80 percent of all basic trade union bodies are organized on an enterprise basis.[9]

Craft or industrial unions comparable to those in the United States are rare. The form of industrial union that exists is an industrywide federation of enterprise unions within a particular industry. The federations are loosely organized and primarily serve to bolster contact among the enterprise unions. The federations typically do not engage in collective bargaining, although they can bargain and order strikes for local enterprise unions desiring them. At the federation's scheduled conferences, however, it is likely that the discussion will focus on industrial problems in a general context.

Additional Data

In addition to the industrial federations, there are four major organizations or national centers to which Japanese unions may belong. In 1982, the number of union members affiliated with the four major national trade union centers (Sohyo, Domei, Shinsanbetsu, and Churitsuroren) totaled 8,250,000, or 65.9 percent of total organized labor.[10] These major national centers differ in both employment of the workers of the affiliated unions and political orientation. Recent efforts to unite labor further have been successful. On December 14, 1982, Zenmin Rokyo was inaugurated. It is composed of unions from all four national centers. Further unification is anticipated by first uniting private sector unions (with consent of the four national centers) and ultimately integrating the private sector unions with public sector unions in a national confederation. The hope in unification is to obtain a powerful labor voice in social and economic issues.[11]

Because the basic unit is the enterprise union, the centralized control and authority found in national unions in the United States do not exist in Japan. The local control facilitates the mix of blue- and white-collar workers. It also means that the leaders are usually full-time employees of the company. Thus, particularly in the smaller unions, there is no professional union representative.

The national labor centers do try to coordinate bargaining activities. Every spring the majority of enterprise unions bargain for wages and benefits. This has become known as the "spring offensive." The hope is to achieve uniform increases for all union members. Strikes during this period are not uncommon. The strike serves to convince the employer of union resolve to encourage serious bargaining. In Japan, both the actual number of strikes and the number of participating members is high.[12] The strikes tend to be short, ranging from a few hours to two or three days.

Stark contrasts exist between the United States and Japan regarding recognition and bargaining rights. Recognition is a simple matter in Japan. When workers, however small or large their number, decide they desire to be in a union, they have only to meet together and then present their demands to the employer. In Japan, employer resistance is considered a social affront as well as a violation of the law. As one Japanese states the case, "No one would be willing to work for such an employer."[13]

Additionally, there is no notion of an exclusive bargaining representative in Japanese private sector labor relations. This is because the constitutional right to bargain is guaranteed equally to all workers. Minority unions share in this right; Japanese employers are obligated to bargain with all competing unions in the enterprise.

The 74,091 trade unions in Japan as of 1982 had a total membership of 12,526,000.[14] The estimated unionization rate was 30.5 percent. The largest number of union members was found in the manufacturing sector—4,121,000 members, or 32.9 percent of the total. This was followed by the transport and telecommunications sector (16.2 percent of the total); the private service sector (13.5 percent); and government service (12 percent). The unionization rate was highest—73.8 percent—in the government service sector. It was followed by a 16.8 percent unionization rate in transportation and telecommunication; 59.3 percent in electricity, gas, water, and steam supply; 51.6 percent in finance, insurance, and real estate; 47.5 percent in mining; and 35.5 percent in manufacturing.

Membership tended to be greater the larger the enterprise. The majority of private sector union membership, or 56.37 percent, were organized in enterprises of 1,000 or more employees. Close to 17 percent were organized in enterprises of 300 to 999 employees. Membership in companies employing 100 to 299 was 11.8 percent, while that in companies with 30 to 99 employees was 5.24 percent. Companies that employed less than 29 workers accounted for .78 percent. The remaining 9.79 percent were in units of unknown size.

The "Evidence"

The specter raised by labor's allegations of the Japanese as antiunion employers may be reinforced by media-reported classes between well-known Japanese companies and the organizing union. Honda, Kawasaki, Sanyo, and Sharp are names familiar to the American public. All vigorously attempted to resist unionization. The organizing union in each instance filed unfair labor practice charges against the company.

Unions believe that these better known cases, together with less publicized ones, are mounting evidence that a major labor law violator has been exported to the United States. They cite a propensity by these firms to engage in practices of union resistance. Especially distressing to unions is the incidence of using management consulting firms, known in labor circles as "union busters." Interviews to select antiunion employees, discriminatory treatment among employees, discharge, and other such practices are noted. The Japanese are also cited for deliberately locating in low-union locales—depressed areas and right to work states.

Two factors make this all the more perplexing to organized labor. One is the fact that it not only welcomed foreign investment it solicited it to create employment.[15] The second factor is that, based on its assessment of union-company relations in Japan, labor did not anticipate resistance to unionization by the Japanese. There, as expressed by a Japanese law professor, "No decent employer dares to deny establishment of a union or to refuse bargaining openly unless they believe that they have some special justification to do so."[16]

Statistics

Are the Japanese systematically antiunion? Statistics from two surveys of Japanese firms in the United States may help to determine if a clear pattern of union avoidance is present.

The following information comes from a study by the Japanese External Trade Organization, which conducted a survey between September 1980 and March 1981 of 238 Japanese-owned factories and operations engaged in manufacturing in the United States.[17] In the survey Japanese companies in the United States were defined as ones in which Japanese hold 10 percent or more of the voting shares. The plants of these companies were the units covered in the survey. JETRO sent staff members from its regional trade centers to the plants.

The facilities surveyed were geographically distributed in 38 states and Puerto Rico. The 10 largest number of facilities were found in the following 17 states: California (73), Alaska (25), Texas (12), Georgia (11), Illinois (10), Michigan (9), Washington, (9), New Jersey (7), Indiana (6), Tennessee (6), Massachusetts (5), New York (5), North Carolina (5), Pennsylvania (5), Florida (4), Oregon (4), and South Carolina (4). Regarding scale of operations, 142 firms had less than 300. The greatest number of firms, 60, employed between 30 and 100. The overall average of employees per plant was about 200.

Considering both number of employees and geographic distribution, the Alaska plants tended to be small in scale and seasonal in nature. This was a function of the concentration of plants in marine seafood processing. Large factories employing 500 or more were most frequently found in California, Arkansas, Alabama, and Tennessee.

The companies represented many industries. Machinery manufacturers were the most numerous with 70 plants. Electronic equipment machinery had 44 plants, transportation equipment 10 plants, and precision machinery registered 8 plants.

The study considered the factors of industry and geographic distribution. In the Pacific Northwest food processing operations were relatively numerous (Alaska included). Metal fabrication was fairly numerous in the Midwest, and electrical machinery production was found in California and the South.

The pace of Japanese investment (since 1950) accelerated from 1970–1980. Two peak periods occurred in 1973–1975 and 1978–1980. Growth was noted particularly in electrical machinery, where a large number of plants had recently opened in the South.

In addition to the traditional factors of locational theory (availability, adequacy, and cost of transportation; quantity, quality, and cost of available labor; taxes; construction costs; and so forth), hospitality and enthusiasm of state and regional officials was considered a factor. This factor favored location in the South and Midwest.

Fifty-five percent of the companies had Japanese directors. In 70 percent of the firms the top position was filled by a Japanese. The remaining division of management showed Americans to be in charge of production, labor matters, and sales. The Japanese occupied positions that involved accounting; liaison with the Japanese parent company, technological matters, and ultimate decisionmaking. The total employment of Japanese nationals at all levels was only 2.5 percent of total employees.

The study found 33 unionized firms, or less than one-fourth of the total. Many of these were in Alaska and many had been acquired with unions intact. Few of the Californian and southern plants had no unions. A 1982 update of the survey stated that 22.7 percent of the survey firms were unionized.[18]

Additional Data

Additional data entered are from a study by the Japan Economic Institute of America.[19] Conducted about the same time as the JETRO study, this study concentrated on the compilation and listing of data rather than analysis. Although the two organizations regard the studies as complementary, the Japan Economic Institute may have conducted a more exhaustive search of facilities.

At the end of 1982, the Institute study found 292 companies in which the Japanese held majority interest (50 percent or more). Twenty-six more were added when companies with 10–50 percent Japanese interest were added. A count of plants with 10 percent of more interest yielded 458. The total number of plants in 1981 was 428, a number significantly larger than JETRO's 258. Some of this difference may be attributed to search techniques and some to definitional variations.

In the Institute study the 10 largest number of facilities were found in the following 14 states: California (116), Alaska (35), New Jersey (23), Georgia (19), Washington (19), Illinois (17), Texas (17), New York (16), North Carolina (16), Michigan (13), Pennsylvania (13), Ohio (11), Tennessee (10), and Indiana (9). Despite absolute differences in the 10 largest numbers of facilities, the relative ranking of states associated with these numbers is quite similar. The JETRO study does not list Ohio. The Institute study does not list Florida, Oregon, and South Carolina, which tied for the 10th position in the JETRO study.

Analysis

Much in these statistics makes it difficult to conclude that any systematic bias against unions is operative. A 1982 update of the JETRO survey cited the unionization rate for the United States in 1980 as 24.5 percent, while 22.7 percent of the Japanese-owned firms were found to be unionized.[20] The majority of the Japanese facilities were in industries (machinery and electronic machinery) that do not have the highest rates of unionization in the United States.

The scale of Japanese operations tended to be small. Although the largest number of firms employed less than 100 workers, the average was 200. The operations also were new. At the time of the survey, 46 percent of the firms were not over five years old.

A study by Jedel and Kujawa concluded that "Length of time in operation and size of work force generally operated in tandem."[21] They found that larger and older firms were more apt to be organized. Since employment typically increased in size over time, they anticipated that as the foreign-owned firms aged and grew it was more likely that they would be successfully organized. Although small at the time, their sample of 14 Japanese-owned firms exhibited the same characteristics as the JETRO sample. Nine of the 14 had been operating for five or fewer years. Ten employed less than 500 workers. If their conclusion is correct, then given the size and age of the majority of the Japanese firms in either study greater numbers should be organized in future years.

No pattern of geographic preference is easily discernable from the data. Looking at the states with the largest number of facilities in the JETRO study, six of 17 are right to work states, and in the Institute study four of 14 are. This does not appear to match charges of locational avoidance. Besides, in the United States in recent years there has been a general industrial movement from the frostbelt to the sunbelt.

Further, the JETRO study pointed out another factor used in location decisions. Some firms (no number) indicated that "the good treatment and enthusiasm of state and regional officials" was considered.[22] This "was frequently mentioned in the cases of firms which located in the South Atlantic states. . . ."[23] With no means to measure, it is conceivable that this treatment variable played as much of a role as any other in locating in right to work states.

In fact, a South Atlantic state commerce department official in the division charged with recruitment of foreign investment was quite emphatic about the importance of enthusiasm and superb treatment of potential foreign investors. He felt that the investor already knew (or could easily be informed) about the state. It was therefore imperative that these individuals felt welcomed.

Concerning the matter of acquired firms, the JETRO study noted that "many of the firms studied existed prior to being purchased by Japanese investors and simply continued their earlier labor organization."[24] One interviewee took this as evidence of a neutral Japanese position on unions. That is, in deciding to acquire a unionized plant, the Japanese investor is aware of that fact and willing to accept it or would not invest.

Perhaps, then, it may tentatively be concluded that, except for isolated instances, the furor over the Japanese as antiunion employers is not substantially founded in fact. Yet closer scrutiny of these same statistics gives cause for reevaluation.

Reevaluation

The comparison the 1982 JETRO study makes of unionization rates may not be valid. The unionization rate given for Japanese firms is the percentage of organized firms to total firms. The study gives no explanation of what their 24.5 percent figure for the United States represents. It is likely, however, that the statistic as usually published is the percentage of the total labor force unionized and therefore not comparable.

Although no geographic preference was easily seen in the historical data the study did point out that in the most recent locations included there was a tendency to prefer the South. It also noted that some machinery plants selected the South based on its supply of inexpensive labor. There is also a locational trend in the South for electronics firms. This could be interpreted as union avoidance. As already mentioned, some of the union officials interviewed believed that recent southern locational pattern was clearly an antiunion tactic. Another interviewee (who really did not believe that this was one of the Japanese decisionmaking factors in location) did allow that the locational decisions of a couple of the more recent firms tended to make one "suspicious" that perhaps it was union avoidance. She regarded this suspicion as even more compelling when viewed in light of executive comments about no need for union representation.[25]

The Jedel-Kujawa study notes that five of the 14 Japanese firms included in their study were unionized, and four of those five were acquisitions.[26] The JETRO study reported that "many of the firms studied existed prior to being purchased by the Japanese investors and simply continued their earlier labor organization pattern."[27] Unfortunately, neither study indicates how many of the unionized firms were acquired or how many of these acquisitions were unionized. In fact, in rereading the quote from JETRO it is not at all clear that the "many" refers to unionized acquisitions. In answer to the argument that the acquired firms were purchased with full knowledge of the existing union, it is possible that the cost of investing in the new plant outweighed the costs of accepting the union.

A final comment must be entered regarding the 1982 JETRO followup survey that indicated the 22.7 percent unionization rate of Japanese-owned firms. No similar figure was published in the 1981 survey. The 1982 survey was a questionnaire mailed to 225 firms, 167 of which responded.[28] The 1981 survey included 258 firms. Because of these differences it is impossible to compare (but legitimate to question) the true extent of unionization. Reference is made in particular to the 1981 survey, which in the section on unionization also noted that "Ten of the 33 unionized firms were Alaska seafood processing operations. Unionization has a long tradition in this industry."[29] This accounts for 30 percent of the unionized firms. In the final analysis, not knowing what percent of unionized firms were acquisitions, little can be said regarding the incidence of unionization at new plants in more traditional industries.

Reasons for Resistance

The evidence presented has not made it possible to establish conclusively whether the Japanese presence in the United States is accompanied by a systematic bias and resolve to remain union free. What remains to be explored is why the Japanese resist unionization at all. There are several possibilities.

The union officials interviewed were of the opinion that the Japanese were being encouraged to exercise antiunion behavior by elements in the United States. Specifically they referred to state government officials, chambers of commerce, and consulting firms. The following analogy was suggested. "It's too uniform to be happenstance. It's too uniform to be by accident. I mean, geez, if you walk into an area and everyone you meet is gay—it didn't happen by accident, it must have come there from somewhere. It's not in the water. Well, every Japanese outfit that you run into is antiunion, so you figure it."

It seems reasonable to believe that chambers of commerce would promote "no union" and that consulting firms wish to solicit business. One union official noted that the American consultants meet with business people in Europe. "They get to these business people before they come to the United States and tell them the problems with the trade union movements." He suspected that this took place in Japan as well. The consultant explained that the Japanese put out feelers in the United States to establish contacts to act as their forerunners. He continued that "any good consulting firm—and that's all a law firm is—knows about that and starts pushing around."

As for state officials, a 1979 *Washington Post* article quoted the then governor of Virginia inviting Japanese industrialists to locate in Virginia because "only a small portion of the state's labor force is organized into unions."[30] The state commerce official interviewed was quite matter of fact, however, in stating that this was not a part of his state's presentation. He said that right to work was not even an issue. His state relies on referral and hospitality.

Perhaps the owners of Japanese firms, the various large investment companies in Japan, possess different attitudes about unionization. This may account for the very different approach of a Sony firm and a Sharp firm. Despite the picture received of very harmonious labor relations in Japan, all is not bliss. In their own way some Japanese firms are more difficult for unions than others.[31] Although it is illegal in Japan to resist unionization, this is not the case in the United States. One union official noted that the Japanese are profit motivated, too, and they certainly realize that unions cost them money. Why pay for something that might be avoided?

Cultural differences may account for attitudes and actions. The Japanese official interviewed believes that the Japanese try hard to adapt to what they perceive to be "the American way." The management consultant found that the Japanese simply do not understand the subtleties of the American culture and tend to be quite clumsy in some matters. The adversarial nature of labor relations in the United States baffles them. They therefore seek help in these matters.

The help the Japanese find includes American managers. The JETRO study reported that it is common in Japanese-owned firms for Americans to be in charge of production, labor matters, and sales.[32] Greer and Shearer found that the majority of foreign-owned firms staffed management positions with Americans.[33] A *Wall Street Journal* article aptly summed up this situation and its implications: "the emerging Japanese-owned operations here are basically American operations. When they establish U.S. units, Japanese auto makers hire American managers. And there's nothing unusual about American businessmen resisting unions."[34]

Conclusion

In closing, mention of a paper by Hanami should prove interesting.[35] Hanami described and analyzed the relationship of labor and the multinational corporation in Japan. It seems that foreign enterprises in Japan, most notably American enterprises, are believed to possess a "general attitude of hospitality towards union activities."[36]

After examining the facts Hanami found no support for this conclusion. Instead, he surmised that even if foreign firms were hostile toward the labor movement this did not necessarily separate them from their Japanese counterparts. Further, foreign firms had a difficult time grasping Japanese employment concepts. They lacked familiarity with Japanese union structure and Japanese labor relations in general. They did not possess the vocabulary to engage in ideological arguments on an equal footing with their Japanese counterparts. Hanami suspected that time would ameliorate these difficulties.

Notes

1. The Railway Labor Act governs labor relations in the railroad and airline industries. The peculiarities of this law as it relates to these industries are not included.
2. U.S. Department of Labor, Bureau of Labor Statistics, *Directory of National Unions and Employee Associations,* 1978 (Washington, D.C.: U.S. Government Printing Office, 1979), p. 73.
3. Audrey Freeman, *Managing Labor Relations* (New York: The Conference Board, Inc., 1975), p. 4.
4. Directory of National Unions and Employee Associations
5. The information that follows is from *The Directory of National Unions and Employee Associations,* p. 19.
6. Constitution of Japan, Article 28, Chapter III.
7. Trade Union Law, Article 7, 1–4.
8. Trade Union Law, Article 25.
9. Arnold R. Weber, "The Structure of Collective Bargaining and Bargaining Power: Foreign Experiences," *The Journal of Law and Economics* (6 October 1963), p. 85.
10. "The 1982 Basic Survey on Trade Unions," *Japan Labor Bulletin* (March 1983), p. 14.
11. Isao Yoshimara, "Leading Actors Promoting Labor Front Unification," *Japan Labor Bulletin* (February 1983), pp. 5–6.
12. Arnold Weber, cited at note 9, p. 109.
13. Quotation is from a video cassette produced by the Communication Workers of America.
14. The following information is from "The 1982 Basic Survey on Trade Unions."
15. See "After Coaxing Japanese Car Makers to U.S., UAW Finds They Resist Union Organization," *The Wall Street Journal,* August 26, 1980, and "Japanese Unions, AFL-CIO Concur on U.S. Job Needs," *AFL-CIO News,* May 30, 1981, p. 2.
16. Tadashi Hanami, "Unfair Labor Practices—Law and Practice," *Japan Labor Bulletin* (June 1983), p. 18.

17. Japan External Trade Organization, *Japanese Manufacturing Operations in the United States* (September 1981).
18. Japan Trade Center/New York, *U.S.-Japan Trade Update,* 1982.
19. Japan Economic Institute of America, *Japan's Expanding Manufacturing Presence in the United States,* 1981.
20. *U.S.-Japan Trade Update,* cited at note 18, p. 5.
21. Michael Jay Jedel and Duane Kujawa, *Management and Employment Practices of Foreign Direct Investors in the United States* (Atlanta: Georgia State University, 1976), p. 14.
22. *Japanese Manufacturing Operations in the United States,* cited at note 17, p. 26.
23. *Ibid.*
24. *Ibid.*, p. 55.
25. See "Japanese-Owned Auto Plants in the U.S. Present a Tough Challenge for the UAW," *The Wall Street Journal,* March 23, 1983.
26. Jedel and Kujawa, cited at note 21, p. 14.
27. *Japanese Manufacturing Operations in the United States,* p. 55.
28. *U.S.-Japan Trade Update,* p. 2.
29. *Japanese Manufacturing Operations in the United States,* p. 55.
30. "Virginia Stresses Non-Union Climate," *The Washington Post,* May 25, 1979, p. D3.
31. Tadashi A. Hanami, "The Multinational Corporation and Japanese Industrial Relations," *International Labor and the Multinational Enterprise,* ed. Duane Kujawa (New York: Praeger Publishers, 1975).
32. *Japanese Manufacturing Operations in the United States,* p. 35.
33. Charles R. Greer and John C. Shearer, "Do Foreign-Owned U.S. Firms Practice Unconventional Labor Relations?", *Monthly Labor Review* 104 (January 1981), p. 45.
34. "After Coaxing Japanese Car Makers to U.S.," cited at note 15.
35. Tadashi A. Hanami, cited at note 31, pp. 173–186.
36. *Ibid.*, p. 174.

ANNOTATED BIBLIOGRAPHY

ANNOTATED BIBLIOGRAPHY

NOTE: *The annotated bibliography is organized into five major sections to allow a more focused literature search.*

I. Attitudes

Adler, N. J. "Expecting International Success: Female Managers Overseas." *Columbia Journal of World Business* 19. 3 (Fall 1984): 79–85.

Personnel managers from sixty American and Canadian corporations were surveyed concerning their attitudes toward sending women abroad. Even though less than 3 percent of all expatriate managers are women, 72 percent of the personnel managers surveyed in 1983 predicted that the number of female expatriate managers sent abroad would increase. While the managers believe that there are qualified women available who are willing to move overseas, they list foreigners' prejudice, dual-career marriages, and the resistance of their own companies as major barriers to women's increased participation in international management. In all cases, companies see that barriers facing women in international management as significantly greater than those facing women pursuing domestic management careers.

Ajami, R. A. "Attitudes of U.S. Workers Toward Foreign–Owned Enterprises." *Management International Review* 23. 4 (1983): 53–62.

The attitude of U.S. workers toward foreign direct investment in the United States is the concern of this study. It was found that the workers believe that foreign direct investment causes loss of control. Moreover, the results suggest that the cognitive and effective components of U.S. workers' attitudes toward foreign investment are not favorable, but the behavioral components of their attitudes, suggest something else. Workers desiring to maintain economic validity and in need of employment will, nevertheless, choose to work for a foreign–owned enterprise.

Badr, Hamed A., Edmund R. Gray, and B. L. Kedia. "Personal Values and Managerial Decision Making: Evidence from Two Cultures." *Management International Review* 22. 3 (1982): 65–73.

This article describes an empirical study of the relationship between personal values and managerial decision making in a cross-cultural context—especially as regards the United States and Egypt. The results indicate that while the personal value structures of the two groups studied (American and Egyptian graduate business students) were different, the managerial decisions of each group were basically consistent with their respective value structures. It was hypothesized, therefore, that this relationship may be "culture-free" although, clearly, further study is needed. Implications for managers in multinational firms are also discussed.

Brady, Donald C., and William O. Bearden. "The Effect of Managerial Attitudes on Alternative Exporting Methods." *Journal of International Business Studies* 10. 3 (Winter 1979): 79.

The salient attributes of direct and indirect exporting methods of distribution were identified. Attitudes of three groups of executives toward the attributes were assessed. These attitudes were analyzed using Anova. The findings suggest that the three groups of executives hold significantly different attitudes about the attributes. The findings: (1) imply that executives using indirect exporting methods and nonexporting executives are most alike in their attitudes; (2) explain the tendency of executives to begin exporting with indirect methods and to switch to direct methods as importing experience increases; and (3) identify the attitudes that each group of executives is most likely to hold.

Chang, Samuel K. C. "American and Chinese Managers in U.S. Companies in Taiwan: A Comparison." *California Management Review* 27. 4 (Summer 1985): 144–55.

In summary, the goal of the research was to answer the following questions: Would American expatriate managers and Chinese managers in U.S.-owned companies and joint ventures in Taiwan have significantly different attitudes toward their jobs? How would the two groups differ in their feelings of job satisfaction in the Taiwanese cross-cultural environment? Would the Chinese managers be more likely than the Americans to exhibit a paternalistic value orientation toward their companies? What ethnocentric expectations would the Chinese managers have for American expatriate managers? And how would American managers react to such expectations?

Doz, Y., and C. K. Prahalad. "Controlled Variety: A Challenge for Human Resource Management in the MNC." *Human Resource Management* 25. 1 (Spring 1986): 55–71.

In this article, we examine some of the issues facing human resource management and the contribution that it can make to help diversified MNCs meet the challenge of controlled variety. We start by analyzing the most critical dimensions along which strategic variety must be maintained in a diversified MNC in order for it to remain responsive to environmental and competitive demands. We then briefly discuss the nature of the need for strategic control and the difficulties of maintaining such control in a complex, diversified MNC. In a second section we discuss what capabilities managers in these companies must develop in order to maintain both strategic variety and strategic control. In particular, we discuss the need for individual managers to be sensitive to both the local idiosyncracies and the global priorities in reaching strategic decisions. We then discuss several complementary approaches to developing such managers. Finally, we outline tentative implications for human resource management in diversified MNCs, both for human resource professionals and for top management.

Geyikdage, Yasar M. "Attitudes Towards MNS: The Middle East in the World Context." *Management Decision* 22. 3 (1984): 14–21.

The purpose of this article is to examine the evolution of the attitudes of Middle Eastern countries toward foreign direct investment and, more specifically, toward multinational corporations. It is important from the point of view of both the multinationals and the host countries to know whether the climate is becoming more favourable for foreign direct investment. Such a situation would mean less risk for the foreign investor and, other things being equal, a lower cost of capital, which would reduce costs for both the foreign investor and the host country.

Jenner, Stephen R. "The British Roots of Business Ideology." *Journal of General Management* 10. 1 (Autumn 1984): 44–56.

This paper explores the ideology of business management in the United Kingdom, the United States, and Australia, based on a survey of middle-to-senior-level managers. The results show a great deal of a similarity between the attitudes, beliefs, and opinions of Anglo managers. However, the U.S. executives differ significantly in the areas of labor management relations, privacy, the role of government, and career development.

Mendenhall, M., and G. Oddou. "The Dimensions of Expatriate Acculturation: A Review." *Academy of Management Review* 10. 1 (January 1985): 39–47.

A review of empirical studies that directly investigated the overseas adjustment of expatriate managers revealed four dimensions that were related to successful expatriate acculturation: (1) the "self-oriented" dimension; (2) the "others-oriented" dimension; (3) the "perceptual" dimension; and (4) the "cultural-toughness" dimension. The study's implications for expatriate selection and training procedures in multinational corporations are discussed.

Miller, E. L., B. J. Bhatt, B. Kumar, J. Cattaneo, and R. E. Hill. "Influence of Expatriate Nationality and Regional Location of the Overseas Subsidiary on Participative Decision Making." *Management International Review* 21. 3 (1981): 31–46.

American and German expatriate managers' perceptions of the capabilities of their supervisors and subordinates were examined. On a regional basis, differences were found in the expatriates' perceptions and attitudes. The preferred style of management differed between the expatriates' approach for managing their subordinates and their superiors.

Miller, Edwin L., and R. Julian Cattanio. "Some Leadership Attitudes of West German Expatriate Managerial Personnel." *Journal of International Business Studies* 13. 1 (Spring/Summer 1982): 39.

This investigation provides data about West German expatriate managers' leadership attitudes. The results indicate that the managers' perceptions about their subordinates' qualifications are an important variable influencing participative management. In addition, regional location appears to influence the managers' attitudes concerning their subordinates.

Morgan, P. V. "International HRM: Fact or Fiction?" *Personnel Administrator* 31 (September, 1986): 43–47.

This article is a general overview of the status of international HRM and discusses why it should be recognized and treated differently from "traditional" HRM. Topics covered were: What is international HRM? Why is IHRM different? IHRM recognition: what needs to be done?

Oddou, G., and M. Mendenhall. "Seven Questions to Ask Before Sending an Employee Overseas." *Training and Development Journal* 40 (May 1986): 24–26.

1. How open-minded and diplomatic is the employee about opinions, attitudes, and behaviors that differ from his or her own?

2. How well does the employee relate to a variety of audiences?

3. Does the employee genuinely like people—of all types, shapes, sizes, and colors?

4. How cohesive is the employee's family?

5. How supportive is the employee's spouse and children of the idea to work and live abroad?

6. How easily and how quickly has the employee adapted to changes in the domestic workplace?

7. How well does the employee cope with unexpected stress?

Orpen, Christopher. "Management Attitudes to Industrial Democracy: An International Assessment." *Management International Review* 20. 1 (1980): 111–27.

To test the hypothesis that management attitudes toward four common forms of employee participation (worker, directors, collective bargaining, job enrichment, employee meetings) are strongly influenced by factors stemming from the socio-political environment, 201 British and 187 South African managers attending Employers Conferences completed measures assessing (a) their experience with each firm, (b) their feelings—positive or negative—with each firm, and (c) their willingness to take steps to implement each firm. They also indicated their attitudes to six main goals of industrial democracy and the extent to which they felt each firm was likely to result in the attainment of these six goals. The results showed strong differences between the two groups of managers, with the British managers being more positively disposed to each form of participation.

Prasad, S. B. "Managers' Attitudes in Brazil—Nationals vs. Expatriates." *Management International Review* 21. 2 (1982): 78–85.

Studies of beliefs, attitudes, and values of managers in a cross-national context have progressed in a systematic way despite methodological limitations. While earlier studies focused on the degree of industrializations as a factor, later studies have assessed the impact of culture. The findings of the exploratory study reported here suggest that the recent changes in the world of business have ushered in a number of contextual variables. These variables have yet to be identified in measurable terms.

Pucik, V., and J. H. Katz. "Information, Control, and HRM in MN Firms." *Human Resource Management* 25. 1 (Spring 1986): 121–32.

This paper discusses the interdependencies of three global organizational systems—control, information transfer, and human resources—based on a linkage between the information processing view of organizational control and human resource management literature.

Reichel, A., and D. M. Flynn. "Values in Transition: An Empirical Study of Japanese Managers in the U.S." *Management International Review* 23. 4 (1983): 63–73.

The purpose of this study was to clarify what effects working in the United States would have on Japanese managers. The 162 upper-level managers working for Japanese firms in the United States hold different organizational values than what might have been expected of Japanese managers in Japan. The results of this study suggest that the personal and organizational variables are as significant as the cultural values in the determination of work-related values.

______. "Seven Prejudices Against MNs." *Across Board* 22. 3 (March 1985): 16–17.

Excerpted from the recent report of the President's Task Force on International Private Enterprise.

Ugur, Yavas, Attila Yaprak, and Glen Riecken. "A Note on the Perception of MNCs." *Management International Review* 24. 4 (1984): 72–78.

Both global and domain-specific attitudinal orientations appear to be a part of the growing worldwide hostility toward MNCs. There seems to be a widespread feeling that the power bases of foreign companies should be closely guarded or regulated by the local governments. This study specifically explores Turkish and American students' perceptions of global (nationalism) and domain-specific attitudinal correlates relative to foreign companies. In addition, socio-economic correlates are included to help categorize respondents into groups holding similar attitudes.

Zeira, T., and M. Banai. "Attitudes of Host-Country Organizations Toward MNCs' Staffing Policies: A Cross-Country and Cross-Industry Analysis." *Management International Review* 21. 2 (1981): 38–47.

This study indicates that attitude surveys of HCOs can assist MNCs operating subsidiaries in Western Europe in their policy-making decisions regarding international staffing management. Despite the innovative method of approaching HCOs and asking them to clarify their expectations, and despite MNC's skepticism concerning the willingness of HCOs to reveal these expectations, our research discloses that the method is not only appropriate, but even applicable. Moreover, the study points out that HCO's collaboration in our research project stems from their desire to promote their own interests as well as that of MNCs.

Zeira, Yoram. "Host-Country Organization and Expatriate Managers in Europe." *California Management Review* 21. 3 (Spring 1979): 40–50.

This article reports the results of a study conducted in five Western European countries of attitudes and expectations of representatives of 110 host-country organizations (HCOs) toward expatriate managers leading subsidiaries in those countries. Findings are classified by the HCOs' positions regarding the following themes: preferred nationality, desired position in the MNC hierarchy, and present and expected personal behavior and interaction with host-country employees. The implications emphasize the importance of changing patterns of personal behavior and improving the selection and training of such managers.

II. Compensation

Beane, S. Robert. "Benefit Plans for TCNs Pose Problems." *Business Insurance* 19 (April 1, 1985): 28.

Whatever their reasons for hiring foreign assignees, multinational companies must provide a compensation program that enables foreign employees to perform their duties without being preoccupied with the possible adverse financial consequences of working in a foreign environment.

Beaumont, P. B. "Concession Bargaining: The British Experience." *Employee Relations* 5. 5 (1983): 13–16.

There is some evidence to suggest that concession bargaining, largely a U.S. phenomenon, has been used in this country in the banking, insurance, and finance industries to weaken existing procedural agreements.

Brooks, B. J. "Long-Term Incentives for the Foreign-Based Executive." *Compensation Benefits Review* 17 (July-August 1985): 46–53.

The author outlines some problems faced by multinational companies seeking to offer equal long-term incentive plans to U.S. and non-U.S.-based executives, and proposes some alternative solutions.

Business International Corporation. "Compensating International Executives: New Perspectives and Practices." (Business International Corporation, 1978), 1–135.

This report evaluates current international personnel policies and practices of major multinational corporations based in the United States and Europe as they affect their nonlocal professional and management work force, and also indicates general trends or courses of action that can guide companies to bettering their programs within the constraints of cost–effectiveness and employee satisfaction.

Domsch, M., T. J. Gerpott, and E. Jochum. "Correlates of General Confidence in the Utility of Formal Performance Appraisal: Results of Cross-Organizational Survey of West German R&D Executives." *Management International Review* 26. 3 (1986): 16–27.

Assuming that the general confidence variable is of critical importance for the effectiveness of performance appraisal systems, the present study was intended to develop a multi-item measure of the general confidence attitude and to identify correlates of this attitude in the light of prior literature in order to facilitate the successful introduction and use of appraisal systems in an R&D context. Based on the results of a cross-organizational survey of 222 West German R&D executives, it was concluded that the

Landy et al. (1978) model of perceived appraisal fairness may hold true across organization hierarchy levels and across nations. Furthermore, results indicate that agreement with different appraisal purposes is not always positively related to general confidence in formal performance appraisal procedures.

Frith, Stan W. "The Expatriate Dilemma: How to Relocate and Compensate U.S. Employees Assigned Overseas." (Chicago: Nelson-Hall, 1981), pp. 1–177.

This book is designed to bring the elements of expatriate administration into sharp focus, identify critical problems, and outline a practical program to increase the expatriate's contribution to corporate profits. The aim has been to make the book useful not only to expatriate compensation administration, but also to financial analysts, to managers, and to expatriates themselves.

Joyce, Brian, and Robert J. Kohne. "The Management of the International Executive Compensation and Benefits Process." *Journal of International Business Studies* 14. 3 (Winter 1983): 37.

Scant attention has been given to the organizational locations of the various tasks that comprise the management process responsible for the international compensation and benefits program of particular international firms. The organizational locations of three managerial tasks associated with these compensation and benefits programs are examined in this article: development of policies and procedures; financing; and supervision and control. The article examines the management of U.S. expatriate and third-country management programs based on the reported practices of U.S.-based firms representing a variety of industries. Management and theoretical implications of the findings are discussed.

Kastiel, D. L. "Benefit Networks Offer Variety of New Products," *Business Insurance* 19 (October 21, 1985): 3, 36, 38.

International employee benefit networks are branching out to further their growth.

The networks, which have traditionally provided benefits for large multinational companies, are not offering their services to more midsized and small employers with as few as twenty employees.

In addition, the networks are offering their clients new options to improve their cash flow, such as flexible premium payment schedules and the opportunity to reinsure benefit coverages with captive insurance companies.

Networks are hoping these innovations will not only allow them to compete more effectively with their rivals, but also allow them to continue to grow.

Almost all of the eleven international benefit networks surveyed by Business Insurance *reported some growth in the past year, and most predict that growth will continue into 1986.*

However, some observers say that network growth has already peaked.

Kuhne, R. J., and B. Joyne. "Who Manages the International Compensation and Benefit Function?" *Compensation Review* 17. 1 (First Quarter 1985): 34–41.

A study of top corporations reveals where certain decisions are best handled—at home or abroad. When defined in their broadest terms, three tasks encompass the entire international compensation and benefits management function. They are (1) the development of policies and procedures; (2) the financing of the programs; and (3) supervision and control. We devised a study to determine the locations at which these tasks are performed and to examine how these locations corresponded with various factors inside and outside the organization. Our purpose was to arrive at a general, yet comprehensive, understanding of the management process controlling, and the influences affecting, this international function.

Reen, Jeremiah J. "Executive Compensation: The Trend Is Up in Europe," *Columbia Journal of World Business* 4. 6 (Winter 1969): 55–62.

The Swiss executive gets top compensation and enough take-home pay to live graciously. By the same standards, British and Dutch executives do less well. These are the conclusions of the latest AMA Executive Compensation Survey. For the four other countries surveyed (France, Italy, Belgium, and Germany), the differences in both gross and net remuneration are now surprisingly small. If these trends continue, and they probably will, it could mean increasing mobility among European managers.

Stone, R. J. "Pay and Perks for Overseas Executives." *Personnel Journal* 65 (January 1986): 64–69.

Premiums and benefits that make up a typical expatriate compensation package: foreign service premium; hardship on-site allowance; cost of living allowances. U.S.-style medical benefits are inappropriate overseas.

Teague, Burton W. "Compensating Foreign Service Personnel." (A Research Report from the Conference Board, 1982), 1–26.

It can be observed from these results that the prevalence of four of the five basic elements of the foreign service compensation package has grown to the point where they are almost universal. The use of the foreign service premium has declined, although it is retained by a significant majority. Another notable difference is the degree to which companies are moving toward eliminating the distinction in treatment of the compensation of U.S. expatriates and third-country nationals.

It may also be noted from the results of the current survey that the basic patterns of compensation are becoming more uniform and are being adopted almost universally. There are, however, distinctions in design and administration, the details of which are discussed in the chapters that follow.

Vivian, John M., et al. "Remuneration and Motivation in Latin America." *Columbia Journal of World Business* 4. 1 (Spring 1969): 41–54.

Exploitation of workers has been the concern of Latin American governments since the time of the conquistadores. Some have enacted the most broadly based social legislation that exists in the world today. Social security and labor laws benefits, however, are expensive to administer and at best are no more than an uneven base on which truly effective programs can be built. The authors review the complexities, but they suggest that it would be even more profitable to identify the factors that motivate the workforce and attune patterns of remuneration and benefits directly to the interests and desires of the workers.

III. Labor markets

Adams, Faneuil, Jr. "Developing an International Workforce." *The Columbia Journal of World Business* 20 (20th Anniversary Issue, 1985): 23–25.

Workforce is usually not international to a satisfactory degree. Two approaches were adopted: (1) emphasis on developing the candidates in the host country for the affiliate management positions; (2) emphasis on developing country affiliate managers. Illustrative example of Japanese firms are given.

Alder, Nancy J. "Women in International Management." *California Management Review* 26. 4 (Summer 1984): 78–89.

In view of the dramatic increases in international business by North American firms, the need for sophisticated international managers can be expected to increase. This article examines the current distribution of female managers sent in expatriate positions by 686 Canadian and American firms. This survey reveals that only 3 percent of all expatriate managers in the responding firms are women. Although women are being sent overseas in managerial and professional capacities by a broad range of industries, gender remains a significant factor in understanding the distribution of North Americans working overseas.

Almaney, Adnan. "Intercultural Communication and the MNC Executive." *Columbia Journal of World Business* 9. 4 (Winter 1974): 23–28.

Effective communication in a foreign culture involves awareness of the modes of thought and patterns of communication expressed by a culture. The author explains and discusses the importance of understanding both verbal and nonverbal communications.

Appleyard, J. R., and J. Gross. "Collective Bargaining in Western Europe." (London: 1973), Institute of Personnel Management, IPM Information Report 13, 7–119.

Following the IPM Information Report on the arrangements for employees to participate in decision making within the undertaking, "Workers' Participation in Western Europe," the institute considered it important that personnel managers should have an insight into collective bargaining practices in Western Europe. This report covers the countries of the enlarged European community and also Norway and Sweden, so that venders have the benefit of Scandinavian experience.

Desatnick, Robert L., and Margo L. Bennett. "Human Management in the Multinational Company." (Hants, England; Gower Press, 1977), pp. 1–407.

The emphasis of this book is on the improvement of productivity and human satisfaction through adaptation to the foreign environment. The key to success is based on the local manager and his crucial relationship with the present company. The corporate boss may be thousands of miles away from the day-to-day operations of the foreign subsidiary, agent, factory, customer, or representative. Hence, the proper selection of the local manager, and his training and development, is critical. Where the local manager is not selected or acquired, perhaps through a takeover, suggestions are made on how to educate him in the new corporate and management style.

Dworkin, James B., Charles J. Hobson, Ekkehart Frieling, and David M. Oaks. "How German Workers View Their Jobs." *Columbia Journal of World Business* 18. 2 (Summer 1983): 48–54.

In this paper, the authors present data on how German workers evaluate their jobs and the codetermination system. The authors evaluate major aspects of the codetermination system in the light of these empirical findings.

Ghosh, Pradip, and Mark Van de Vall. "Workers' Participation in Management—Applied to India." *Management International Review* 18. 3 (1978): 55–68.

The authors propose to examine some aspects of the organization and functions of joint management councils in India in the context of historical forces and the social environment in which it is contained. The main purpose of this study is to illustrate an approach to a sociological and organizational analysis of workers' participation.

Harbison, Frederick H. "Human Resources as the Wealth of Nations." (New York: Oxford University Press, 1973), pp. 3–173.

The author attempts to present an approach to national development based on the simple idea that human resources are the ultimate basis of the wealth of nations. From this perspective, the goals of development are the maximum possible utilization of human beings in productive activity, and the fullest possible development of the skills, knowledge, and capacities of the labor force. If these goals are pursued, then others such as economic growth, higher levels of living, and more equitable distribution of income are thought to be the likely consequences.

Leksell, Laurent, and Ulf Lindgren. "The Board of Directors in Foreign Subsidiaries." *Journal of International Business Studies* 13. 1 (Spring/Summer 1982): 27–38.

This paper addresses the following questions: What role does the board of directors play in wholly owned and partly owned foreign subsidiaries in MNCs? What is the composition and responsibility of the subsidiary boards? What are the potential determinants of the role and effectiveness of the board? Three different roles are identified. The research indicates that certain strategic, structural, and environmental variables may explain differences in board functioning in different MNCs.

Micou, Ann M. "The Invisible Hand at Work in Developing Countries." *Across The Board* 22. 3 (March 1985): 8–15.

It's time to monitor the multinationals, which are everywhere: shutting down plants; fleeing to low-wage havens; violating workers' rights; ignoring health and environmental responsibilities; undermining third-world development; aided and abetted by favorable government policies, while avoiding taxes.

Murray, F. T., and A. H. Murray. "SMR Forum: Global Managers for Global Businesses." *Sloan Management Review* 27 (Winter 1986): 75–80.

The increasing globalization of business produces a need for effective overseas managers. Among Japanese overseas managers the failures are quite low, while failures among American expatriate managers are quite common. What is the reason for this? What can be done about it? In this paper, the authors review the factors that make expatriate managers successful and outline how targeted training programs, modeled after the systematic and thorough approach of Japanese companies, can reduce the failure rate and improve performance. Training in effectiveness and coping skills not only produces successful overseas managers, but also successful overseas businesses.

Nelson, James A., and John A. Reeder. "Labor Relations in China." *California Management Review* 27. 4 (Summer 1984): 13–32.

This article explores labor relations in the state-owned industrial enterprises of China: where they are now and where they appear to be heading. Both the theory and practice of labor relations in the People's Republic of China are currently undergoing substantial changes. It is questionable whether some desired goals can be achieved under current policies and procedures.

Ondrack, Daniel. "International Transfers of Managers in North American and European MNEs." *Journal of International Business Studies* 16 (Fall 1985): 1–18.

Abstract. Global-scale MNEs require a network of managers to direct and control operations around the world. Managerial resources for these jobs can be managers from the headquarters country, host, and third countries. International transfers can be for specific staffing needs, for management development, and for organization development. The general hypothesis examined in this paper was that global scale MNEs would operate in a regional or geocentric fashion with full integration of the world pool of managerial resources for all international transfers. Case studies were done on two North American and two European MNEs in the chemicals and electronics industries.

Tung, Rosalie L. "Corporate Executives and Their Families in China: The Need for Cross-Cultural Understanding in Business." *The Columbia Journal of World Business* 21. 1 (Spring 1986): 21–25.

This paper discusses the most common problems encountered by American and Western corporate executives living and working in China. It then recommends strategies that companies can use to cope with the situation, and, thus, enhance the incidence of success in operating in China.

Welge, M. K. "A Comparison of Managerial Structures in German Subsidiaries in France, India, and the United States." *Management International Review* 21. 2 (1981): 5–21.

This paper presents part of the results of empirical research into the organizational effectiveness of foreign subsidiaries of German MNCs. More specifically, the relationships between the internal organizational structures of the subsidiaries and organizational effectiveness—economic as well as social—have been analyzed in fifteen foreign affiliates. Comparing delegation of decision-making and coordination mechanisms employed across the countries studied, contextual and socio-cultural factors are identified as factors explaining the structural differences. Relating the finding to performance, it could be observed that a positive correspondence between differentiation and integration did not necessarily lead to above-average effectiveness, as has been suggested before. The findings show how this relationship has to be specified according to the cultural context of the company.

Zamet, J. M., and M. E. Bovarnick. "Employee Relations for Multinational Companies in China." *The Columbia Journal of World Business* 21. 1 (Spring 1986): 13–19.

In China, human resource management poses considerable challenges for foreign companies which must deal with a communist power structure that pervades all aspects of society, as well as extreme cultural differences and an underdeveloped economy. The power structure creates a novel problem for managing local workforces, while the culture and the lack of modern conveniences make for unusually difficult living and working conditions for expatriate personnel. Coming to terms with these issues, companies may find that basic principles are put to the test.

Zeira, Yoram. "Overlooked Personnel Problems of Multinational Corporations." *Columbia Journal of World Business* 10. 2 (Summer 1975): 96–103.

Through surveys of MNC subsidiary managers and personnel directors, Professor Zeira finds that important misconceptions can inadvertently appear in personnel offices regarding the problems of host and parent country to the company as a whole. Several suggestions alleviate these problems.

IV. Motivation

Buera A., and W. F. Glueck. "The Need Satisfaction of Managers in Libya." *Management International Review* 19. 1 (1979): 113–22.

This paper reports on a study of the need satisfactions and need importance of 176 Libyan top executives. In a test of Maslow's hierarchy of need theory in a non-Western, non-Christian setting, our findings agree with many others that the hierarchy's order was different from Maslow's. Maslow himself warned that the hierarchy theory was tentative and should not be widely accepted without more research.

Ritsuko, Miyajima. "Organization Ideology of Japanese Managers." *Management International Review* 26. 1 (1986): 73–76.

Ten Japanese expatriate managers were asked to fill "Harrison's Organizational Ideology Scale." The findings from this exploratory study show that those managers shared, to a considerable extent, their ideology with one another and that the predominant culture that emerged was task oriented.

The Japanese, moreover, tended to value a boss who is strong but protective and generous, and a subordinate who is responsible and reliable.

They viewed the ideology of their British colleagues as more power oriented and less person oriented than their own.

V. Selection and Training

______. "Acculturation for Foreign Managers." *Training* 23 (April 1986): 19, 65–68.

Training and acculturation in the United States is a common way for international companies to groom foreign managers. But the experience can turn into a disaster for the foreign employee.

The aspects of American business that tend to trouble foreign employees most include: initiative, preoccupation with work, action orientation, promoting yourself, directness, strictly business, delegation and specialization, language, different scales. Objective standards to be adopted in a performance appraisal system: S = specific; M = measurable; A = attainable; R = results-oriented; T = time-related.

Aiken, Thomas. "The Multinational Man: The Role of the Manager Abroad." (London: George Allen and Union Ltd, 1973), pp. 13–173.

This book examines the role of one particular type of multinational man: the manager, director, or managing director of a wholly owned foreign subsidiary of an international company. A few individuals among them do achieve the intellectual growth to take an interest in international affairs, and periodically, the professionals do exchange ideas internationally by means of specialized journals and the convocation in international conferences. These are exceptions to the custom of each national professional group of barring its foreign or even local counterparts from practicing within the confines of its preserve. The losers in this situation are the people of most countries.

Andre, R. "The Effects of MN Business Training: A Replication of INSEAD Research in an Institute in the U.S." *Management International Review* 25. 3 (1985): 4–15.

First, we investigate the general attitudes of nationalities toward each other during the managerial experience. The INSEAD study found important differences in how nationalities were perceived regarding their mixing with other students, and in their receiving from and contributing to the learning process. The INSEAD study was initiated in part because, while German students were considered to be less mixed with students from other nationalities, several individual German students behaved differently from the majority of their countrymen and mixed readily. This individual predisposition to mixing was believed to be related to prior international experience. We explore these national and individual variables in mixing within the training setting and also within the host culture, and compare our findings with those of the INSEAD studies.

Second, we investigate attitudes toward treatment of a top manager as reflected in students' judgments of a case study. Weinshall has related these judgments to the "anti-mobility value."

Baker, J. C. "Foreign Language and Predeparture Training in U.S. Multinational Firms." *Personnel Administrator* 29 (July 1984): 68–72.

A survey finds that more emphasis is needed. A study was conducted to determine the extent and type of language training and predeparture orientation programs utilized by U.S. multinationals (MNCs) for the managers they send to foreign posts. The analysis included an attempt to measure the importance placed on these programs by U.S. MNCs.

Baker, James C., and John M. Ivancevich. "The Assignment of American Executives Abroad: Systematic, Haphazard, or Chaotic?" *California Management Review* 23. 3 (Spring 1971): 39–44.

As American business corporations have expanded their operations into overseas locations, the demand for qualified executive personnel has risen sharply. The focus of the article is on the procedures for staffing overseas positions used by American firms and the frequently disorganized staffing programs being used by some of the corporate giants of American industry.

Baliga, G. M., and J. C. Baker. "Multinational Corporate Policies for Expatriate Managers: Selection, Training, Evaluation." *S.A.M. Advanced Management Journal* 50 (Autumn 1985): 31–38.

This paper will first review the qualities that expatriate managers should possess. Second, it will consider the training process employed by MNCs after expatriate managers are chosen and assigned. Third, it will address the evaluation process that is used to appraise the performance of these managers. Finally, it will discuss what MNCs should do differently, how their selection, training, and evaluation practices can be improved, and what the payoff may be for MNCs who take these research findings seriously.

Blake, David H. "How to Get Operating Managers to Manage Public Affairs in Foreign Subsidiaries." *Columbia Journal of World Business* 16. 1 (Spring 1981): 61–67.

Operating managers of MNCs have a critical role to play in the management of public affairs at the subsidiary level. However, often their past experiences and current job pressures make it difficult to focus their attention on this area. This article identifies ways to institutionalize the external relations function, and discusses several examples of the way MNCs have attempted to enhance the public affairs awareness and skill level of their managers.

Chang, Samuel K. C. "American and Chinese Managers in U.S. Companies in Taiwan: A Comparison." *California Management Review* 27. 4 (Summer 1985): 144–56.

Two hundred top-level American and Chinese managers of U.S.-owned companies and joint ventures in Taiwan were surveyed on their attitudes toward their work. On most of the items assessing job attitudes, the two groups of managers showed no differences, indicating a positive impact of mutual adaptation in the cross-cultural environment. However, American managers felt more satisfied with their job security and opportunities for advancement, while Chinese managers had a greater interest in company paternalism. Although American and Chinese managers had different attitudes on certain ethnocentric issues, the two groups were clearly moving toward a common understanding. This article recommends the American subsidiaries in Taiwan adopt various policies to reduce the remaining differences and make the managerial styles of the two groups more compatible.

Copeland. L. "Training Americans to Do Business Overseas." *Training* 21. 7 (July 1984): 22–30.

The United States no longer calls the shots in international trade; in fact, savvy competition from many nations is quickly eroding our share of the market. One step toward regaining our competitive edge: language and cultural training for employees going abroad.

Daniels, John D. "The Education and Mobility of European Executives in U.S. Subsidiaries: A Comparative Study." *Journal of International Business* 5. 1 (Spring 1974): 9–24.

Although U.S. firms operating abroad must have managers largely from the same labor force as host country companies, this study indicates that the profile of the subsidiary managers differs substantially from that in the local companies.

Daniels, John D. "The Non-American Manager, Especially as Third Country National, in U.S. Multinationals: A Separate But Equal Doctrine?" *Journal of International Business* 5. 2 (Fall 1974): 25–40.

Foreign managers with U.S. international companies perceive that they are effectively excluded from the so-called better jobs and that U.S. nationals generally receive better treatment and opportunity, especially when cross-national transfers may be involved. This could in the future affect the ability to attract qualified local managers abroad.

Fayerweather, John. "Attitudes Toward Foreign Firms Among Business Students, Managers, and Heads of Firms." *Management International Review* 15. 6 (1975): 19–28.

This article reports the results of attitude studies in Japan, Korea, the Philippines, France, Britain, and Canada. Three aspects of attitudes toward foreign firms are analyzed. Rankings of criteria for appraising performance of foreign firms show that effects on control of national affairs and economic impact are consistently rated most important, with benefits for workers and managers secondary and other points, including cultural impact, of lesser concern. As to quality of effects, the overall impact of foreign firms is generally seen favorably. The control and economic effects evoked strong to moderately adverse judgments as compared to generally favorable assessments of cultural impact. Correlation analysis produced a quite mixed pattern with control, economic, and cultural effects all showing a fairly strong relation to overall appraisals.

Franko, Lawrence G. "Who Manages Multinational Enterprise?" *Columbia Journal of World Business* 8. 2 (Summer 1973): 30–42.

The use of expatriate managers in foreign subsidiary operations of multinational enterprises seems to follow a constantly repeating cycle that varies in its details for each individual company, but whose overall pattern seems surprisingly consistent. International staffing changes tend to coincide with predictable stages through which companies evolve. Nevertheless, few firms have developed clear, rational staffing strategies.

Haire, M., Edwin E. Ghiselli, and Lyman W. Porter. "Managerial Thinking: An International Study." (New York: John Wiley and Sons, Inc., 1966), pp. 1–298.

It is the conviction of the authors that present conditions and trends demand that we all know more about the rest of the people in the world with whom we live and deal. These two themes give shape to the effort: the need for international knowledge and a belief in certain paths to knowledge.

Harari, Ehud, and Goram Zeira. "Training Expatriates for Managerial Assignments in Japan." *California Management Review* 20. 4 (Summer 1978): 56–62.

This study examines perceptions of existing and desired patterns of organizational behavior in MNCs in various countries. The major finding is that despite the numerous differences in organizational behavior patterns between Japan and other nations, four critical managerial patterns are perceived identically by Japanese and non-Japanese employees: leadership, decision making, communication, and group behavior. These findings enable the authors to cite types of training needed for subsidiaries in Japan and for interaction between subsidiaries and their environment.

Harris, Philip R., and Robert T. Moran. "Managing Cultural Differences." (Houston: Gulf Publishing Company, 1979), pp. 1–411.

The first part of this book is concerned with the manager, broadly defined. Material is presented that highlights how the role of the manager is constantly changing under the impact of increased international exchanges. The manager who knows only his or her own country is doomed to become obsolete. Most organizations can no longer afford to employ culturally myopic managers. The cosmopolitan manager is required—one who is an intercultural communicator and transmitter. There are new areas of competence, most of which are not adequately reflected in the course offerings of many of the academic institutions involved in teaching managers.

Harvey, Michael G. "The Executive Family: An Overlooked Variable in International Assignments." *The Columbia Journal of World Business* 20. 1 (Spring 1985): 84–92.

One of the major problems associated with conducting business in foreign markets is training executives to function effectively during their assignment. MNCs have directed their training programs to the expatriate employee and seldom have assisted family members. This paper examines the stress associated with foreign assignments on all family members and illustrates a means to minimize the threat of early return through preliminary screening and selection criteria.

Harvey, Michael C. "The Other Side of Foreign Assignments: Dealing with the Repatriation Dilemma." *The Columbia Journal of World Business* 17. 1 (Spring 1982): 53–59.

MNCs have recognized the need to train executives for foreign assignments for some time. Recently MNCs have discovered an equally pervasive problem: the repatriation "shock" experienced by executives returning to the domestic organization. Repatriation shock manifests itself in disorientation to corporate procedures and practices, reduced productivity and morale, and increased turnover. This article examines a means of planning for more effective repatriation of executives.

Hays, Richard D. "Ascribed Behavioral Determinants of Success-Failure Among U.S. Expatriate Managers." *Journal of Internal Business Studies* 2. 1 (Spring 1971): 40–46.

Myriad factors have important effects on the performance of the multinational corporation. In addition to the normal business issues faced by its domestic counterpart, the MNC faces many added opportunities and problems simply because it operates in more than one country. One set of factors that is important to the success of multinational firms includes the unique human and behavioral problems encountered by a firm operating in several cultural and national environments. One of these behavioral issues which is particularly vital to the MNC is the performance of persons of one nationality who are assigned to positions in another cultural environment.

Hays, Richard D. "Expatriate Selection: Insuring Success and Avoiding Failure." *Journal of International Business* 5. 1 (Spring 1974): 25–38.

The experience of expatriate selection and assignment has been a mixed success for multinational firms. Several selection strategies have been used, but failure situations in individual assignment cases are known to be in nearly every MNC. New research has indicated that the problem of insuring success for an expatriate is quite different from the problem of avoiding failure. A different set of factors is critical to each of these two problems. When this distinction is made, the variables related to the expatriate selection and assignment problems are considerably more ordered and operable.

Illman, Paul E. "Developing Overseas Managers—And Managers Overseas." (AMACOM, 1980), 1–298.

Who might benefit or gain a few ideas that would be helpful in the whole matter of developing overseas managers? First, there is the home-office executive who is responsible for selecting and preparing the U.S. manager who is to go overseas. Second, there is the U.S. manager himself. Third, the book may help the local national manager who is the subject of the American company's development efforts. Finally, but to a lesser degree, it may help the foreign national who visits or is transferred to a post in the United States.

Lee, James A. "Developing Managers in Developing Countries." *Harvard Business Review* 46 (November-December 1968): 55–65.

Attempts to identify, select, and train future business leaders in the developing nations of Africa, Asia, and South America must take into account the fundamental differences in management development conditions between the United States and the emerging countries. The author pinpoints five key environmental problem areas and suggests a straightforward program of techniques for coping with them.

Luck-Nunke, B. "Recruiting European Nationals to Return to Their Home Countries." *Personnel Administrator* 29 (July 1984): 41–45.

Tips and key differences on college recruiting in the United States and Europe.

Masionroughe, Jacques G. "The Education of a Modern International Manager." *Journal of International Business Studies* 14. 1 (Spring/Summer 1983): 141–46.

This article is based on a speech delivered by Mr. Jacques G. Masionroughe, senior vice president, IBM Corporation, and Chairman of the Board, IBM World Trade Corporation. In his speech he illustrates the traits of successful managers, qualities of success, and the symptoms of failure.

Miller, Edwin, and Joseph Cheng. "A Closer Look at the Decision to Accept an Overseas Position." *Management International Review* 18. 3 (1978): 25–34.

A sample of 135 expatriate American upper middle managers were asked to make ratings regarding the importance of certain variables they considered when they decided to accept their current overseas assignments. A factor analysis identified different dimensions underlying the decision spaces between experienced and inexperienced expatriate managers. In the inexperienced expatriate, the overseas assignment represents a necessary stepping stone for advancement in the parent company hierarchy. The experienced expatriate manager chooses an additional assignment for related but not the same motives as the inexperienced expatriate. In the experienced expatriate, he has made a career choice to remain in international business.

Perlmutter, Howard V., and David A. Keenan, "How Multinational Should Your Top Managers Be?" *Harvard Business Review* 52 (November–December 1974): 121–32.

It may be easier to talk to your person in Rio if he or she speaks your language, but insisting on that may cause MNCs to lose some top people, not to mention profits.

The authors' article surveys executives in MNCs and determined what attitudes toward foreign ideas most executives think ought to prevail. Nearly all executives think a global attitude retains talented foreigners and helps business abroad. The authors also assert that the CEO's commitment to multinationalize is paramount if change is to occur. They also state that some radical structural changes may help an MNC attain true multinationalism.

Sethi, Prakash S., and Carl L. Swanson. "Hiring Alien Executives in Compliance with U.S. Civil Rights Laws," *Journal of International Business Studies* 10. 2 (Fall 1979): 37.

As foreign direct investment in the United States increases, foreign MNCs are bringing with them their own management style and organizational ethics. The infusion of these values into the domestic employment practices of their U.S. subsidiaries can be in conflict with U.S. civil rights laws. This article analyzes the legal, managerial, and intercultural implications of this conflict as illustrated by a Title VII lawsuit currently pending before a U.S. District Court involving C. Itah and Company (American), Inc.

Simmonds, Kenneth. "Multinational? Well, Not Quite." *Columbia Journal of World Business* 1. 4 (Fall 1966): 115–22.

Global installations and global marketing, but a top headquarter management that is virtually closed to foreign forces. This situation, standard in many international companies, may be profoundly damaging to corporate effectiveness. Yet little remedy is in sight: planned internationalization of parent management is, if anything, waning as companies rush to embrace the centralized strategy formulation that pushes resources affiliate managers still farther from the big decisions.

Stephens, D. B. "Cultural Variation in Leadership Style: A Methodological Experiment in Comparing Managers in the U.S. and Peruvian Textile Industries." *Management International Review* 21. 3 (1981): 47–85.

This study is a cross-cultural comparison of various aspects related to the leadership style of managers in the United States and Peru. Its purpose is to make such a transnational comparison while controlling methodological and conceptual weaknesses common to earlier research efforts.

Yun, Chul Koo. "Role Conflicts of Expatriate Managers: A Construct." *Management International Review* 13. 6 (1973): 105–13.

A construct will be presented here as a framework to investigate the role conflicts of expatriate managers of multinational corporations. The construct will reveal that it is almost impossible for the managers to avoid role conflicts, since their role is built in such a way that it is easily vulnerable to potential conflicts. While their conflicts can be detrimental to the international managers' mental health and to the effective functioning of the company, they could be sources of challenges and opportunities.

The problem implied in the construct for MNC is not to attempt to eliminate the potential sources of role conflicts of expatriate managers, since that is next to impossible. The task of MNCs is to see the role conflicts problems from an integrated point of view and to find ways to manage them constructively.